# Hands-on Ansible Automation

*Streamline your workflow and simplify your tasks with Ansible*

**Luca Berton**

www.bpbonline.com

**FIRST EDITION 2023**



**ISBN: 978-93-55515-599**



## Distributors:

**BPB PUBLICATIONS**
20, Ansari Road, Darya Ganj
New Delhi-110002
Ph: 23254990/23254991

**DECCAN AGENCIES**
4-3-329, Bank Street,
Hyderabad-500195
Ph: 24756967/24756400

**MICRO MEDIA**
Shop No. 5, Mahendra Chambers,
150 DN Rd. Next to Capital Cinema,
V.T. (C.S.T.) Station, MUMBAI-400 001
Ph: 22078296/22078297

**BPB BOOK CENTRE**
376 Old Lajpat Rai Market,
Delhi-110006
Ph: 23861747

**To View Complete BPB Publications Catalogue Scan the QR Code:**

Published by Manish Jain for BPB Publications, 20 Ansari Road, Darya Ganj, New Delhi-110002 and Printed by him at Manipal Technologies, Manipal

www.bpbonline.com

# Disclaimer

Any opinions or personal views I express in this book are my own and not those of Red Hat Inc. or JPMorgan Chase & Co.

Ansible®, Red Hat® Ansible® Automation Platform, Red Hat®, JBoss®, OpenShift®, Fedora®, Hibernate®, CloudForms®, RHCA®, RHCE®, RHCSA®, Ceph®, Gluster®, the Red Hat® logo and "A" logo in a shaded circle are trademarks or registered trademarks of Red Hat, Inc. or its subsidiaries in the United States and other countries. **https://www.redhat.com/en/about/brand/standards/trademarks**

"JPMorgan," "JPMorgan Chase," "Chase," the JPMorgan Chase logo, and the Octagon Symbol are trademarks of JPMorgan Chase Bank, N.A. JPMorgan Chase Bank, N.A., is a wholly-owned subsidiary of JPMorgan Chase & Co. **https://www.jpmorgan.com/**

Linux is a registered trademark of Linus Torvalds.

Certified Kubernetes®, Certified Kubernetes Administrator®, Certified Kubernetes Application Developer®, Certified Kubernetes Security Specialist®, CloudEvents®, CloudNativeCon®, CNCF®, containerd®, etcd®, KubeCon®, Kubernetes®, LSB®, Open Container Initiative®, Prometheus®, The Linux Foundation®, Xen Project®, Cloud Native Computing Foundation logo, Kubernetes and Cloud Native Associate and Design (color), OpenTelemetry and Design (black and white), Fluentd and Design of a Carrier Pigeon (color - horizontal) are registered trademarks of The Linux Foundation in the United States and / or other countries. The marks CRI-O™, LF™, LinuxCon™, Linux Foundation™, OpenGitOps™, OpenTelemetry™, Open Container Format™, Open Virtualization Alliance™, Virtual Kubelet™, World of Open Source™ have registrations pending or trademarks in use of The Linux Foundation in the United States and/or other countries. The Linux Foundation logo. US Reg. no. 5166331 (The Linux Foundation geometric design (black and white)), The Linux Foundation logo. US Reg. no. 5166330 (The Linux Foundation geometric design (color)), Certified Kubernetes logo. US Reg. no. 5734733, Community Data License Agreement logo. US Reg. no. 5852265, fluentd logo. US Reg. no. 4734498, Kubernetes logo. US Reg. no. 4816320, Kubernetes and Cloud Native Associate and Design (color) US Reg. 6949718, SupplyChainSecurity and Design (black and white) US Reg. No. 6949717 are registered trademarks for the following logo marks in the United States and/or other countries. **https://www.linuxfoundation.org/trademark-usage/**

UNIX® is a registered trademark of The Open Group.

Python, PyCon, PyLadies, and Python logos (in several variants) are registered trademarks of the Python Software Foundation. **https://www.python.org/psf/trademarks/**

Azure, Microsoft®, Microsoft® 365, Microsoft Teams, PowerPoint®, Outlook®, OneDrive®, SharePoint®, The Microsoft ® Store, Windows® and Windows® 10, Windows, Vista, XP, NT are registered trademarks or trademarks of Microsoft Corporation in the U.S.A. and other countries. **https://www.microsoft.com/en-us/legal/intellectualproperty/trademarks**

Apple, Mac, Mac OS, Macintosh, Pages, and TrueType are either registered trademarks or trademarks of Apple Computer, Inc. in the United States and/or other countries. **https://www.apple.com/legal/intellectual-property/trademark/appletmlist.html**

IBM is a registered trademark of International Business Machines Corporation. **https://www.ibm.com/legal/us/en/copytrade.shtml**

Celeron, Celeron Inside, Centrino, Centrino logo, Core Inside, Intel Core, Intel Inside, Intel Inside logo, Itanium, Itanium Inside, Pentium, Pentium Inside, VTune, Xeon, and Xeon Inside are trademarks or registered trademarks of Intel Corporation or its subsidiaries in the United States and other countries. **https://www.intel.com/content/www/us/en/legal/trademarks.html**

Amazon Web Services, AWS, the Powered by AWS logo, and any other AWS Marks used in this book are trademarks of Amazon.com, Inc. or its affiliates. This book is not endorsed by or affiliated with Amazon in any way **https://aws.amazon.com/trademark-guidelines/**

Google, Chrome™ browser, Chromium™ open source project, Cloud TPU™ integrated circuit, GCP™ infrastructure platform, GKE™ software service, Gmail™ email service, Google App Engine™ platform, Google Cloud Platform™ service, Google Cloud Storage™ service, Google Cloud™ enterprise services, Google Compute Engine™ service, Google Container Engine™ container management system, Google Dashboard™ interface, Google Photos™ photo storage and organizing platform, Google™ search or search engine, Go™ programming language, Kubeflow™ open-source machine learning platform, Optimized Chip™ processor chip, SPDY™ protocol, YouTube™ video community, are trademarks of Google LLC and this book is not endorsed by or affiliated with Google in any way. **https://about.google/brand-resource-center/**

HashiCorp®, Vagrant, Packer, Terraform, HashiCorp products, name & logo are trademarks of The HashiCorp, Inc. **https://www.hashicorp.com/trademark-policy**

All other trademarks are the property of their respective owners.

# Dedicated to

*My son* ***Filippo*** *- the joy of my life*

# About the Author

**Luca Berton** is an Ansible Automation Expert who has been working with JPMorgan Chase & Co. He previously worked with the Red Hat Ansible Engineer Team for three years. He is a published author of the best-selling books "Ansible for VMware by Examples" and "Ansible for Kubernetes by Examples" as part of the Ansible By Example(s) practical book series. Luca is also the creator of the Ansible Pilot project.

With over 15 years of experience as a System Administrator, he possesses extensive expertise in Infrastructure Hardening and Automation. He is an avid supporter of the Open Source community and shares his knowledge at various public events. A geek by nature, Luca's inclination is towards Linux, particularly Fedora.

# Acknowledgement

I would like to express my gratitude to my son, family, and friends who make life worth living and whose support and encouragement have made this work possible.

I also want to extend my appreciation to all those whom I've worked with over the years and who shared their ideas for this book: Thank you all for the knowledge you've shared.

# Preface

Welcome to "Hands-on Ansible Automation," a comprehensive guide that will take you on a journey through the world of automation using Ansible. In today's fast-paced digital landscape, where efficiency and scalability are paramount, Ansible has emerged as a leading automation tool that empowers organizations to streamline their operations and achieve remarkable results.

This book is designed to equip beginners and developers alike with the knowledge and skills needed to harness the full potential of Ansible. Whether you are a system administrator, network engineer, developer, or manager, this book will provide you with the necessary tools and techniques to automate routine tasks, enhance configuration management, and orchestrate complex deployments.

As an Ansible automation expert with years of experience, I have meticulously crafted this book to provide you with a practical, step-by-step approach to mastering Ansible. Each chapter is enriched with real-world examples and hands-on exercises, covering everything from the fundamentals of Ansible's architecture and installation to advanced topics such as leveraging the Ansible Automation Platform and Morpheus.

Throughout the book, you will discover how Ansible can transform your infrastructure operations, enabling you to achieve Infrastructure as Code and unlock the benefits of multi-cloud environments. You will learn how to develop playbooks, manage variables, handle conditional statements, and utilize Ansible modules effectively.

Moreover, this book goes beyond just Ansible by delving into the integration of Morpheus. It explores topics such as configuration management, graphical user interfaces, role-based access control, and more. You will not only gain insights into troubleshooting common issues but also acquire best practices to optimize your Ansible workflows.

By the end of this book, you will have developed a solid understanding of Ansible and the confidence to automate tasks, accelerate deployments, and improve overall efficiency in your IT operations. Whether you are a beginner seeking a comprehensive introduction or an experienced user looking to expand your knowledge, this book serves as your ultimate guide to mastering Ansible automation.

I invite you to embark on this exciting journey with me as we delve into the world of Ansible and discover how it can revolutionize your automation practices. Let's automate everything and unlock the true power of Ansible.

Happy automating!

**Chapter 1: Introduction to Ansible Automation-** In this chapter, we will lay the foundation by introducing Ansible and guiding you through the installation process on Linux, macOS, and Windows. You will gain an understanding of Ansible's architecture and learn how to execute basic ad-hoc commands to manage remote hosts effectively.

**Chapter 2: Ansible Basics and Core Concepts-** In this chapter, we will delve into the core language of Ansible. You will learn how to work with Ansible inventory, create powerful playbooks, utilize variables, leverage facts, and harness the flexibility of conditional statements and loops.

**Chapter 3: Extending Ansible's Capabilities-** Building upon the core language, this chapter explores advanced concepts such as Ansible Vault for securely storing sensitive data, utilizing handlers to trigger actions, harnessing the power of roles and collections for code reusability, and employing filters, templates, and plugins to enhance your automation capabilities.

**Chapter 4: Managing Linux Systems with Ansible-** This chapter will focus on configuring Linux target hosts and performing everyday system administration tasks. You will learn how to ensure host availability, edit files, create text files, and execute rolling updates, among other essential Linux-specific automation tasks.

**Chapter 5: Automating Windows Infrastructure with Ansible-** In this chapter, we shift our focus to Windows target hosts. You will discover how to configure Windows hosts, test their availability, manipulate files, create text files, and perform rolling updates, enabling seamless automation in a Windows environment.

**Chapter 6: Troubleshooting Ansible Deployments-** Troubleshooting is an integral part of any automation journey. In this chapter, we will equip you with the knowledge to diagnose and resolve common issues you may encounter while working with Ansible. From connection failures and syntax errors to missing module parameters, you will learn effective troubleshooting techniques.

**Chapter 7: Scaling Up with Ansible Enterprise-** This chapter explores Ansible for Enterprise features and its integration with Ansible Automation Platforms and Morpheus. It covers a range of topics, including GitOps, Configuration Management (CM), Graphical User Interfaces (GUIs), and Role-based Access Control (RBAC).

**Chapter 8: Advanced Ansible Techniques-** In this final chapter, we will explore Ansible's advanced features and third-party integration within Cloud Providers and Kubernetes. We will showcase real-world Ansible use cases and orchestration scenarios.

## Development environment

The code included in this book can be used with any text editor or integrated development environment (IDE). An IDE is a software tool that provides comprehensive features and tools for software development, including code editing, debugging, compilation, and project management.

The base environment for reproducing the examples is:

- A text editor: terminal (VIM, Emacs, Nano, Pico, etc.) or GUI (VS Code, Atom, Geany, etc.)
- A workstation with the ansible or ansible-core installed packages

The recommended IDE and editor is Visual Studio Core which can be downloaded for free at **https://code.visualstudio.com**.

## Conventions used in the book

Inside this book, you will find numerous examples and terminal commands. The Ansible language primarily uses YAML and INI formats syntax. Assume the file format is YAML when not specified in the text. The code follows the latest YAML 1.2.2 specification. YAML (YAML isn't a Markup Language) is a human-readable data serialization format known for its simplicity, readability, and broad compatibility with programming languages and tools. It allows for a concise representation of complex data structures and is widely used for configuration files and data exchange. It's very similar to JSON and can be used as an XML alternative, but it uses Python-style indentation and a more compact format for lists and dictionary statements.

The INI format is often used for inventory and the Ansible configuration file. It is a simple configuration file format that uses key-value pairs and sections to store settings and preferences in a human-readable manner.

Many terminal commands are well-known Linux commands and are marked inline (for example, ansible [command]) or in a code block (with or without line numbers) like:

```
cat /proc/cpuinfo
```

The provided terminal commands follow POSIX conventions and are compatible with Unix-like systems, including Linux, macOS, and BSD. Each command assumes usage by a standard user account when prefixed with the $ (dollar) symbol or by the root user when prefixed with the # (number sign) symbol.

We are going to see the code from the installation in our first steps in the Ansible language and later in our automation journey. Each Playbook, Role, and Collection follow the latest Ansible best practices verified with the latest release of the Ansible Linter.

However, certain code snippets, especially in the troubleshooting section, specifically break the best practices rule to reproduce a behavior or a use case.

# Code Bundle and Coloured Images

Please follow the link to download the
***Code Bundle*** and the ***Coloured Images*** of the book:

## https://rebrand.ly/e716c2b

The code bundle for the book is also hosted on GitHub at **https://github.com/bpbpublications/Hands-on-Ansible-Automation**. In case there's an update to the code, it will be updated on the existing GitHub repository.

We have code bundles from our rich catalogue of books and videos available at **https://github.com/bpbpublications**. Check them out!

# Errata

We take immense pride in our work at BPB Publications and follow best practices to ensure the accuracy of our content to provide with an indulging reading experience to our subscribers. Our readers are our mirrors, and we use their inputs to reflect and improve upon human errors, if any, that may have occurred during the publishing processes involved. To let us maintain the quality and help us reach out to any readers who might be having difficulties due to any unforeseen errors, please write to us at :

**errata@bpbonline.com**

Your support, suggestions and feedbacks are highly appreciated by the BPB Publications' Family.

## Piracy

If you come across any illegal copies of our works in any form on the internet, we would be grateful if you would provide us with the location address or website name. Please contact us at **business@bpbonline.com** with a link to the material.

## If you are interested in becoming an author

If there is a topic that you have expertise in, and you are interested in either writing or contributing to a book, please visit **www.bpbonline.com**. We have worked with thousands of developers and tech professionals, just like you, to help them share their insights with the global tech community. You can make a general application, apply for a specific hot topic that we are recruiting an author for, or submit your own idea.

## Reviews

Please leave a review. Once you have read and used this book, why not leave a review on the site that you purchased it from? Potential readers can then see and use your unbiased opinion to make purchase decisions. We at BPB can understand what you think about our products, and our authors can see your feedback on their book. Thank you!

For more information about BPB, please visit **www.bpbonline.com**.

# Join our book's Discord space

Join the book's Discord Workspace for Latest updates, Offers, Tech happenings around the world, New Release and Sessions with the Authors:

**https://discord.bpbonline.com**

# Table of Contents

# CHAPTER 1
# Introduction to Ansible Automation

## Introduction

Ansible is a key technology to standardize and homogenize different tool chains and obtain excellent results in deliverability and customer satisfaction in any organization. Ansible is a simple language to learn, and its standard code block makes the learning process smooth, as we proceed in our journey.

## Structure

In this chapter, we shall cover the following topics:

- Modern datacenter
- Introduction to Ansible
- Ansible community
- Ansible architecture
- Ansible installation
- Ansible ad-hoc commands

# Objectives

In this chapter, we are going to familiarize ourselves with the context of using the Ansible automation technology, understand the architecture, set up Ansible in our machines, and execute the first command on a target host.

# Modern datacenter

Every company nowadays relies on an efficient and modern Information Technology department. It is important to maintain the highest quality in order to meet business demand, and being competitive in the global market is extremely important.

A modern data center is a centralized location where an organization's IT infrastructure is housed and managed. This can include servers, storage systems, networking equipment, and other hardware and software components that support the organization's computing needs.

One of the key characteristics of a modern data center is that it is designed to be scalable, flexible, and highly available. This means that it can easily be expanded or adapted as the organization's computing needs change and that it is able to continue operating even if one or more components fail.

A modern data center may also be designed to be energy efficient, using advanced cooling and power management systems to reduce energy consumption. It may also include features such as redundant power and networking infrastructure in order to ensure high levels of uptime and reliability.

In addition to traditional hardware and software components, a modern data center may include cloud-based services, such as **Infrastructure as a Service** (**IaaS**) and **Platform as a Service** (**PaaS**). These services allow organizations to access computing resources on demand without purchasing and maintaining their own hardware.

In IT infrastructure, we have many applications running to meet the needs of the business stakeholders.

Application deployment refers to the process of delivering and installing a software application to a production environment, where it can be accessed and used by end users. This process typically involves building the application, testing it to ensure it is functioning properly, and then releasing it to a live environment where it can be accessed by users over the internet or a local network.

There are many ways to deploy an application, depending on the type of application and the target environment. Some common methods include:

- **Manual deployment**: This involves installing an application on each device or server by executing manual steps. This can be time-consuming and error-prone but is often used for small applications or for applications that are not expected to be used by many users.

- **Scripted deployment**: This involves using scripts or automated tools to install the application on multiple devices or servers simultaneously. This can be faster and more reliable than manual deployment but requires more upfront work to set up scripts and automation tools. This technique of using script-based approach for automation is called "Imperative Approach".
- **Container-based deployment**: This involves packaging the application and its dependencies into a container, which can then be deployed to any device or server that is capable of running the container. Containers allow applications to be deployed quickly and consistently, making it easier to scale them up or down as needed.
- **Cloud deployment**: This involves hosting the application on a cloud platform such as **Amazon Web Services** (**AWS**) or Microsoft Azure. Cloud platforms provide a variety of tools and services to make it easy to deploy, scale, and manage applications in a live environment.

Overall, the goal of application deployment is to make it easy to get the application up and running in a production environment, so that end users can access and use it as needed. We can also automate the deployment process using Ansible in our deployment tool chain, for example, combined with Jenkins. Learn more about CI/CD pipeline in *Chapter 6, Ansible Troubleshooting*, section *Troubleshooting tools*.

A container is a lightweight, stand-alone, and executable package that includes everything an application needs to run, including the application code, libraries, dependencies, and runtime. Containers allow applications to be easily packaged and deployed on any platform, including on-premises servers, cloud infrastructure, and hybrid environments.

One of the key benefits of containers is that they allow applications to be isolated from their surroundings and run consistently across different environments. This makes it easier to develop, test, and deploy applications, and it also helps ensure that applications run correctly when deployed in production.

Containers are typically run on top of the container runtime, such as Docker, Podman and CRI-O (also used by Kubernetes), which is responsible for managing and scheduling the containers. The container runtime provides a consistent interface for interacting with the containers, regardless of the underlying operating system or infrastructure.

Containers have become increasingly popular in recent years as a way to deploy and manage applications in a cloud-native manner, and they are widely used in DevOps and microservices architectures.

Modern IT infrastructure offers self-healing, intelligent scheduling, service discovery, horizontal scaling, automated rollouts and rollbacks, load balancing, Secrets, Config Maps and automation, using configuration management. When the number of machines is too high, we need a reliable patch management system to keep the systems updated and apply faster patches and security updates.

# Introduction to Ansible

Ansible is an open-source software platform for automating and managing IT infrastructure, including deploying applications and configuring systems. It allows us to write "playbooks" which are sets of tasks written in YAML (a human-readable language), that describe how to perform Automation steps (tasks) on one or more remote servers. *Figure 1.1* shows the Ansible logo:

***Figure 1.1:*** *The Ansible logo*

Ansible uses a client-server architecture, with a central control server (known as the Ansible Control Node) and managed nodes (that is, the servers that we want to automate tasks on). The control machine connects to the managed nodes over SSH (a secure network protocol) and runs the playbooks on them.

**Note: Control/Controller Node, Control/Controller Host, Control/Controller Machine or Control/Controller Server are various ways of referring to Ansible Central Control Node. On the other hand, Managed Node, Managed Host, Managed Machine or Managed Server are various ways of referring to devices where Ansible Control node will perform automation.**

One of the key benefits of Ansible is that it uses a simple, easy-to-learn syntax and does not require any special programming skills. This makes it an appealing choice for IT professionals who need to automate various regular repetitive work, but may not have much programming experience. Ansible is a declarative language, and the scripts are usually written as procedural. The advantage is that it is focused on the final status of the system rather than on the step to achieve the status.

Ansible can be used to automate a wide range of tasks, including the deployment of applications, the configuration of systems, the provisioning of cloud infrastructure, and the management of security and compliance. It is commonly used in DevOps (a software development methodology that emphasizes collaboration between development and operations teams) to automate the build, test, and deployment of applications.

Ansible connects to target machines using the following protocols:

- OpenSSH for Unix-like operating systems: Linux, macOS, and so on.
- WinRM for Windows operating systems.

The following *Figure 1.2* represents the Ansible architecture:

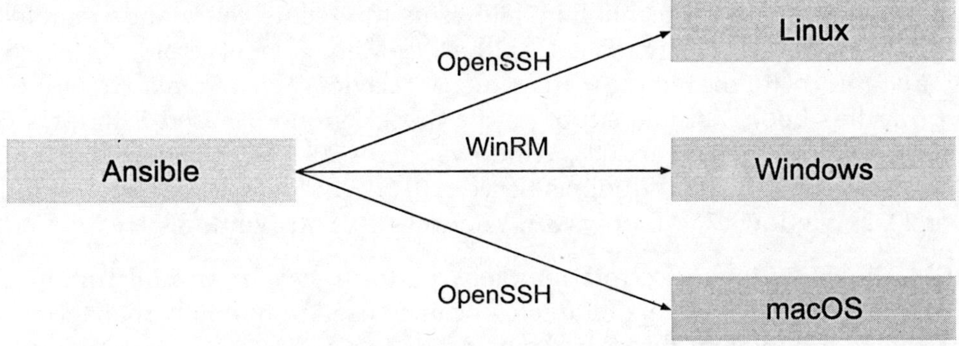


***Figure 1.2:*** *The Ansible architecture*

Ansible in the preceding diagram is a "central controller node", and Linux, Windows and macOS are "managed nodes" where the automation will be performed.

# Linux and MacOS target

Ansible connects to any POSIX, Unix-like operating system in managed hosts using the OpenSSH protocol. The long list includes any Linux distributions, Unix, macOS, and any flavor of BSD, and so on. OpenSSH is a free, open-source implementation of the **Secure Shell** (**SSH**) protocol. It is a network protocol that provides secure communication between computers, allowing us to remotely log in to another computer, execute commands, and transfer files securely over a network.

The SSH protocol uses encryption to secure the connection between the client (our computer) and the server (the remote computer). It authenticates the client and server using public key cryptography and establishes a secure channel over which data can be transmitted.

OpenSSH is widely used to access remote servers and systems, and it is the default SSH implementation on most Linux and Unix-based systems. It is also available as third-party software on other operating systems, such as Windows and macOS.

OpenSSH provides various tools and utilities for managing SSH connections, such as SSH for establishing an SSH connection, SCP for securely transferring files between computers, and SFTP for transferring files over an SSH connection. It also includes a **Secure Copy** (**SCP**) utility for transferring files between computers and a **Secure File Transfer Protocol** (**SFTP**) for transferring files over an SSH connection.

## Windows target

Ansible connects to Windows-managed hosts using **Windows Remote Management** (**WinRM**). This Microsoft technology allows us to execute commands remotely on a Windows machine. This is based on the WS-Management protocol, which is a standard protocol for the remote management of devices and systems. At the moment of writing this book, Ansible supports the most commonly used Windows client and servers: Windows Server 2008, Windows Server 2008 R2, Windows Server 2012, Windows Server 2012 R2, Windows Server 2016, Windows Server 2019, Windows Server 2022, Windows 7, Windows 8.1, Windows 10, and Windows 11.

WinRM allows us to run scripts remotely, perform system administration tasks, and manage Windows servers remotely. It can be used to remotely manage a single machine or a group of machines in a network.

To use WinRM, we need to enable it on the remote machine and then use a tool such as Windows PowerShell or a third-party tool like Ansible to connect to the remote machine and execute commands.

Overall, WinRM is a useful tool for remotely managing and automating tasks on Windows machines. It can save time and effort by allowing us to manage multiple machines from a single location. It can be especially useful in large organizations where there may be hundreds or thousands of servers to manage.

Ansible nowadays expanded its connection capabilities to storage and network devices, container technologies, virtualization (VMware), orchestration technologies (Kubernetes), and cloud providers.

**Tip: We can run our Ansible Playbook in the current machine using the setting "ansible_connection" variable to the "local" value.**

## Ansible community

The Ansible community (refer to *Figure 1.3*) refers to individuals and organizations that are using, developing, and contributing to the Ansible automation tool. Ansible is an open-source automation tool that helps users manage their IT infrastructure and application deployments by automating configuration management, application deployment, and orchestration tasks. Please refer to the following figure:

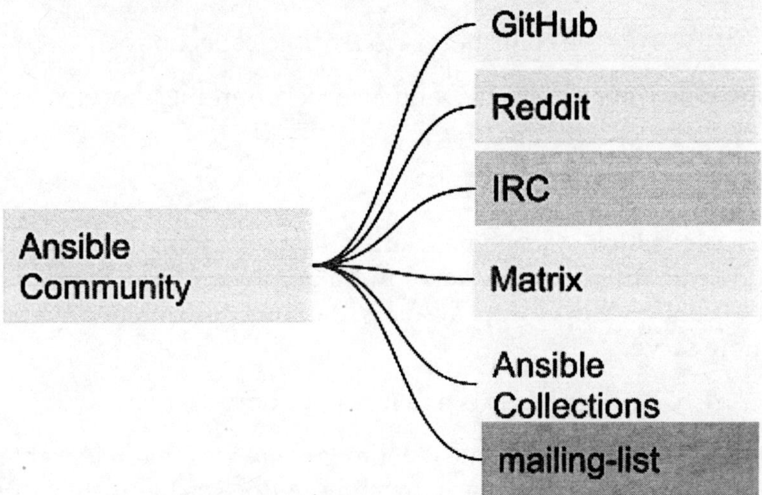


***Figure 1.3:** The Ansible Community channels*

The Ansible community is made up of users, contributors, and developers who share their knowledge, experience, and code through various channels. These channels include online forums, mailing lists, social media groups, and meet ups. The community also provides documentation, tutorials, and training materials to help users learn and get started with Ansible.

One of the key features of the Ansible community is its collaborative nature. Users and developers work together to improve the tool by contributing code, reporting bugs, and providing feedback. The community also creates and maintains thousands of Ansible modules, playbooks, roles, and collections that users can use to automate various tasks.

The Ansible community is supported by Red Hat, the company behind Ansible, and other organizations and individuals committed to open-source software and automation. The community is constantly growing and evolving, with new contributors and users joining every day.

To get an idea of the magnitude of the Ansible Community at the moment of writing this book, refer to the following points:

- Nearly half a million people monthly visit the documentation website (ref: **docs.ansible.com**),
- 800+ monthly comments on **reddit.com/r/ansible**

- 300+ monthly questions tagged Ansible on Stack Overflow
- 200+ monthly of posts to the ansible-project mailing list
- 800+ active GitHub contributors
- 400+ active Ansible contributors to Ansible collections
- Strong daily presence of IRC and Matrix communication systems

# Ansible architecture

Ansible is a configuration management and automation tool that allows us to manage and control a large number of systems in an automated and standardized way. It can be used to configure operating systems, deploy applications, and perform other tasks on remote servers.

The architecture of Ansible consists of a few key components:

- **Control machine**: This is the machine where we run the Ansible commands and playbooks. It can be any machine with Ansible installed, such as our local desktop or laptop. This machine is the heart of Ansible ecosystem.
- **Managed nodes**: These are the machines managed by Ansible control machine to perform automation.
- **Inventory**: The inventory is a list of the systems that Ansible will manage. It can be a static file or a dynamic inventory that is generated at runtime.
- **Modules**: Modules are the building blocks of Ansible. They are small programs that perform a specific task, such as installing a package or starting a service.
- **Playbooks**: Playbooks are written in YAML and contain a series of tasks to be executed. They can be used to automate complex processes and are a key component of Ansible's automation capabilities.
- **Plugins**: Plugins are small programs that extend Ansible's core functionality. They can be used to modify the behavior of Ansible modules or to add new features.

Overall, Ansible connects to the systems in our inventory and runs the tasks specified in our playbooks. It uses a simple, human-readable syntax and can be easily extended with custom modules and plugins.

Let us break down these components one by one. An Ansible controller is simply any computer with Ansible installed on it. For information about the installation, please refer to the following section "*Ansible Installation*". Once Ansible is successfully installed, we can check the running version with the command:

```
$ ansible --version
```

Please note that the Ansible platform includes the Ansible engine, the command-line utilities (for example: "**`ansible`**", "**`ansible-playbook`**", "**`ansible-galaxy`**", "**`ansible-inventory`**", and so on) and the Ansible collections ("**`ansible.builtin`**").

The list of target hosts is stored in the inventory text file. The default location for this file is **`/etc/ansible/hosts`**, but we can override for each execution, specifying the "**`-i`**" parameter in every Ansible command. The Ansible Inventory support files in INI, JSON, and YAML format. We can also have multiple files and combine them together in execution time. A very powerful feature is the dynamic inventory, and the ability to execute a script to return an inventory. This is very useful in a fast-paced environment, for example, virtual machines or cloud computing providers, where the enumeration of running services is critical and fast-changing.

An Ansible module performs every Ansible action of a managed host. There are so many Ansible modules that it is easy to perform any action without reinventing the wheel.

When we would like to concatenate multiple tasks, save data in a data structure, or execute a loop or conditional, we need the Ansible playbook. It is a YAML format document defining what and when to execute our automation steps. It is very powerful, especially combined with reusable code packed as a role or collection. We can write our own reusable code or use it from vendors or third-party libraries.

Ansible has a great plugin structure that allows us to extend the core functionality. It is possible to create plugins for a lot of tasks. There are different types of plugins based on the type of integration that we would like to achieve.

We can distribute our code and plugins to our IT department or the Internet. There is a great selection of roles and collections on the Ansible Galaxy website at **https://galaxy.ansible.com**.

# Ansible installation

To install Ansible on our local machine (assuming we are running a Unix-like operating system such as Linux or MacOS), we need to have Python 3.6 or later already installed. The machine with Ansible installed is called Ansible controller.

First of all, we can check if Ansible is already installed using the following command:

```
$ ansible --version
```

It verifies if Ansible has already been successfully installed and should display the version of Ansible in our system.

```
ansible [core 2.15.0]
```

For example, in our system, the latest installed version is Ansible core 2.15.0. Here, 2 is called major, 15 minor, and 0 patch versions.

When the result is:

```
command not found: ansible
```

The output **`command not found`**, means that it is not installed in our system.

Installing Ansible is the first step to executing our automation. There are several ways to achieve this result. It supports all modern operating systems, and so we usually only need to type "**`install ansible`**" in our operating system. In the following section, we can see the installation step by step in the most popular operating systems.

# Ansible core versus Ansible community packages

Since 2021, the Ansible project has distributed two different packages of the Ansible software, from version 2.10 onward. The Ansible core package and the Ansible Community package are distributed. Ansible Core is a command-line tool primarily for developers and users who want to install only the bare minimum content they need. It contains a minimal amount of modules and plugins and allows other collections to be installed. Similar to Ansible 2.9, though without any content that has since moved into a collection. Ansible core is distributed as an **`ansible-core`** package, that is, the main building block and architecture for Ansible, and includes the following:

- CLI tools such as **`ansible-playbook`** and **`ansible-doc`**, and others for driving and interacting with automation.
- The Ansible language uses YAML to create a set of rules for developing Ansible Playbooks and includes functions such as conditionals, blocks, includes loops, and other Ansible imperatives.
- An architectural framework that allows extensions through Ansible collections. The Ansible core team releases a new major release approximately twice a year.

Another way of installing Ansible is using the Ansible community package. Each major release of the Ansible community package accepts the latest released version of each included collection and the latest released version of **`ansible-core`**. Major releases of the Ansible community package can contain breaking changes in the modules and other plugins within the included Collections and/or in core features.

The **ansible** package depends on the **ansible-core** package. Ansible 3.0.0 and the following contain more collections thanks to the wider Ansible community reviewing collections against the community checklist. The Ansible community team typically releases two major versions of the community package per year on a flexible release cycle that trails the release of **ansible-core**.

Some operating system package managers prefer to distribute only the **ansible-core** package, and some distribute both packages (**ansible-core** and **ansible**). Please check what is available with our favorite distribution.

At the moment of writing the book, the latest release of the **ansible-core** package is 2.14.3 on 27th February 2023, and for **ansible,** the package is 7.3.0, released on 28th February 2023.

# Linux

Linux is the first citizen operating system for Ansible. All the distributions have an Ansible package in their repository. Whenever we would like to install the latest version of Ansible, we could use the PIP command line utility instead (see the related section).

In most Linux distributions, the user experience of configuring an Ansible controller is to open the terminal and install the package by the distribution package manager.

A good recommendation is always to update the package manager's package list.

We can use the apt package manager in a Debian or Ubuntu-compatible operating system to install Ansible via the DEB package system, as shown in the following *Figure 1.4*.

We can perform the following steps:

1. Update the package cache by running the following command:

   ```
   $ sudo apt update
   ```

2. Install the necessary dependencies by running the following command:

   ```
   $ sudo apt install Ansible
   ```

Refer to the following *Figure 1.4:*

***Figure 1.4:*** *Result of execution of Ansible installation in Ubuntu 22.10*

In the same way, we could install the additional command line **ansible-lint** Ansible utility, as shown in the following *Figure 1.5:*

***Figure 1.5:*** *Result of execution of ansible-lint installation in Ubuntu 22.10*

We can use the YUM/DNF package manager in Fedora, Red Hat Enterprise Linux, Oracle Linux, Rocky Linux, Alma Linux, Amazon Linux, CentOS and other distributions that use the RPM package system to install Ansible. Please note that CentOS 7 and 8 are the final releases of CentOS Linux. The **End-Of-Life** (**EOL**) dates for CentOS 7 are June 30, 2024, and 8 December 31, 2021.

We can perform the following steps:

3. Update the DNF package cache by running the following command:

```
$ sudodnf update
```

4. Install the necessary dependencies by running the following command:

```
$ sudodnf install Ansible
```

Refer to the following *Figure 1.6:*

***Figure 1.6:*** *Result of execution of Ansible installation in Fedora 37*

# Pip

Ansible is written in the Python language, and it is possible to install it using Python-native tools and repositories. This is also an option if we want to consume the latest released version of Ansible. Sometimes Linux distributions need some time to incorporate the latest Ansible releases according to the distribution release cycle.

Install Ansible using the pip tool and the Python package manager by running the following command. It interacts with the **Python Package Index** (**PyPI**) internet archive (ref: **https://pypi.org/**).

In a Debian or Ubuntu operating system, we can perform the following steps:

1. Update the package cache by running the following command:

   ```
   $ sudo apt update
   ```

2. Install the necessary dependencies by running the following command:

   ```
   $ sudo apt install python3-pip
   ```

3. Install the Ansible package:

   ```
   $ pip3 install Ansible
   ```

4. Verify that Ansible has been successfully installed by running the following command:

   ```
   $ ansible --version
   ```

The last command displays the version of Ansible that we have installed (as shown in *Figure 1.7*).

Please note that in some distributions, the `pip` command could be used by typing the `pip3` command, which means that the PIP tool is specifically for Python version 3. In some cases, we can also be more specific, for example, pip 3.9 for Python version 3 using Python 3.9. This use case is typical for the **Red Hat Enterprise Linux** (**RHEL**) distributions.

Refer to the following *Figure 1.7*:

***Figure 1.7:** Result of execution of Ansible installation via PIP*

Once Ansible is installed, we can use it to manage our infrastructure and automate tasks on multiple servers or devices. We will need to create an Ansible inventory file, specifying the servers or devices we want to manage, and write Ansible playbooks, which are written in the YAML language and define the tasks we want to automate.

# MacOS

The MacOS operating system is UNIX System-V compliant, and hence, is fully compatible with Ansible.

In order to install on macOS (either Intel or Apple Silicon processor), it is handy to use the Homebrew Package Manager, as shown in *Figure 1.8*. The Homebrew is a super convenient way to install and maintain additional up-to-date software on MacOS.

The Homebrew is a Ruby-based software that we could install with a simple command in our macOS terminal (for more reference, **https://brew.sh/**):

```
$ /bin/bash -c "$(curl -fsSL https://raw.githubusercontent.com/Homebrew/install/HEAD/install.sh)"
```

Open the terminal and update the package manager's package list by running the following command:

```
$ brew install ansible
```

Refer to the following *Figure 1.8*:

```
lberton@Lucas-MBP ~ % brew install ansible
==> Fetching dependencies for ansible: sqlite
==> Fetching sqlite
    Downloading https://ghcr.io/v2/homebrew/core/sqlite/manifests/3.41.1
######################################################################### 100.0%
    Downloading https://ghcr.io/v2/homebrew/core/sqlite/blobs/sha256:fedac4380affc3aa80c2
    Downloading from https://pkg-containers.githubusercontent.com/ghcr1/blobs/sha256:feda
######################################################################### 100.0%
==> Fetching ansible
    Downloading https://ghcr.io/v2/homebrew/core/ansible/manifests/7.3.0
Already downloaded: /Users/lberton/Library/Caches/Homebrew/downloads/8abde3dff30d5f40dee3
9f30248a558f50232653b325325b924a206bf6cfb3ad--ansible-7.3.0.bottle_manifest.json
    Downloading https://ghcr.io/v2/homebrew/core/ansible/blobs/sha256:11869f8ad5ad1d3ba34
Already downloaded: /Users/lberton/Library/Caches/Homebrew/downloads/8e11fbfc581c55381e47
db1a2da0391de4b61a030fc31169f24b65a21a9be5bf--ansible--7.3.0.arm64_ventura.bottle.tar.gz
==> Installing dependencies for ansible: sqlite
==> Installing ansible dependency: sqlite
    Pouring sqlite--3.41.1.arm64_ventura.bottle.tar.gz
🍺  /opt/homebrew/Cellar/sqlite/3.41.1: 11 files, 4.5MB
==> Installing ansible
    Pouring ansible--7.3.0.arm64_ventura.bottle.tar.gz
🍺  /opt/homebrew/Cellar/ansible/7.3.0: 29,252 files, 378.6MB
    Running `brew cleanup ansible`...
Disable this behaviour by setting HOMEBREW_NO_INSTALL_CLEANUP.
```

***Figure 1.8:*** *Result of execution of Ansible installation on macOS via Homebrew*

In the same way, we could install the additional command line **`ansible-lint`** Ansible utility as shown in the following *Figure 1.9*:

```
lberton@Lucas-MBP ~ % brew install ansible-lint
    Downloading https://formulae.brew.sh/api/formula.jws.json

    Downloading https://formulae.brew.sh/api/cask.jws.json

==> Fetching ansible-lint
    Downloading https://ghcr.io/v2/homebrew/core/ansible-lint/manifests/6.14.2
######################################################################## 100.0%
    Downloading https://ghcr.io/v2/homebrew/core/ansible-lint/blobs/sha256:04daf6b64c58f0
    Downloading from https://pkg-containers.githubusercontent.com/ghcr1/blobs/sha256:04da
######################################################################## 100.0%
    Pouring ansible-lint--6.14.2.arm64_ventura.bottle.tar.gz
🍺  /opt/homebrew/Cellar/ansible-lint/6.14.2: 1,351 files, 14.1MB
    Running `brew cleanup ansible-lint`...
Disable this behaviour by setting HOMEBREW_NO_INSTALL_CLEANUP.
Hide these hints with HOMEBREW_NO_ENV_HINTS (see `man brew`).
Removing: /Users/lberton/Library/Caches/Homebrew/ansible-lint--6.14.0... (3.7MB)
lberton@Lucas-MBP ~ %
```

***Figure 1.9:*** *Result of execution of ansible-lint installation on macOS via Homebrew*

# Windows

The Windows operating system is not officially supported as an Ansible control node by Ansible engineer team. Alternatively, the Windows operating system is officially supported as a target node. The main problem is that Windows is not a POSIX-compliant operating system, and many Ansible modules have been deeply coded in that way.

There are two possible workarounds, none of which are officially supported:

- Cygwin
- **Windows Subsystem for Linux** (**WSL**)

Cygwin is additional software that adds a Unix-like environment and command-line interface for Microsoft Windows. Even if it sounds good on paper, sometimes the execution simply breaks.

Windows Subsystem for Linux is the modern feature of Windows to run a Linux environment in a separate sandbox environment. It works better because it runs a native Linux operating system inside our Windows system. The supported Linux distributions are Ubuntu, OpenSUSE, Kali, Debian, Arch Linux, and so on. It requires Windows 10 version 2004 and higher (Build 19041 and higher) or Windows 11. We can install the WSL using the following command in a PowerShell with the option "**Run as administrator**":

```
wsl --install
```

After a successful installation of WSL, we can proceed with the standard Linux installation. The result is shown in *Figure 1.10*:

***Figure 1.10:*** *Ansible installation on Windows 11 WSL*

# Ansible ad-hoc commands

Ansible ad-hoc command is a quick and simple way to perform a one-time task on a group of hosts. It allows us to execute a single command or a short script on one or multiple hosts using the Ansible command-line tool.

Ad-hoc commands are useful for performing quick tasks such as checking the uptime of servers, installing packages, or restarting services. They are also helpful for testing or troubleshooting a specific configuration or setting on a host or a group of hosts.

The syntax for the Ansible ad-hoc command is as follows:

```
ansible <hosts> -i<inventory-file> -m <module> -a <arguments>
```

Here:

- **<hosts>**: The target hosts on which we want to run the command. We can specify a single host or a group of hosts using a pattern.
- **<inventory-file>**: The location of the inventory file that contains the list of hosts.
- **<module>**: The Ansible module to run on the hosts. Modules are pre-written scripts that perform specific tasks, such as managing packages, copying files, or running shell commands.
- **<arguments>**: The arguments passed to the module to perform the desired task.

One of the first Ansible modules that we might encounter is the "**ping**" module. The "**ping**" module is part of the "**ansible.builtin**" Ansible collection.

The purpose of the "**ping**" module is to check whether a host is available to execute any automation. It is completely different from the network ping command. In the Ansible "**ping**" module, we are going to verify the connection to the target host (usually via OpenSSH connection) and execute some simple Python code that returns a "**ping: pong**" message. We can customize the return message, but it is not important. The core part is the ability to check the availability of executing code in our target host. We should use the "**win_ping**" module for the Windows target instead.

Another useful Ansible module is the "**command**" module. Moreover, the "**command**" module is part of the "**ansible.builtin**" Ansible collection. We can combine the "**command**" module with any Linux command. The only limitation is that the "**command**" module does not allow the usage of the shell extension, like the ***** (star), **|** (pipe), **>** (redirect) operators. If we need any of this, Unix twinkle redirects to the "**shell**" module instead, which is also arguably, more dangerous.

For example, to check the "**uptime**" Linux command of a group of hosts, we can run the following ad-hoc command:

```
$ ansible webservers -i inventory.ini -m command -a "uptime"
```

This command will run the **uptime** command on all hosts in the **webservers** group defined in the **inventory.ini** file. A group of hosts is helpful when we want more than one target for our automation. We simply define a group of hosts and use it in our automation.

There are many Ansible modules included in the default installation of Ansible. The list is very long and gets longer and longer every day. In the next chapter, we are going to explore the most useful.

```
$ ansible webservers -i inventory.ini -m ping
```

The Ansible **ping** module is one of the most well-known because it tests the target host's availability. It has nothing related to the network **ping** command. It connects to the target host via the SSH connection with the username and password specified in the inventory files (or using the SSH Key authentication) and executes some commands using the native Python interpreter. This is the reason why the target host needs only a modern operating system and Python installed.

When we would like to execute multiple steps, there is another key component in Ansible automation: the Ansible Playbook (discussed in *Chapter 2, Ansible Language Core*).

Ansible is used to apply DevOps principles to worldwide organizations using human readable YAML files called Ansible Playbook.

We are going to explore the Ansible programming language in the upcoming chapter deeply. The Ansible Playbook enables us to use data structure, and the typical programming language constructs to execute code only when needed.

# Conclusion

Ansible is a modern infrastructure automation tool that enables us to standardize the script and reduce human errors. It only requires a connection to the target host without any agent installed. Automating our day-to-day tasks is beneficial for every IT department nowadays. Ansible can interact with a plethora of different operating systems, services, applications, and cloud providers. It is a Swiss knife to always have in our pocket.

In this chapter, we started deep in the Ansible architecture and executed some simple Ad-Hoc commands. In the next chapter, we are going to expand on how to execute multiple tasks one after another and take advantage of the full Ansible language and data structures.

# Points to remember

- The Ansible control machine executes the automation against the target host.
- Ansible uses modules to execute a common operation to target hosts.
- Ansible automates Unix-like operating systems (Linux, MacOS, and so on) and Windows.
- Ansible ad hoc executes one module or commands against to target host(s).

# Key terms

- **Control machine:** This is the machine where we run the Ansible commands and playbooks. It can be any machine with Ansible installed, such as our local desktop or laptop.
- **Inventory:** The inventory is a list of the systems that Ansible will manage. It can be a static file or a dynamic inventory that is generated at runtime.
- **Modules:** Modules are the building blocks of Ansible. They are small programs that perform a specific task, such as installing a package or starting a service.
- **Playbooks:** Playbooks are written in YAML and contain a series of tasks to be executed. They can be used to automate complex processes and are a key component of Ansible's automation capabilities.
- **Plugins:** Plugins are small programs that extend Ansible's core functionality. They can be used to modify the behavior of Ansible modules or to add new features.

# Multiple choice questions

1. **What <u>is not</u> a characteristic of a modern data center?**
    a. Scalability
    b. None of these
    c. Flexibility
    d. High availability
2. **What protocol is used by Ansible to communicate with Linux target hosts?**
    a. OpenSSH for Unix-like operating systems: Linux, MacOS, and so on.
    b. WinRM for Windows operating systems
    c. We can use "`ansible_connection=local`" for current hosts
    d. None of these
3. **Is it possible to use Windows as an Ansible controller?**
    a. True
    b. False

4. **What is the expected output of the "ping" Ad-Hoc command?**
    a. `ping: ping`
    b. `no route to host`
    c. `ping: 1`
    d. `ping: pong`

# Answers

1. **b**
2. **a**
3. **b**
4. **d**

# Questions

1. What is Ansible inventory?
2. How to connect to the Ansible community?
3. Explain the purpose of the ad-hoc command.

## Join our book's Discord space

Join the book's Discord Workspace for Latest updates, Offers, Tech happenings around the world, New Release and Sessions with the Authors:

**https://discord.bpbonline.com**

# CHAPTER 2
# Ansible Basics and Core Concepts

## Introduction

Ansible helps us streamline multiple tasks to target hosts. As it has an easy learning curve, we can also code the Ansible language in a so-called Ansible playbook. This file could also contain data structures, loops, and conditionals to execute tasks only when some conditions are present. In this chapter, we are going to learn the basic principles of Ansible language and how to write our first successful Ansible playbook.

## Structure

In this chapter, we shall cover the following topics:

- Ansible inventory
- Ansible playbook
- Ansible variables
- Ansible facts
- Ansible magic variables
- Ansible conditional
- Ansible loop

# Objectives

By the end of this chapter, the reader will know/be able to understand the Ansible language and create a successful list of actions in an Ansible Playbook.

# Ansible inventory

Ansible itself runs only on the control machine, so we do not need to install Ansible on target machines. Ansible works by placing temporary Python scripts in POSIX target machines based on the modules we specify. Some of these modules have prerequisites, and so we may need to install specific Python packages on POSIX target machines. For the Windows target, the connection is performed using the WinRM protocol using some PowerShell scripts in a mechanism similar to the Python scripts for POSIX target machines.

## Inventory

An Ansible inventory is the list of hosts where we target our automation. Accordingly, a list of hosts managed by Ansible is called inventory. We can organize our inventory with groups or patterns to select the hosts or groups where we would like to target our Ansible automation. We can also use group name to target the execution.

# INI inventory

The INI inventory is the simplest inventory type. We could list all our hosts or IP addresses. The default location is **/etc/ansible/hosts**, but we can also customize it with the **-i** parameter. The most straightforward Ansible inventory format is INI. The INI format has been around in the IT industry for years and is very popular for configuration files. It is simply a text file that could have some **name=value** fields inside. The **name** is the name of the property, and the **value** is the property's value. Moreover, it is possible to define sections inside, specifying the section name between brackets, using **[section]**.

Let us see a simple example using the **simple_inventory.ini** file as follows:

```
server01.example.com

[web]

server02.example.com

server03.example.com
```

As shown in *Figure 2.1*, the Ansible inventory file lists three hosts under the **example.com** domain:

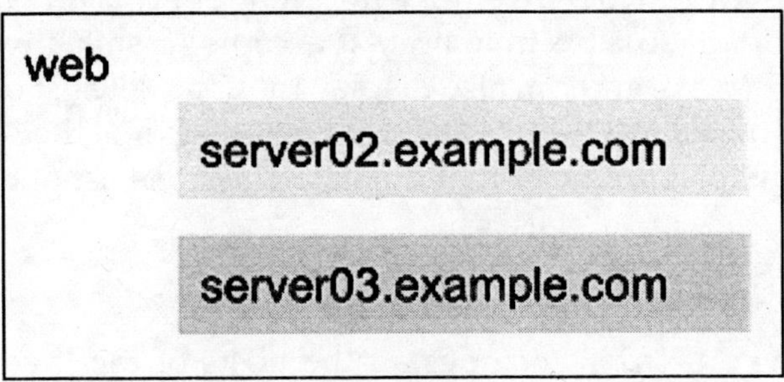


***Figure 2.1:*** *The simple_inventory scenario*

Specifically, the **server01.example.com** host is ungrouped. The **server02.example.com** and **server03.example.com** hosts are grouped as **web**.

## YAML inventory

The YAML format is a simple human-readable format that is often used for Ansible inventories. Please be very careful about the indentation of the code. The YAML format could be used instead of the INI format to code an Ansible inventory. The complete list of host names or IP addresses must be under the **all** node. Each host must be under the **hosts** field. We can specify the groups like the INI format in the YAML format under the **children** keywords. The simple INI inventory of the previous section could be expressed in the code as follows:

```
---
all:
  hosts:
    server01.example.com:
  children:
    web:
      hosts:
        server02.example.com:
        server03.example.com:
```

As shown in *Figure 2.1*, the **server01.example.com** is ungrouped, but the **server02.example.com** and **server03.example.com** hosts are grouped as **web**.

# The ansible-inventory tool

The **ansible-inventory** command-line tool is included in every Ansible installation and shows the current Ansible inventory information. It is advantageous to verify the current status of our Ansible inventory. It accepts Ansible inventory files in INI, YAML, and JSON formats, and can also display the complete list of parameters using **--help**. The most popular option is the parameter **–list** that displays the list of the host and the **-graph** parameter that displays the same list of hosts in a tree view.

# The "all" keyword

The particular keyword **all** includes all the hosts of the Inventory used in any group. The only exception is **localhost**, which we need to specify. The **all** keyword is important and will be required in our Ansible usage. If we do not specify any specific host that is to be the of our automation, Ansible targets the automation against **all**.

# List view

The list view of the **ansible-inventory** command is useful for displaying a JSON of the current inventory used by Ansible, on-screen. The more our inventory becomes complex, the longer the list is. Let us suppose we have a simple **inventory.ini**, which is an INI inventory file with one host **server.example.com**, as shown in *Figure 2.2*:

```
server.example.com
```

***Figure 2.2:*** *The inventory scenario*

We can have the list view output specifying the following command:

```
ansible-inventory -i inventory.ini --list
```

Where:

- **ansible-inventory** is the command to work with Ansible inventory.
- **-i inventory** parameter specifies the source inventory file in the current directory.
- **--list** parameter requests the output in list view format.

The result of the execution of the **ansible-inventory -list** command is as follows:

```
{
    "_meta": {
        "hostvars": {}
    },
    "all": {
        "children": [
            "ungrouped"
        ]
    },
    "ungrouped": {
        "hosts": [
            "server.example.com"
        ]
    }
}
```

## Graph list view

The graph view of the **ansible-inventory** command is useful for displaying a tree view of the current inventory used by Ansible, on-screen.

Let us suppose we have a simple INI inventory file, as shown in the preceding *Figure 2.2*.

We can have the list view output, by specifying the following command:

```
ansible-inventory -i inventory.ini --graph
```

Where:

- **ansible-inventory** is the command to work with Ansible inventory.
- **-i inventory** parameter specifies the source **inventory** file in the current directory.
- **--graph** parameter requests the output in graph view format.

The result of execution of the **ansible-inventory -graph** command is as follows:

```
@all:
  |--@ungrouped:
  |  |--server.example.com
```

## Ranges of hosts

Group members could also be defined using ranges by numbers or letters. In the field by numbers, we could specify a stride as the increment between a sequence of numbers. The **range_inventory.ini** file looks like the following:

```
[web]

server[01:10].example.com
```

In this INI example **range_inventory.ini**, the **web** group contains all hosts from **server01.example.com** to **server10.example.com**. We can extend the range as much as needed, specifying the start and end elements of the servers.

We can test the Ansible inventory using the list view parameter of the **ansible-inventory** command:

```
ansible-inventory -i range_inventory.ini --list
```

The command produces the following output:


```
{
    "_meta": {
        "hostvars": {}
    },
    "all": {
        "children": [
            "ungrouped",
            "web"
        ]
    },
    "web": {
        "hosts": [
            "server01.example.com",
            "server02.example.com",
            "server03.example.com",
            "server04.example.com",
            "server05.example.com",
            "server06.example.com",
            "server07.example.com",
            "server08.example.com",
```

```
        "server09.example.com",
        "server10.example.com",
    [...]
```

## Host in multiple groups

The hosts could be present in multiple groups inside an inventory. This feature is highly useful in production, where we can classify systems from different angles.

```
server01.example.com
[web]
server02.example.com
server03.example.com
[prod]
server02.example.com
[dev]
server03.example.com
```

In this INI example, the hosts **server02.example.com** and **server03.example.com** are in the web group. **server02.example.com** is present on the **web** and in the **prod** groups. **server03.example.com** is present on the **web** and **dev** groups.

We can verify the list view using the command:

```
ansible-inventory -i groupsmultiple_inventory.ini--list
```

The output of the **groupsmultiple_inventory.ini** inventory command is as follows:

```
{
    "_meta": {
        "hostvars": {}
    },
    "all": {
        "children": [
            "ungrouped",
            "web",
            "prod",
            "dev"
        ]
    },
```

```
    "dev": {
        "hosts": [
            "server03.example.com"
        ]
    },
    "prod": {
        "hosts": [
            "server02.example.com"
        ]
    },
    "ungrouped": {
        "hosts": [
            "server01.example.com"
        ]
    },
    "web": {
        "hosts": [
            "server02.example.com",
            "server03.example.com"
        ]
    }
}
```

As we can see for each group name, there is a list of the host(s) inside of it.

## Host and group variables

We are going to explore some examples of host variables and group variables in the following Ansible variable section. Please refer to *Chapter 4, Ansible for Linux,* for the usage of host and group variables in an Ansible inventory for Linux target hosts and *Chapter 5, Ansible for Windows,* for usage in the Windows target hosts.

## Local inventory

Targeting automation against **`localhost`** is quite a special place for Ansible because we need some special parameters. Please remember that **`localhost`** is usually excluded from the **`all`** keyword.

One particular case in inventory is with **localhost**. We need to specify the connection type as **local**. Otherwise, Ansible presumes using the default SSH connection.

This is a classic Ansible **localhost_inventory.ini** file example in the INI format:

```
localhost ansible_connection="local"
```

We can obtain the list view of this inventory using the command:

```
ansible-inventory -ilocalhost_inventory.ini --list
```

That produces the following output:

```
{
    "_meta": {
        "hostvars": {
            "localhost": {
                "ansible_connection": "local"
            }
        }
    },
    "all": {
        "children": [
            "ungrouped"
        ]
    },
    "ungrouped": {
        "hosts": [
            "localhost"
        ]
    }
}
```

## Multiple inventories

It is possible to use multiple inventory files for each execution. Let us reuse some Ansible inventories that we defined before, for this scope.

For example, we could specify the **simple_inventory.ini** and the **localhost_inventory.ini** inventories, setting two times the **-i** parameter.

```
ansible-inventory -ilocalhost_inventory.ini -i simple_inventory.ini  --list
```

The result is a combined output of the two Ansible inventories, **`localhost_inventory.ini`** and **`simple_inventory.ini`**:

```
{
    "_meta": {
        "hostvars": {
            "localhost": {
                "ansible_connection": "local"
            }
        }
    },
    "all": {
        "children": [
            "ungrouped",
            "web"
        ]
    },
    "ungrouped": {
        "hosts": [
            "localhost",
            "server01.example.com"
        ]
    },
    "web": {
        "hosts": [
            "server02.example.com",
            "server03.example.com"
        ]
    }
}
```

# Dynamic inventory

When our target host is moving fast, we might find it useful to generate our Ansible inventory dynamically. Typical use cases are virtual machines hypervisor, container orchestrators, public cloud providers, and so on. Ansible Dynamic Inventory is a way to run some code to generate on the fly, an Ansible Inventory. The generated Ansible inventory is coded in JSON format, and the generation code is usually Python. The dynamic inventory code usually requires a configuration file with credentials to connect to our infrastructure or cloud provider. We are going to share some examples of Ansible dynamic inventories in *Chapter 8, Ansible Advanced,* section *Third-party integrations, fragility and agility.*

## Windows inventory

Windows target hosts require a special configuration that we are going to see in *Chapter 5, Ansible For Windows.*

**Note: From now onward, we suppose to execute our code against an inventory containing the server01.example.com server. It is only an example, and we can substitute the inventory with our use case, as learned in the Ansible inventory section.**

# Ansible playbook

An Ansible playbook is a set of plays to be executed against an inventory. Tasks form each play. We are going to learn from a simple Ansible playbook, from the basic syntax, and add more skills. Most Ansible playbooks and Ansible modules are idempotent. Idempotence with Ansible means running the same automation as many times as we want and still obtaining the same result.

## YAML syntax

The Ansible playbook is coded in the YAML format. The YAML format is a human-readable programming language with a shallow learning curve. Please take a look at the following YAML example file (not an Ansible playbook):

```
---
# This is a YAML comment
some data # This is also a YAML comment
this is a string
'this is another string'
"this is yet another a string"
with_newlines: |
Example Company
123 Main Street
New York, NY 10001
without_newlines: >
```

```
This is an example
of a long string,
that will become
a single sentence.
yaml_dictionary: {name1: value1, name2: value2}
yaml_list1:
- value1
- value2
yaml_list2: [value1, value2]
...
```

The content of the Ansible playbooks reflects the schema shown in *Figure 2.3*:

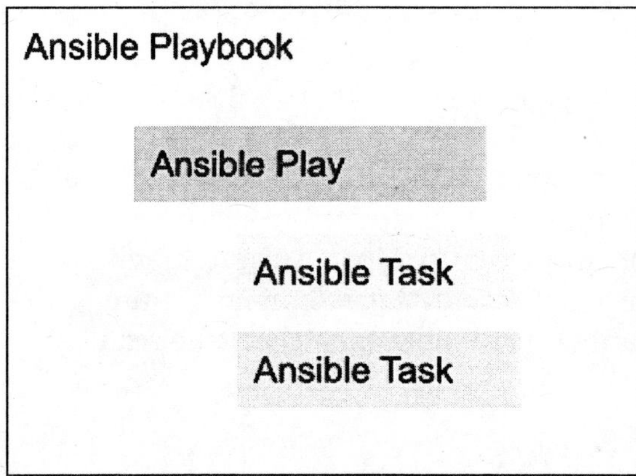


***Figure 2.3:*** *Ansible playbook schema*

Every playbook is based on YAML syntax, making the file easy and human-readable. YAML is a text format, and we can easily recognize the presence of the three dashes (`---`) symbols at the beginning and three dots (`...`) at the end. The three dots (`...`) are optional, and so, many people omit them. This file type is susceptible to the spacing between element aspects of the same level and must be in the same indentation, despite some programming languages.

**Tip: YAML is very sensitive to indentation. Always double-check the indentation because it is often the root cause of so many code errors. Learn more in Chapter 6, Ansible Troubleshooting.**

We could use the sharp symbol (#) for comments, even on the lines with some previous code. The string is significant; we could specify it directly or with a single or double quote. We recommend using a double quote as a general rule. Using the pipe ("|" symbol) and major (">" symbol) statements, we could define multi-line strings.

The first statement will keep the newlines. The second will not. Other valuable data structures are dictionaries and lists.

**Tip: Always put one empty line at the end of the Ansible file. It is not a fatal error, but we obtain a warning message when we omit the empty line at the end of the Ansible playbooks or if we put more than one.**

# First playbook

This is the first Ansible playbook that displays a simple Hello World message on the screen using the **debug** module. In the following code snippet, we can see the complete Ansible code:

```
---
- name: Hello World sample
  hosts: all
  tasks:
    - name: Hello message
      ansible.builtin.debug:
        msg: "Hello World!"
...
```

Let us navigate line by line through the Ansible playbook:

- Beginning of the file (`---`)
- Name of the Play
- Target hosts of execution (all of the inventory)
- Beginning of tasks
- The first task is named "**`Hello message`**"
- Module **`ansible.builtin.debug`** (to display messages onscreen)
- The argument "**`msg`**" of module debug (the message that we would like to display)
- End of file (`...`)

We can execute the Hello World Ansible playbook using the following **`ansible-playbook`** command:

```
ansible-playbook -i inventory helloworld.yml
```

Here:

- **ansible-playbook** is the command line utility included in every Ansible installation.
- The **-i** parameter specifies which inventory file to use. In this case, the **inventory** file is in the current directory. Let us assume that the **inventory** file consists of the **server01.example.com** target host.
- The **helloworld.yml** parameter is the name of the Ansible playbooks file.

The command produces the following output:

```
PLAY [Hello World sample] ***********************************************
************************

TASK [Gathering Facts] **************************************************
************************

ok: [server01.example.com]

TASK [Hello message] ****************************************************
************************

ok: [server01.example.com] => {

    "msg": "Hello World!"

}

PLAY RECAP **************************************************************
****************

server01.example.com: ok=2    changed=0    unreachable=0    failed=0
skipped=0    rescued=0    ignored=0
```

Each line of the output highlights a step of the execution.

In the output of the execution of the **helloworld.yml** via the command **ansible-playbook**. The first parameter is the inventory file, and the second is the playbook.

The play executes against the target host **server01.example.com** node. The output is self-explanatory in the step-by-step implementation.

When the command is successful, the outcome highlights in green color. The orange color is an indicator of a warning message, and the red color for an error. We can customize the colors using **ansible.cfg** file, more details in *Chapter 3, Ansible Language Extended,* section *Ansible Configuration Settings.*

Let us go line by line.

- In the beginning, the Play name is prefixed by the PLAY text. It simply means that the following tasks are related to the "Hello World sample" Play for easy debugging of the code. The following line in the output is the first TASK called **`Gathering Facts`** which means acquiring some system information (facts in Ansible jargon) from the remote hosts.

- The result of the operation is an "**`ok`**" status followed by the target node name, **`server01.example.com`**, in this case. The green color confirms that the operation was successful.
- The second task is one that we defined in the code, displaying the "**`Hello World!`**" message on the screen. We usually see the "**`ok`**" status and the **`localhost`** target node.
- The last line is a **`PLAY RECAP`** table that summarizes the target host(s), and the task reported status. In this case, only two "**`ok`**" statuses against **`server01.example.com`**. Please notice that more statuses are possible.

**Tip: The most attentive we have noticed is an extra task called Gathering Facts, which Ansible performs to acquire information about the target node. It will be beneficial. The entire performance includes two tasks.**

# Check

The check option enables us to execute read-only operations on the target host. Not all modules supports the check module.

Using the **`-check`** option allows us to perform a read-only operation on the target node:

```
ansible-playbook --check helloworld.yml
```

Using the **`helloworld.yml`** Ansible playbook, we obtain the same result. Still, with modules that alter the status of the target node, the result is the usage in a read-only way. As usual, we can execute the command in our terminal widget as follows:

```
---
- name: Hello World sample
  hosts: all
  tasks:
    - name: Hello message
      ansible.builtin.debug:
          msg: "Hello World!"
...
```

An advantageous option is using **`-check`** for the **`ansible-playbook`** command. This option is used to perform a dry run on the playbook execution. Ansible report changes would have occurred if the playbook were executed but did not make any actual changes to managed hosts.

# Debug

The Ansible debug module allows us to print text on the screen during the execution. While this practice is extremely useful in the development phase, it is annoying during production. Some developers used to delete any debug messages before moving to production, but they lost the opportunity to dive deep into the code in the future. A better approach is to keep all the particular debug messages in place and specify the "verbosity" parameter to show only when the execution is performed in verbose mode. We can set four verbosity levels, from zero to three, as shown in *Table 2.1:*

| Levels | ansible-playbook parameter |
|---|---|
| 0 | no parameter |
| 1 | `-v` |
| 2 | `-vv` |
| 3 | `-vvv` |
| 4 | `-vvvv` |

***Table 2.1:** Ansible verbosity levels*

For example, let us set the verbosity to two in the following playbook:

```
---
- name: Hello World sample
  hosts: all
  tasks:
    - name: Hello message
      ansible.builtin.debug:
        msg: "Hello World!"
        verbosity: 2
...
```

Let us analyze the line by line the Ansible code.

1. The beginning of the YAML document (`---`)
2. Name of the Play
3. Target hosts of the execution

4. List of tasks
5. One task is named **Hello message**
6. Ansible module **debug** in the **ansible.builtin** collection
7. Argument **msg** of module **debug**
8. Argument **verbosity** is **2**.

Specifying the **verbosity** parameter, we can keep the debug code in our playbook and enable the execution only when needed.

When we execute the Ansible playbook without specifying any verbosity level, it is assumed that the verbosity level zero:

```
ansible-playbook helloworld_debug.yml
```

The expected execution result using the verbosity level zero is a skipping state on the debug message, with a verbosity higher than that. This is the expected output in this execution:

```
PLAY [Hello World sample] ***********************************************
*******************************

TASK [Gathering Facts] **************************************************
****************************

ok: [server01.example.com]
TASK [Hello message] ****************************************************
**************************

skipping: [server01.example.com]
PLAY RECAP **************************************************************
****************

server01.example.com: ok=1    changed=0    unreachable=0    failed=0
skipped=1    rescued=0    ignored=0
```

The output of **helloworld_debug.yml** reports that the execution of the "**Hello message**" is skipped with verbosity level zero, which means that it is not in debug mode. We can try the execution using the Playbook code as follows:

```
---
- name: Hello World sample
  hosts: all
  tasks:
    - name: Hello message
      ansible.builtin.debug:
```

```
        msg: "Hello World!"
        verbosity: 2
...
```

The only way to display the debug message is to execute the code specifying a higher verbosity level (in this scenario, level two). We can execute the playbook by adding the **-vv** parameter to the usual **ansible-playbook** command. Please notice the two **v** that enable verbosity level two execution:

```
ansible-playbook -vvhelloworld_debug.yml
```

The output of **helloworld_debug.yml**, when executed with verbosity level two mode, now shows onscreen the **Hello message** and much more information about the execution.

```
[...]
PLAYBOOK: helloworld_debug.yml*****************************************
***********************************

1 plays in helloworld_debug.yml
PLAY [Hello World sample] **********************************************
*******************************

TASK [Gathering Facts] *************************************************
****************************

task path: /test/helloworld_debug.yml:2
ok: [server01.example.com]
META: ran handlers
TASK [Hello message] ***************************************************
**************************

task path: /test/helloworld_debug.yml:5
ok: [server01.example.com] => {
    "msg": "Hello World!"
}
META: ran handlers
META: ran handlers
PLAY RECAP *************************************************************
****************

server01.example.com: ok=2    changed=0    unreachable=0    failed=0
skipped=0    rescued=0    ignored=0
```

# Multiple play

Let us consider a scenario of Linux servers with Nginx on frontend machines and PostgreSQL on the backend, as shown in *Figure 2.4*:

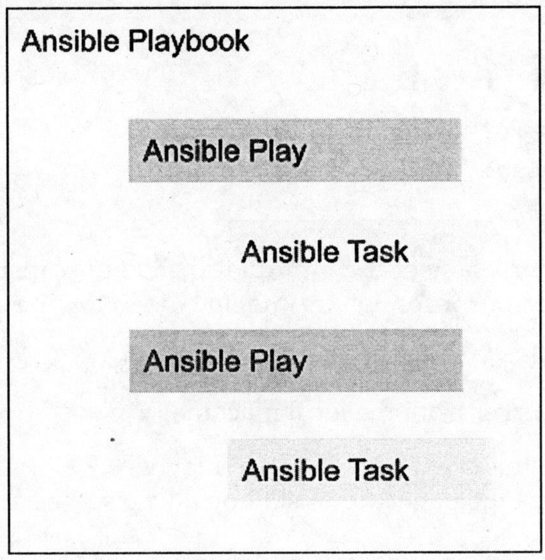


***Figure 2.4:*** *Ansible playbook and Play Schema*

We can change the name of the service on the frontend machines as well as the type of database for the backend. The Ansible playbook needs to take care of the following steps:

1. Install the Nginx webserver in the frontend machines.
2. Install the PostgreSQL database in the backend machines.

We can specify only one target node for every list of tasks (Ansible Play). We have two options: write two different Playbooks (one for the frontend target hosts and one for the backend target hosts) or write one Playbook with two Play inside of it. Let us highlight that we could specify multiple Ansible Play in an Ansible playbook.

```
---
- name: webserver
  hosts: web
  become: true
  tasks:
  - name: Nginx installed
    ansible.builtin.apt:
      name: nginx
```

```
      state: present
- name: db
  hosts: db
  become: true
  tasks:
  - name: PostgreSQL installed
    ansible.builtin.apt:
      name: postgresql
      state: present
```

As we can see, another usage of the multiple Ansible play inside the same Ansible playbook is for testing purposes. Let us imagine the following scenario:

1. Install the web server on the frontend machine.
2. Test the webserver from the local machine.

We could implement this scenario in a single Playbook using two Ansible Play. For example, we could test the page after installing a web server on a target machine.

```
---
- name: webserver
  hosts: web
  become: true
  tasks:
  - name: Nginx installed
    ansible.builtin.apt:
      name: nginx
      state: present
- name: test page
  hosts: web1.example.com
  tasks:
  - name: Test page
    ansible.builtin.uri:
      url: http://server01.example.com
```

# Includes

It is possible to speed up the code development by taking advantage of the code reuse within our team or from other creators. We can execute within our team using the inclusion or import of single tasks, handlers, and playbooks or using third-party code via Ansible roles and Ansible collections. We will discuss more about this in *Chapter 3, Ansible Language Extended* in the *Code Reuse* section.

# Ansible variables

Storing and retrieving data into variables is a crucial task in every computer programming language. It enables us to perform data modification or access some content. In Ansible, this task is very important because the data contains our datacenter information. We can store the data in all the Python data structures: string, integer, boolean, lists, dictionaries, and so on. All these data types enable great flexibility and the ability to perform complex data operations in a blink of an eye.

Inside the variables, we can store the list of user accounts of our systems, the information about the operating systems, the usage of the machine resources, and so much more.

Ansible variables store dynamic values for a given environment.

In our Playbook, it is an excellent practice to use variables to store all the dynamic values we need. By editing variables, we could reuse our code in the future, only parameterizing accordingly to our business needs.

# Unpermitted variable names

Variables names are permitted, but remember that a good habit is always to use meaningful names. The following *Table 2.2* summarizes the invalid variable names for the Ansible variables:

| Unpermitted | Example |
|---|---|
| No white spaces between the name | `variable name` |
| No dots between the name | `variable.name` |
| Does not start with the number | `3rdvariable` |
| Do not contain special character | `variable$1` |

***Table 2.2:*** *Unpermitted Variable Names*

Ansible allows all the combinations of letters and numbers in variable names. If we plan to use numbers, be aware that we cannot use them initially, like in other programming languages. The four main limitations in variable names are: no white spaces are allowed, no dots, do not start with numbers, and do not contain special characters. In the right column, we see some examples of invalid variable names.

In the following sections, we are going to explore:

- User-defined variables
- Extra variables
- Host and group variables
- Array variables
- Registered variables

# User-defined variables

The user-defined variables are the most popular and are similar to those in many programming languages. The variables could have the data types summarized in *Table 2.3*. The declaration is performed using the **vars** statement followed by the list of each variable and value. Core variable types are the ones permitted by Python, such as, string, number, boolean, list, dictionary, and so on. We can easily retrieve the variable value in any part of our Ansible playbook specifying the **name** between double brackets, like this: **{{ name }}**. Please refer to the following table:

| Type | Example |
|---|---|
| string | `message: "Hi!"`<br>`memory: 2Gb` |
| numeric integer | `cpus: 2` |
| numeric float | `bandwidth: 123.45` |
| boolean (true/false or yes/no) | `verify_ssl: true`<br>`connected: no` |

***Table 2.3:*** *Scalar Data Types*

The following example declares a variable **operatingsystem**, assigns the value **Linux**, and prints onscreen using Ansible debug module:

```
---
- name: Variable print sample
  hosts: all
  vars:
```

```
    operatingsystem: "Linux"
  tasks:
    - name: Print variable
      ansible.builtin.debug:
        msg: "Print the value of variable {{ operatingsystem }}"
```

The **variableprint.yml** file has:

1. YAML beginning **---**
2. Name of the play
3. Target hosts (**all**)
4. List of the user-defined variables **vars**
5. The **operatingsystem** is the variable name
6. List of tasks
7. One task is named "**Print variable**"
8. Ansible module **debug** of the **ansible.builtin** collection
9. The argument **msg** of the module **debug** with printing the value of **operatingsystem**

The **variableprint.yml** playbook is similar to the **helloworld.yml** playbook. The syntax and the structure of the element are very similar except for the presence of the variable **operatingsystem**. Variables store information such as strings, numbers, and more complex data structures like lists, dictionaries, and so on. In this case, the variable has the name **operatingsystem** and the value **Linux**. In this case, the **debug** module will concatenate the text **Print the value of the variable** with the value of the variable **operatingsystem**. Please note the double bracket that means the importance of the variable. It is a best practice always to include the double brackets within the double quote in the code.

The previous code produces the following message on the screen:

```
msg: "Print the value of the variable Linux."
```

We can execute the Ansible playbook using the **ansible-playbook** command included in every Ansible installation. The full command is as the following:

```
ansible-playbook variableprint.yml
```

The output of the command is as follows:

```
PLAY [Variable print sample] *****************************************
************************
```

```
TASK [Gathering Facts] ************************************************
************************

ok: [server01.example.com]

TASK [Print variable] *************************************************
************************

ok: [server01.example.com] => {
    "msg": "Print the value of variable Linux"
}

PLAY RECAP ************************************************************
****************

server01.example.com: ok=2    changed=0    unreachable=0    failed=0
skipped=0    rescued=0    ignored=0
```

The output of the "**variableprint.yml**" execution is very similar to that of the "**helloworld.yml**" file. Please note that the print of the message "**Print the value of variable Linux"** is obtained by combining the string with the variable's value. Moreover, this execution is thriving, as seen in the play recap area and the green color. The total execution amount to two tasks.

# Multiline

Many scenarios require us to break a string over multiple lines: for better code readability and compliance with columns number, multiline strings, and so on.

To break a string over multiple lines in Ansible, we can use the following operators:

- **Literal Block Scalar (|):** This operator tells Ansible to treat the string as a literal block scalar. This means that Ansible will preserve the newlines in the string. For example, the following code will create a variable called **my_variable** that contains the following string:

  ```
  my_variable = |

  This is a

  multiline string
  ```

- **Folded Block Scalar (>):** This operator tells Ansible to treat the string as a folded block scalar. This means that Ansible will collapse all the newlines in the string into a single space. For example, the following code will create a variable called **my_variable** that contains the following string:

  ```
  my_variable = >

  This is a

  multiline string
  ```

The main difference between the literal block scalar and the folded block scalar operators is that the literal block scalar operator will preserve the newlines in the string, while the folded block scalar operator will collapse all the newlines in the string into a single space.

Both operators support the adding of the "-", a minus to remove any newline at the end of the strings. The two operators with new line removal become:

- "|-": Literal block scalar without a new line.
- ">-": Folded block scalar without a new line.

# Extra variables

The extra variable is a way to pass the value from the command line. It is advantageous when we are trying to integrate Ansible into our current tool chain or simply would like to parameterize our playbook from the command line. Let us execute the same code as the previous example, but we would like to change the value of the variable **operatingsystem** from **Linux** to **Windows** without changing the code. We simply specify the **-e** parameter of the command line **ansible-playbook**, followed by the variable name and value. In this case, **-e operatingsystem=Windows** allows us to specify the variable's value from the command line.

The full command is as the following:

```
ansible-playbook -e "operatingsystem=Windows"variableprint.yml
```

The output of the command is the following:

```
PLAY [Variable print sample] *******************************************
*********

TASK [Gathering Facts] *************************************************
*********

ok: [host1.example.com]

TASK [Print variable] **************************************************
*********

ok: [host1.example.com] => {
    "msg": "Print the value of variable Windows"
}

PLAY RECAP *************************************************************
*********

host1.example.com    : ok=2    changed=0    unreachable=0    failed=0
skipped=0    rescued=0    ignored=0
```

We can override the playbook variables to specify the value from the command line. Variables set on the command line are called extra variables. The output of the execution of the **`variableprint.yml`** is very similar to the previous one. Please note the print of the message "**`Print the value of variable Windows`**" obtained by combining the string with the variable's value. The value passed from the command line overrides any playbook value.

# Host and group variables

We can also define some variables in the inventory file. Variables defined at the host level are called host variables. Likewise, variables defined at the group level are called group variables.

We are going to see examples of:

- host variable in INI inventory
- group variable in INI inventory
- host variable in the file system
- group variable in the file system

## Host variable in the INI inventory

Specifying the login used to the server assigning the value **`ansible_user`** followed by the username in a host variable is valid.

This is an example inventory of having the login user **`devops`** for the server **`host1.example.com`**. In this way, we could specify a different user for each target host.

## Host variables

A host variable sets the value for a single host in the Ansible inventory. Let us define the variable **`ansible_user`** to **`devops`** for a single host.

```
[servers]

host1.example.com ansible_user=devops
```

## Host variable in the file system

We can obtain the same Ansible inventory by separating the inventory file from the variable file.

We need to create an inventory file that looks like the following file:

```
[servers]
host1.example.com
```

Then, a host variable file with the exact name of the host is under the **host_vars** directory. The file **host_vars/host1.example.com** contains the variables for the host **host1.example.com**.

```
ansible_user=devops
```

## Group variables

A group variable sets the value for a group of hosts in the Ansible Inventory. We could specify a group variable that sets the **ansible_user** variable to **foo** for all target hosts in the **servers** group:

```
[servers]
host1.example.com
host2.example.com
[servers:vars]
ansible_user=foo
```

The group variable is applied to **host1.example.com** and **host2.example.com** with the same **foo** value.

## Group variable in the file system

Similarly, we could apply group variables to the inventory group via the file system. Let us suppose we have an inventory with a **servers** group inside like this:

```
[servers]
host1.example.com
host2.example.com
```

The group variable file with the group's exact name is the **group_vars** directory. The file **group_vars/servers** contains the variables for the group **servers**.

```
ansible_user=foo
```

We can achieve the same result using directories to populate host and group variables. As we can see, the result will be the same as the previous host and group inventory, but using more files.

## Array variables

Array variables are instrumental when we want to specify some properties that apply to objects. Let us suppose we have users containing **foo** and **bar**. Each of them has its own **username** and **homedir** variables.

The Ansible playbook begins like this the following code. Please notice the **users** array variable structure under the **vars** statement:

```
---
- name: Array sample
  hosts: all
  vars:
    users:
      foo:
        username: foo
        homedir: /users/foo
      bar:
        username: bar
        homedir: /users/bar
  tasks:
    - name: print foo's username
      ansible.builtin.debug:
        var: users.foo.username
```

Like in Python programming language, we can access each property using dot (`.`) or bracket notation ([]).

- dot notation

  The code "`users.foo.username`" print the value of **foo**

- bracket notation

  The code "`users['foo']['username']`" print the value of **foo**

We could organize the information in a hierarchical data structure. A handy data structure in this case, is the Array. For example, the list of users is easily readable by **foo** and **bar**. Each list element has two properties: **first name** and **home dir**. We could access the data with dot notation or square brackets. In both cases, we obtain the same result as we collide.

The full command to execute the **array.yml** file is as the following:

```
ansible-playbook array.yml
```

The output of the command is the following:

```
PLAY [Array sample] ****************************************************
************************

TASK [Gathering Facts] *************************************************
```

```
************************
ok: [server01.example.com]
TASK [print foo's username] ********************************************
********************
ok: [server01.example.com] => {
    "users.foo.username": "foo"
}
PLAY RECAP ***********************************************************
****************
server01.example.com: ok=2    changed=0    unreachable=0    failed=0
skipped=0    rescued=0    ignored=0
```

The output of the execution of the **array.yml** is very similar to the previous one. Ansible accessed the variable array value, as shown in the output, as expected. We could notice the production of "**Print foo's first name: foo.**"

# Registered variables

Another functional data structure is registered variables. We could save the output of any commands inside registered variables. In this example, print the result on the screen.

```
---
- name: Install a package and prints the result
  hosts: all
  become: true
  tasks:
    - name: Install the package
      ansible.builtin.yum:
        name: wget
        state: installed
      register: install_result
    - name: debug
      ansible.builtin.debug:
        var: install_result
```

At first, the **yum** module verifies the presence of the package; if missing, proceed with the installation. The output of the setup process is stored inside a registered variable that prints on the screen. The result of the execution of the **registeredvariables.yml** shows some tasks executed.

The full command is as the following:

```
ansible-playbook registeredvariables.yml
```

The output of the command is the following:

```
PLAY [Installs a package and prints the result] ************************
************************

TASK [Gathering Facts] *************************************************
************************

ok: [server01.example.com]
TASK [Install the package] *********************************************
************************

ok: [server01.example.com]
TASK [debug] ***********************************************************
******************

ok: [server01.example.com] => {
    "install_result": {
        "cache_update_time": 1660746334,
        "cache_updated": false,
        "changed": false,
        "failed": false
    }
}
PLAY RECAP *************************************************************
****************

server01.example.com: ok=3    changed=0    unreachable=0    failed=0
skipped=0    rescued=0    ignored=0
```

See the further section *Temporary Facts* in the *Ansible Facts* section, to create a new variable manipulating the output of a command.

## Writing a variable to a file

There are two main ways to write a variable to a file in Ansible:

- Use the Ansible copy module
- Use the Ansible template module

The Ansible copy module is a simple way to write a variable to a file. To use it, we specify the name of the variable, the path of the destination file, and the content of the file. For example:

```
- name: Write variable to a file
  ansible.builtin.copy:
    path: ./myfile.txt
    content: "{{ operatingsystem }}"
    state: present
```

This will create a file called **myfile.txt** that contains the value of the **operatingsystem** variable.

The Ansible template module is a more flexible way to write a variable to a file. It allows us to use Jinja2 templates to generate the contents of the file. For example:

```
---
- name: Array sample
  hosts: all
  vars:
      operatingsystem: Linux
  tasks:
  - name: Write variable to a file
    Ansible.builtin.template:
      src: mytemplate.j2
      dest: myfile.txt
```

The **mytemplate.j2** file looks like the following:

```
{{ operatingsystem }}
```

This will create a file called **myfile.txt** that contains the following text:

```
Linux
```

The main advantage of using the Ansible template module is that it allows us to use Jinja2 templates to generate the contents of the file. This can be useful if we need to create files that contain complex or dynamic content.

On the other hand, the main disadvantage of using the Ansible template module is that it can be more difficult to use, than the Ansible copy module. If we are not familiar with Jinja2 templates, we may find it difficult to write a template that produces the desired output.

In general, the Ansible copy module is a good option if we need to create a simple file that contains a static value. The Ansible template module is a good option if we need to create a file that contains complex or dynamic content.

# Ansible facts

Ansible facts are variables related to remote hosts. Variables related to remote systems are called facts. They are powerful because we can obtain a comprehensive vision of the current host, the operating system, the distribution used, the IP address, the networking configuration, the storage configuration, and so on. With facts, we can use the behavior or state of one system as a configuration on other systems.

# Ansible ad-hoc

The best way to understand Ansible facts is to list them ourselves using this simple Ansible ad-hoc command.

```
ansible -m setup host1.example.com
```

Adapt the command to the target host; obviously, **host1.example.com** is just for our laboratory.

Facts are handy, because they contain the following information about hardware and software and some target host specified by the operating system.

The most used is the current hardware configuration: architecture, processor, RAM, available memory, storage configuration, operating system, Linux distribution used, IP address, networking configuration, storage configuration, and so on.

It is only the beginning of the long list obtained using the previous command. The **ansible** command produces the following output:

```
[...]
        "ansible_architecture": "arm64",
        "ansible_date_time": {
            "date": "2023-04-05",
            "day": "05",
            "epoch": "1680726722",
            "epoch_int": "1680726722",
            "hour": "22",
            "iso8601": "2023-04-05T20:32:02Z",
            "iso8601_basic": "20230405T223202059078",
            "iso8601_basic_short": "20230405T223202",
"iso8601_micro": "2023-04-05T20:32:02.059078Z",
            "minute": "32",
"month": "04",
```

```
            "second": "02",
            "time": "22:32:02",
            "tz": "CEST",
            "tz_dst": "CEST",
            "tz_offset": "+0200",
            "weekday": "Wednesday",
            "weekday_number": "3",
            "weeknumber": "14",
            "year": "2023"
        },
        "ansible_default_ipv4": {
            "address": "192.168.58.46",
            "broadcast": "192.168.58.255",
            "device": "en0",
[...]
```

Just note down the name of the Ansible fact we are interested in, because we will use it in our Ansible playbook.

## Facts in playbook

We could access the same amount of data from the Ansible playbook. In this simple example, we will list all the Ansible facts for all the inventory hosts. The expected result will be the same as the previous ad-hoc execution.

Please note that requires **gather_facts** enabled. The statement **gather_facts** is necessary to acquire Ansible facts from target machines and use them inside Ansible playbook.

**Pro tip: Disable gather_facts to speed up Ansible execution when not needed.**

```
---
- name: facts_printall
  hosts: all
  gather_facts: true
  tasks:
  - name: Print all facts
    ansible.builtin.debug:
      var: ansible_facts
```

The execution results in printing the content of the variable **ansible_facts** list and values on the screen. For example, a small portion shows the variable **architecture** with the value **x86_64**, as shown:

```
    "ansible_facts": {
        "architecture": "x86_64",
[...]
```

The output of the execution of the **facts_printall.yml** shows the contents of the **localhost** node as the target host. The result is very long, with all the facts re-obtained automatically by Ansible in the task **Gathering Facts**.

# Single fact

We could easily interact with facts specifying the exact fact name. Customize the code to the ansible facts that better fit our needs. In this example, we are listing the managed nodes' architecture. The **facts_printone.yml** file looks like the following:

```
---
- name: facts_printone
  hosts: all
  gather_facts: true
  tasks:
  - name: Print a fact
    ansible.builtin.debug:
      msg: "architecture: {{ ansible_facts['architecture'] }}"
```

We can execute the **facts_printone.yml** Playbook file using the **ansible-playbook** command included in every Ansible installation. The full command with the inventory is like the following:

```
ansible-playbook facts_printone.yml
```

The execution of the previous command is as follows:

```
TASK [Print a fact] *******************************************************
************************
ok: [server01.example.com] => {
    "msg": "architecture: x86_64"
}
PLAY RECAP ****************************************************************
server01.example.com: ok=2    changed=0    unreachable=0    failed=0
skipped=0    rescued=0    ignored=0
```

# Temporary facts

We can define some temporary facts using the **ansible.builtin.set_fact** module.

The **set_fact** module in **ansible.builtin** is used to add new Ansible facts. It is primarily useful to transform data from registered outputs and existing facts into a new structure. The created facts are available for all subsequent tasks.

The following **facts_temporary.yml** Ansible playbook creates a temporary fact when the **ansible_distribution** fact has value **Red Hat Enterprise Linux**. Basically, we are overwriting the **ansible_distribution** fact with the value **'rhel'** when the condition is verified:

```
---
- name: Temporary Facts
  hosts: all
  tasks:
    - name: Set mydistribution
      ansible.builtin.set_fact:
          mydistribution: >-
            "{{ 'rhel' if (ansible_distribution == 'Red Hat Enterprise
Linux')
            else ansible_distribution }}"
    - name: Print mydistribution
      ansible.builtin.debug:
        var: mydistribution
```

We can learn more about the **if** statement in the *Ansible Conditional* section. The usage of the folded block scalar operator (**>-**) was introduced in the *Multiline* section under the *Ansible Variables* section.

As usual, we can execute the **facts_temporary.yml** Playbook file using the **ansible-playbook** command using the full command:

```
ansible-playbook facts_temporary.yml
```

The execution on a MacOS operating system produces the following output:

```
TASK [Print mydistribution] ******************************************
*********************************
ok: [server01.example.com] => {
    "mydistribution": "\"MacOSX\""
}
```

Whereas the execution on a Red Hat Enterprise Linux operating system produces:

```
TASK [Print mydistribution] *********************************************
*********************************

ok: [server01.example.com] => {
    "mydistribution": "\"rhel\""
}
```

# Custom facts

In addition to the default facts created by the **setup** module (part of **ansible.builtin**) and temporary facts created by the **set_fact** module, Ansible also supports creating custom facts.

We can define custom facts on the target machine in a directory called **/etc/ansible/facts.d**. All fact files have a **.fact** extension. If the fact file is executable, Ansible will run it. Otherwise, Ansible will try to treat it as INI or JSON format. The custom facts are loaded by the "**setup**" module (part of **ansible.builtin**).

Custom facts are placed in a separate dictionary called "**ansible_local**" organized by the filename of the custom fact: **ansible_local['fact file name']**.

Custom facts are not automatically loaded as soon as they are installed, and so we need to wait for the next play or re-run "**setup**" ourselves.

The **/etc/ansible/facts.d/infrastructure.fact** file looks like the following:

```
[system]
type=dr
```

We can access all the Ansible custom facts in our playbook with the task:

```
- name: display ansible_local
  ansible.builtin.debug:
    var: ansible_local
```

Or access any specific properties using any property in the custom fact:

```
- name: print system type
  ansible.builtin.debug:
      msg: "The system type is
{{ ansible_local.infrastructure.system.type }}"
```

The output of the code displays the "**dr**" system type on the screen.

# Ansible magic variables

The Ansible magic variables contain some information about the target hosts. Magic variables are internal variables of Ansible that come in handy sometimes.

Sometimes beginner users confuse the Ansible facts with magic variables.

The main difference is that magic variables do not require the **`gather_facts`** enabled at the beginning of the Ansible playbooks as the Ansible facts require.

## Common magic variables

These are the five most common magic variables:

- **`hostvars`**: With the **`hostvars`** (host variables) magic variable, we can access variables defined for any host in the play. It is advantageous when we would like to access one host's property from another. We could combine the host variable with Ansible facts to access the property of another host.
- **`groups`**: The **`groups`** magic variable lists all the groups in the inventory. We could use **`groups`** and the host variables' magic variables together, in order to list all the IP addresses of the hosts in a group.
- **`group_names`**: The **`group_names`** list which groups are the current hosts.
- **`inventory_hostname`**: The **`inventory_hostname`** magic variable contains the host's name configured in the inventory.
- **`ansible_version`**: The **`ansible_version`** magic variable contains version information about Ansible.

## Ansible version

The following example prints on the screen, the current Ansible version used. Underneath, it relies on the **`ansible_version`** magic variable. The **`ansible_version.yml`** file looks like the following:

```
---
- name: ansible_version print
  hosts: all
  tasks:
    - name: ansible_version display
      ansible.builtin.debug:
        var: ansible_version
```

The output of the execution is the following. As we can see, the result displays the full version **2.13.3**, major **2**, minor **13**, and revision **3**, as well as the entire string **2.13.3**.

We can execute the code using the **ansible-playbook** command included in every Ansible installation. The full command is as the following:

```
ansible-playbook ansible_version.yml
```

The output of the command is the following:

```
TASK [ansible_version display] *****************************************
**********************

ok: [server01.example.com] => {

    "ansible_version": {

        "full": "2.13.3",

        "major": 2,

        "minor": 13,

        "revision": 3,

        "string": "2.13.3"

    }

}
```

Ansible magic variables are instrumental in our Ansible playbook, especially when we need to execute some operations that impact all hosts in the inventory. We could apply the loop or other statements we will explore in the following lessons. For example, generate a custom **/etc/hosts** file for all hosts involved in the list.

# Ansible conditional

A conditional statement checks a condition and changes the program's behavior accordingly. In every computer programming language, we almost always need the ability to check conditions and change the program's behavior accordingly. Conditional statements give us this ability. The Ansible form is the **when** statement. Ansible uses Jinja2 tests and filters in conditionals. Ansible supports all the standard tests and filters and adds some unique ones.

## Basic conditionals with "when"

The **when** statement defines whether a task will be executed. We can use the **when** statement in every Ansible playbook task or block. Simply add the **when** statement with the condition.

In the real world, we can use:

- Complex expression using parenthesis `()`
- Comparison operators `==`, `>=`, `<=`, `!=`
- Use Ansible facts (**`ansible_facts['os_family'] == "Debian"`**)

In the following example, a simple Boolean variable controls the execution. Obviously, we need a **`true`** status to execute the task. The **`conditional_basic_false.yml`** file looks like the following:

```
---
- name: conditionalbasic
  hosts: all
  vars:
      configure_nginx: false
  tasks:
    - name: reload nginx
      ansible.builtin.service:
        name: nginx
        state: reloaded
      when: configure_nginx
```

The task **`reload nginx`** executes when the **`configure_nginx`** boolean variable is **`true`**.

In this example, the variable is always **`false`**, so we expect this task to skip during execution in the execution output.

We can execute the Ansible playbook using the **`ansible-playbook`** command line utility, that is included in all Ansible installations. The full command is as follows:

```
ansible-playbook conditional_basic_false.yml
```

We can specify the Ansible inventory using the parameter **`-i`** with a local file **`inventory`**. The easiest is the local Ansible inventory. The **`conditional_basic_false.yml`** is the filename of our Ansible playbook.

We expect to see an output one **`skipped`** status for the task, where the statement is **`false`** during the execution.

In the following output, we see a **`skipping`** status in the task **`reload nginx`** and **`skipped=1`** in the final **`PLAY RECAP`**:

```
PLAY [conditionalbasic] ***********************************************
***********************
```

```
TASK [Gathering Facts] *****************************************************
************************
ok: [server01.example.com]
TASK [reload nginx] ********************************************************
************************
skipping: [server01.example.com]
PLAY RECAP *****************************************************************
****************
server01.example.com: ok=1    changed=0    unreachable=0    failed=0
skipped=1    rescued=0    ignored=0
```

The play executes against the **server01.example.com** node in this execution, and the output is highlighted in green and blue colors. As we can see, the task **reload nginx** is displaying a **skipping** status because of our conditional statement.

The following example shows the **configure_nginx** variable to the **true** Boolean value. We expect the execution to execute the task **reload nginx** this time. The **conditional_basic_true.yml** file looks like this:

```
---
- name: conditionalbasic
  hosts: all
  vars:
      configure_nginx: true
  tasks:
    - name: reload nginx
      ansible.builtin.service:
        name: nginx
        state: reloaded
      when: configure_nginx
```

This is the same basic example of usage of the "when" statement in our Ansible playbook, although we changed the variable value from **false** to **true**. The **reload nginx** task executes because of the "**configure_nginx**" Boolean variable is set to **true**. We can execute our playbook using the **ansible-playbook** command:

```
ansible-playbook conditional_basic_true.yml
```

The parameter **conditional_basic_true.yml** is the Ansible playbook filename. The previous **ansible-playbook** command produces the following output:

```
TASK [reload nginx] *****************************************************
***********************

changed: [server01.example.com]
```

As we can see, the task **reload nginx** is read by Ansible and executed successfully status "**changed**" in our conditional statement. In this execution, the play runs against the "**server01.example.com**" node, and the output is highlighted in green color in every line in the ok status.

# Conditionals based on Ansible facts

It is handy to combine conditional and facts, so that we can adapt the execution of our code based on individual host conditions, IP address, operating system, the status of a file system, and many more.

In this example, we will execute the shutdown of the RedHat-like hosts as shown in the **conditional_facts.yml** file:

```
---
- name: conditional_facts
  hosts: all
  tasks:
  - name: Shut down RedHat-like systems
    ansible.builtin.command: /sbin/shutdown -t now
    when: ansible_facts['os_family'] == "RedHat"
```

We can execute our playbook using the **ansible-playbook** command:

```
ansible-playbook conditional_facts.yml
```

The parameter **conditional_facts.yml** is the Ansible playbook filename. Here is the output of the previous command:

```
TASK [Shut down RedHat-like systems] ***********************************
***********************

skipping: [server01.example.com]
```

In this execution, the play executes against the **server01.example.com** node. The target host is not a RedHat-like system because we could notice that the task named "**Shut down RedHat-like systems**" is in the **skipped** status.

For reference, the complete list of values for the Ansible fact stored in the variable **ansible_facts['os_family']** variable is **AIX**, **Alpine**, **Altlinux**, **Archlinux**,

**`Darwin`**, **`Debian`**, **`FreeBSD`**, **`Gentoo`**, **`HP-UX`**, **`Mandrake`**, **`RedHat`**, **`SGML`**, **`Slackware`**, **`Solaris`**, **`Suse`**, and **`Windows`**.

Conditionals are vital because they enable us to create Ansible playbooks that respond to some events, conditions, or Ansible facts. This statement is the foundation of the intelligent Ansible playbook.

# Ansible loop

Like in every programming language, loops are the most important part of executing tasks repeatedly. Ansible has several statements according to the interaction that we would like to achieve.

## Loop statements

Loop statements automate repetitive tasks in our Ansible playbook. Computers are better at repeating identical or similar tasks without errors than humans. The repeated execution of a set of statements is called **iteration**.

Ansible has several statements for iteration:

- **`loop`**
- **`with_items`**
- **`with_file`**
- **`with_sequence`**
- **`with_fileglob`**

We will be focusing on two of the statements only:

- **`loop`** statement
- **`with_items`** statement

The **`with_items`** statement is more versatile and could rely on external plugins.

## The loop statement

A simple loop iterates a task over a list of items. The **`loop`** statement is added to the task and takes as a value the list of items over which the task should be iterated. The **`loop_simple.yml`** file looks like the following:

```
---
- name: Check services
  hosts: all
```

```
tasks:
- name: httpd and sshd are running
  ansible.builtin.service:
    name: "{{ item }}"
    state: started
  loop:
    - apache2
    - sshd
```

Inside our module parameter, we can use the loop variable **item** that will be substituted in Ansible runtime with the current value during each iteration.

We can execute the Ansible playbook using the **ansible-playbook** command line utility included in all Ansible installations.

The complete command is as follows:

```
ansible-playbook loop_simple.yml
```

The parameter **loop_simple.yml** specifies the filename of our Ansible playbook. The execution of the command produces the following output:

```
TASK [print values of data] *******************************************
************************
ok: [server01.example.com] => (item=apache2) => {
    "msg": "apache2"
}
ok: [server01.example.com] => (item=sshd) => {
    "msg": "sshd"
}
```

The loop list should not be a list of simple values. In the following example, each item on the list is a hash or a dictionary.

Each hash or dictionary in the example has two keys, name and groups, and the value of each key in the current item loop variable can be retrieved with the **item.name** and **item.group** variables, respectively. The **loop_hash_or_dict.yml** file looks like the following:

```
---
- name: Users exist and are in the correct group
  hosts: all
  tasks:
```

```
  - name: Users exist and are in the correct group
    ansible.builtin.user:
      name: "{{ item.name }}"
      state: present
      groups: "{{ item.group }}"
    loop:
      - name: foo
        group: wheel
      - name: bar
        group: root
```

As usual, we could execute our playbook using the **ansible-playbook** command:

```
ansible-playbook loop_hash_or_dict.yml
```

With the **loop_hash_or_dict.yml** as the Ansible playbook filename, the command produces the following output:

```
TASK [Users exist and are in the correct group] ************************
***********************
changed: [server01.example.com] => (item={'name': 'foo', 'group':
'wheel'})
changed: [server01.example.com] => (item={'name': 'bar', 'group':
'root'})
PLAY RECAP *************************************************************
****************
server01.example.com: ok=2    changed=1    unreachable=0    failed=0
skipped=0    rescued=0    ignored=0
```

## Siblings of the with_items statement

The **with_items** is not the only statement available in the Ansible language. All the loop statements that begin with "**with_**" are:

- **with_items statement:** Interact with simple lists, lists of strings, or a list of hashes or dictionaries. Flatter to list if lists of lists are provided.
- **with_file statement:** This keyword requires a list of control node file names. The loop variable **item** holds the content of the file.
- **with_sequence statement:** This keyword requires parameters to generate a list of values based on a numeric sequence.

- **`with_fileglob` statement:** This statement list files matching a pattern. For example, we can specify the **`*.txt`** parameter to list all the files with the **`txt`** extension on the target node.

In the following example, we will use the **`with_items`** to loop against a list called **`data`**, containing a list of users in our system. The following example loop between the **`data`** list data type with two items: **`foo`** and **`bar`**. The **`loop_with_items.yml`** file looks like the following:

```
---
- name: Example with_items
  hosts: all
  vars:
    data:
      - foo
      - bar
  tasks:
  - name: Print values of data
    ansible.builtin.debug:
      msg: "{{ item }}"
    with_items: "{{ data }}"
```

We can execute our playbook using the **`ansible-playbook`** command:

```
ansible-playbook loop_with_items.yml
```

The parameter **`loop_with_items.yml`** specify the Ansible playbook filename. It produces the following output:

```
TASK [Print values of data] ********************************************
************************
ok: [server01.example.com] => (item=foo) => {
    "msg": "foo"
}
ok: [server01.example.com] => (item=bar) => {
    "msg": "bar"
}
```

In the **`loop_with_items.yml`** playbook, the variable **`data`** is a list of strings. The task "Print values of data" uses the **`with_items`** to iterate item by item and print on screen.

Loop statements are handy for automating repetitive tasks. Loops are the foundation of a triumphant Ansible playbook.

# Conclusion

Ansible language contains data structure and tasks to achieve a common goal. We learned how to use variables, loops, and conditional on performing any operation in our data center. The Ansible inventory is the heart of our automation, where we define the target hosts and some relevant host(s) or group(s) variables. Some tools such as Ansible facts, magic variables, and the ability to include multiple Plays in a single Playbook enable us for the most successful automation.

In the next chapter, we are going to learn the extension of the Ansible language, how to store sensitive data, use the extension plugin, and how to enable code reuse with role and collection.

# Points to remember

- Ansible inventories are in INI, YAML or JSON format and contain the list of target hosts.
- Ansible playbook combines Ansible play against target hosts with a list of tasks.
- Ansible variables enable us to parameterize and reuse the playbook in a different context.
- Ansible facts contain system information of the target host, and Ansible magic variables are useful for accessing some internal variables.

# Key terms

- **Inventory:** Inventory is usually written in INI, YAML, or JSON format and contains the list of hosts where we will target our execution. We can also add host(s) or group(s) variables to parameterize. We can print a list of graph views for a more graphical overview.
- **Playbooks:** Playbooks are written in YAML and contain a series of tasks to be executed. They can be used to automate complex processes and are a key component of Ansible's automation capabilities.
- **Facts:** Facts are variables related to remote hosts containing system information. They are populated automatically by Ansible in the `Gather Facts` task.

- **Magic variables:** Magic variables are internal Ansible variables that we can use to check the current state of the execution or access data of others hosts in the current inventory.

# Multiple choice questions

1. **What are the formats of Ansible inventories?**
    a. YAML, Python, and Java
    b. INI, YAML, and JSON
    c. INI and YAML
    d. HTML and Python
2. **What variable naming conventions are allowed in Ansible?**
    a. Does not start with the number
    b. Dots between the name
    c. Uses meaningful names
    d. Contains special character
3. **How do we define the `ansible_version` variable?**
    a. User-defined variable
    b. Host variable
    c. Ansible fact variable
    d. Ansible magic variable
4. **What is the Ansible statement for conditional?**
    a. `when`
    b. `with_items`
    c. `with_file`
    d. `loop`

## Answers

1. b
2. c
3. d
4. a

# Questions

1. What are the two ways of displaying an Ansible inventory using the `ansible-inventory` command line tool?
2. What files do we need to create to store host and group variables on the file system?
3. What are the most used parameters of the `ansible-playbook` command line tool?
4. How can we manually list all the Ansible facts?

# CHAPTER 3
# Extending Ansible's Capabilities

## Introduction

After going over the first steps in the Ansible language, we are now going to learn the extension of the Ansible language, how to store sensitive data, use the extension plugin, and enable code reuse with role and collection. All these tools are extremely useful when we would like to share code within our team in the IT department of the organization.

## Structure

In this chapter, we shall cover the following topics:

- Ansible vault
- Ansible handler
- Code reuse
- Ansible role
- Ansible collection
- Ansible filters
- Ansible template
- Ansible plugin

# Objectives

By the end of this chapter, the reader will know / be able to understand the advanced concepts of the Ansible language and take advantage of the code reuse for our project.

# Ansible vault

Ansible vault encrypts variables and files to protect sensitive content and lets us use them with Ansible. Ansible vault stores variables and encrypted files and lets us use them in playbooks or roles. The AES 256 cipher protects files with strong encryption in the latest versions of Ansible. We can manage the Ansible vault using the **`ansible-vault`** command in the terminal included in all the Ansible installations.

## Creating an encrypted file

To create a new encrypted file, use the `create` parameter of the **`ansible-vault`** command. The command prompts the new vault password and opens an empty file using the default editor. The command to create our Ansible vault:

```
ansible-vault create secret.yml
```

The preceding command will create the **`secret.yml`** file. The command does not show any output when we enter the password on the terminal (not even some * symbol).

We need to enter our password twice in the terminal manually:

```
New Vault password:
Confirm New Vault password:
```

The **`ansible-vault`** command opens the default text editor in the terminal, which is most commonly the VIM editor, as shown in *Figure 3.1*:

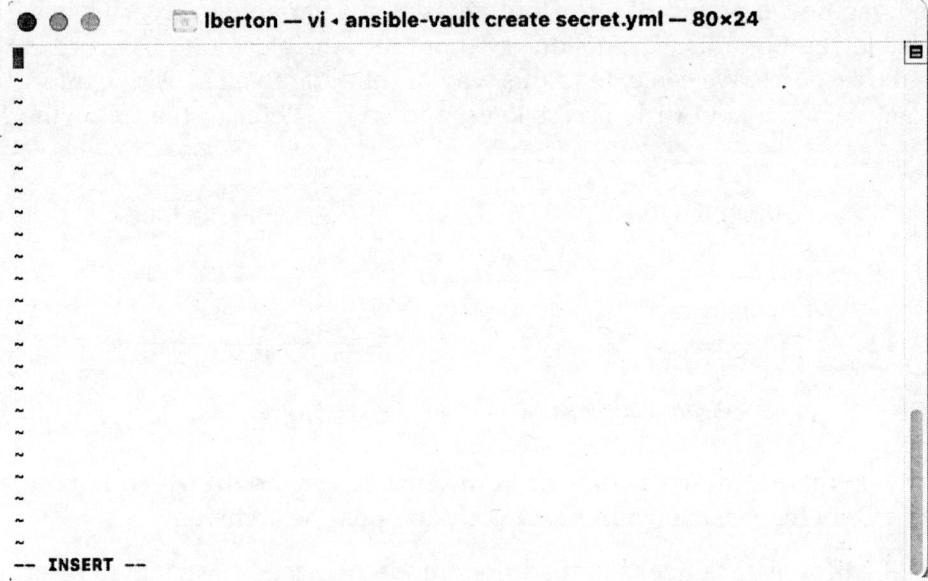


***Figure 3.1:*** *Creation of the secret.yml vault in the VI editor*

The Ansible vault is a YAML document, and so it always begins with `---`. Let us suppose we would like to insert a single variable, password, in the encrypted file with the value **`mypassword`** as shown in the **`secret.yml`** file in *Figure 3.2*:

```
---

password: mypassword
```

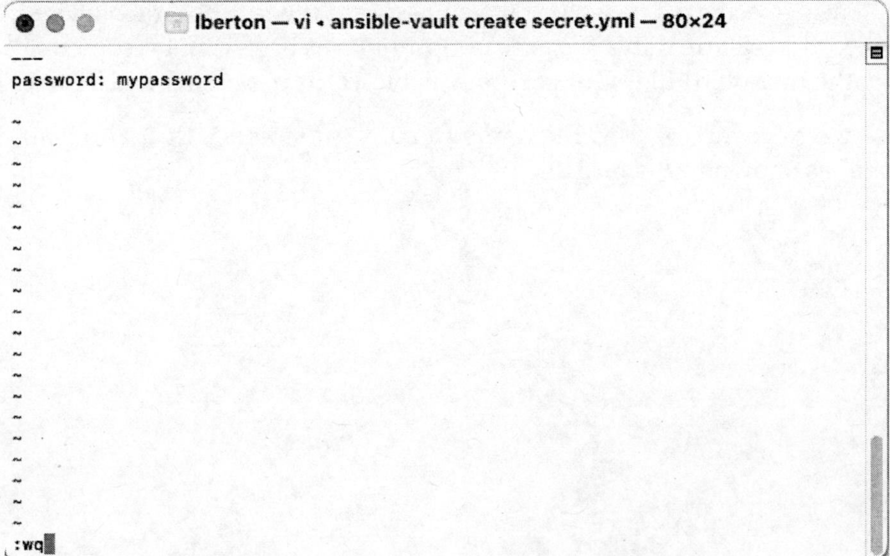


***Figure 3.2:*** *Content of the secret.yml file in the VI editor*

Let us imagine we would like to store a password variable in a secure way using the Ansible vault. In this way, nobody without the Ansible vault password is able to access the resource. We can extend this way of thinking to all sensitive information. For example, secrets, OAuth, access keys, and so on. Refer to the following *Figure 3.3:*

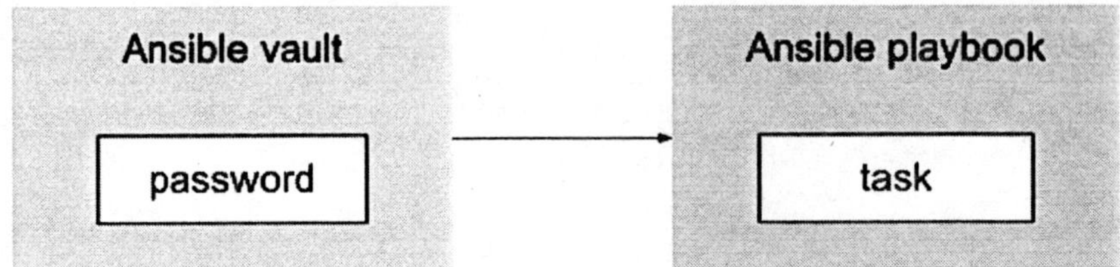


***Figure 3.3:*** *The password is stored in the Ansible vault*

We can use the **`password`** variable in our Ansible playbook, which is now stored securely. Only the Ansible vault password can open the archive.

The VIM editor always opens in read-only mode. We need to switch to insert mode by pressing the key "*I*" on the keyboard. The text "**`-- INSERT --`**" on the screen confirms the insert mode is enabled.

The last step is to actually save the file and exit from the VIM editor by typing the combination "**`:wq`**" after the "**`ESC`**" key. Once the file is saved, Ansible proceeds to the encryption of the file and saves only the encrypted version of it on disk.

# Encrypting using a password file

We could also specify the password via a password file for the Ansible vault. Storing the password in cleartext in a file is a suboptimal solution. What if someone can gain access to the password file? Our secure Ansible vault password will be in danger.

Suppose we have a password file named **`vault-password.txt`** with a simple text "**`example`**" as shown in *Figure 3.4*:

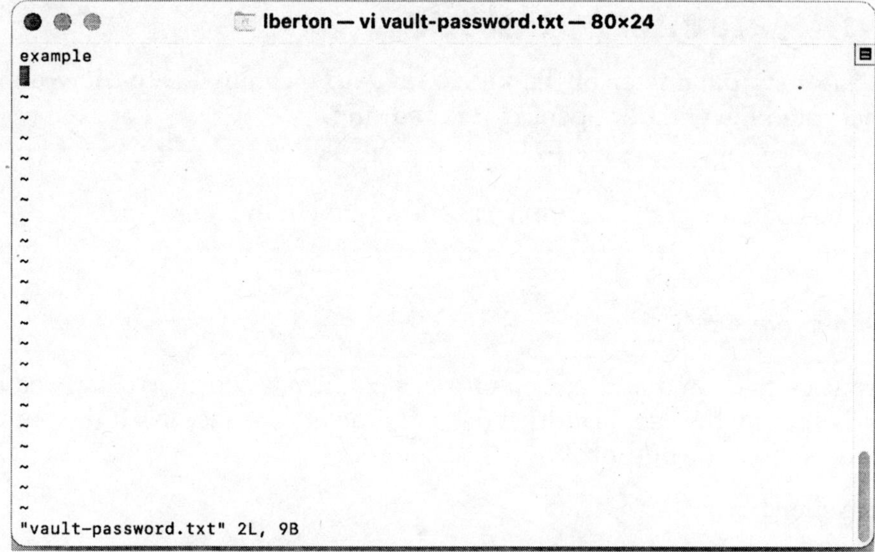


***Figure 3.4:*** *Content of the vault-password.txt file in the VI editor*

We can create the **`vault-password.txt`** file by simply writing the password in a text file and saving it as **`vault-password.txt`**. Now, the **`ansible-vault`** command will use the create parameter combined with the **`--vault-password-file`** parameter, which will be followed by the name of the password file, as shown in *Figure 3.5*.

```
ansible-vault create --vault-password-file=vault-password.txt secret.yml
```

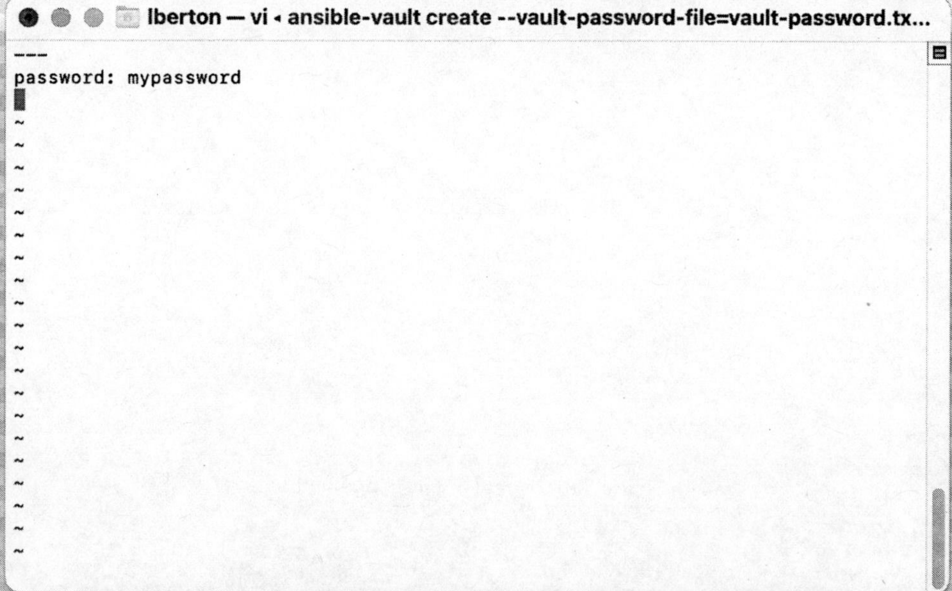


***Figure 3.5:*** *Content of the secret.yml file in the VI editor*

# Viewing an encrypted file

We use the view parameter of the **ansible-vault** command to view an Ansible vault-encrypted file without opening it for editing.

```
ansible-vault view secret.yml
```

Here are the contents of the **secret.yml** file as shown in *Figure 3.5*:

```
---

password: mypassword
```

The output of the command asks us for the Vault password. We can see that the password input by the user is hidden (no * characters are shown). If the password is correct, we can see the output shown in *Figure 3.6*:

```
Vault password:

---

password: mypassword
```

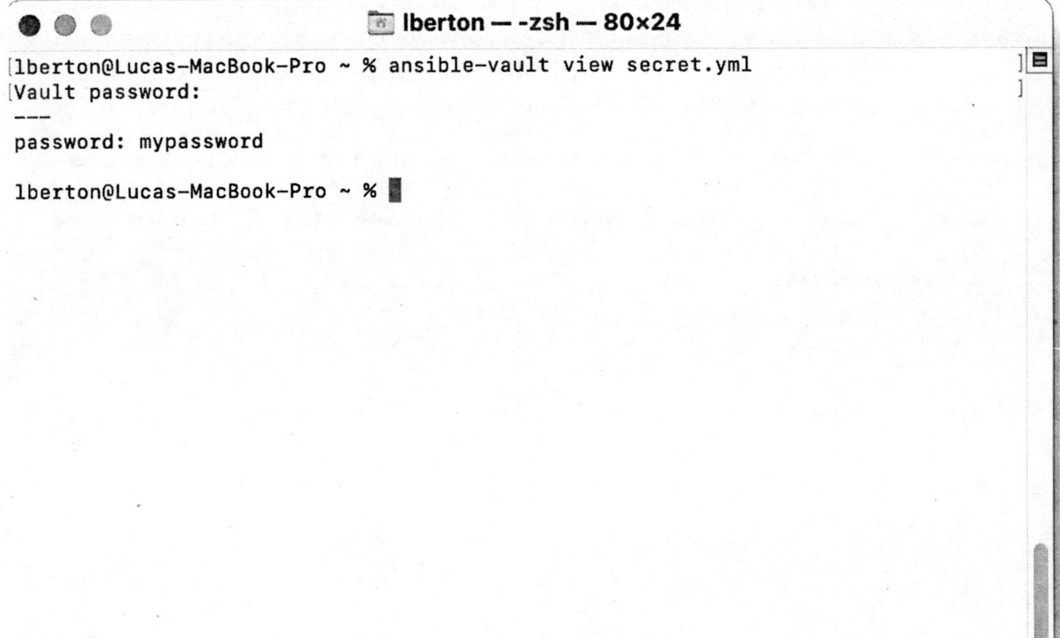


*Figure 3.6: Content of the secret.yml file*

# Editing an encrypted file

We use the edit parameter of the **ansible-vault** command to edit an existing encrypted Ansible vault file. This command decrypts the file to a temporary file and allows us to edit it. When saved, it copies the content to the original file and removes the temporary file. Merge the following sentences in a single paragraph:

```
ansible-vault edit secret.yml
```

The output of the command is displayed in *Figure 3.7*:

```
Vault password:
```

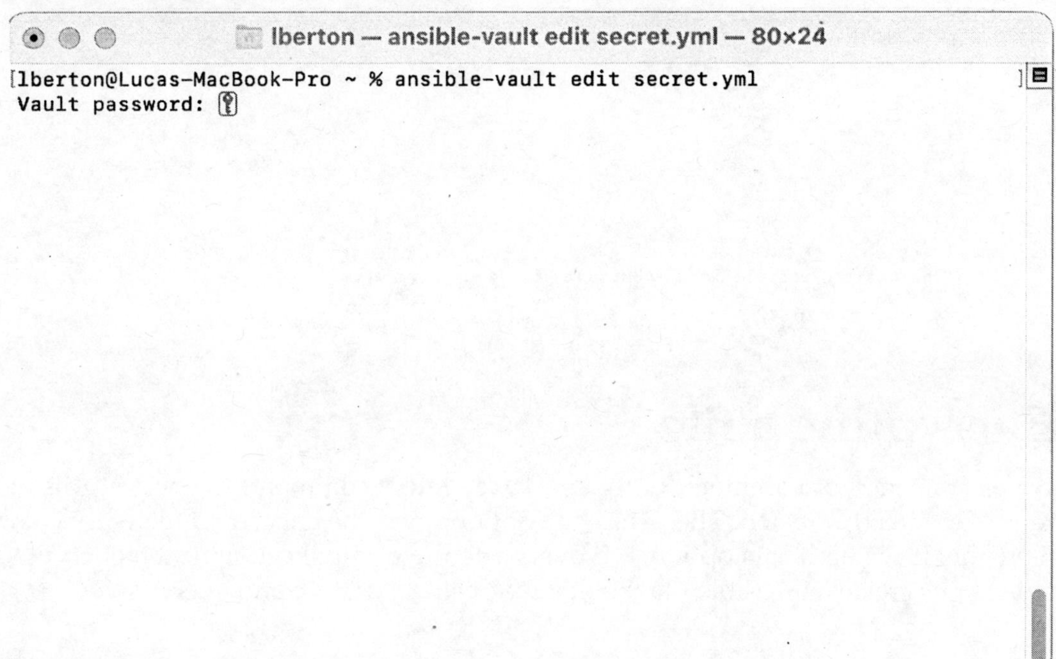


***Figure 3.7:*** *The output of the ansible-vault edit command*

The password of the **secret.yml** encrypted file is the word "**example**" defined in the previous section, as shown in *Figure 3.8*:

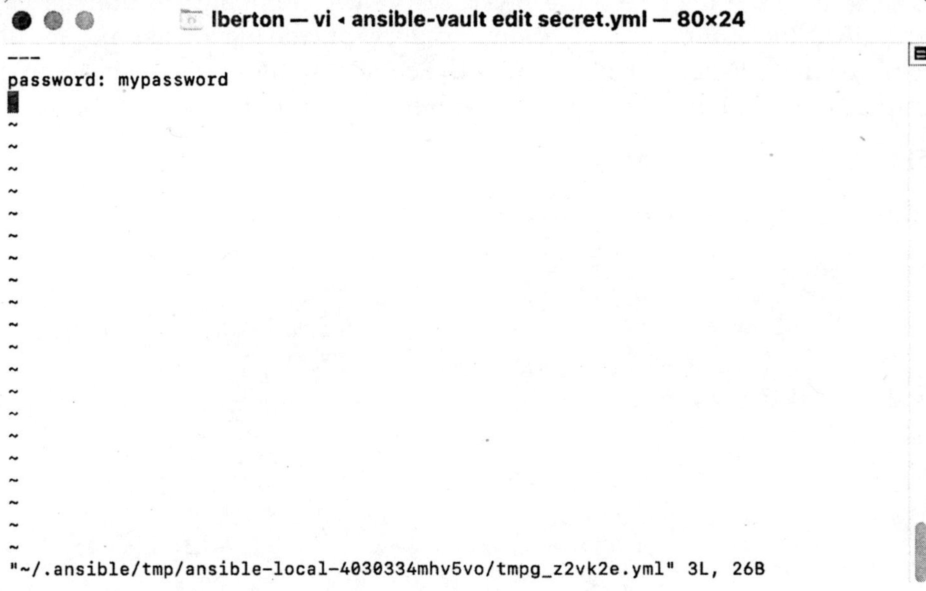


*Figure 3.8: The output of the ansible-vault edit command*

# Encrypting a file

We use the encrypt parameter of the **ansible-vault** command to encrypt Ansible resources already created. The **--output** option saves the encrypted file with a new filename. If we omit this option, we overwrite the original file with the encrypted one. Let us create an Ansible playbook **cleartext1.yml** file and encrypt it.

```
---

password: mypassword
```

The following command will encrypt the Ansible playbook **cleartext1.yml** in the **vault1.yml** file. After the execution, the **cleartext1.yml** still contains the file in clear text, whereas the **vault1.yml** is an encrypted Ansible vault containing the same information.

```
ansible-vault encrypt cleartext1.yml --output=vault1.yml
```

This is the output of the **ansible-vault encrypt** command, as shown in *Figure 3.9*:

```
New Vault password: password

Confirm New Vault password: password

Encryption successful
```

```
lberton — -zsh — 80×24
lberton@Lucas-MacBook-Pro ~ % ansible-vault encrypt cleartext1.yml --output=vault1.yml
New Vault password:
Confirm New Vault password:
Encryption successful
lberton@Lucas-MacBook-Pro ~ %
```

*Figure 3.9: The output of the ansible-vault encrypt command*

# Decrypting a file

We can permanently decrypt an already encrypted file using the **`ansible-vault decrypt`** filename command. When decrypting a single file, we can use the **`--output`** option to save the decrypted file under a different name.

```
ansible-vault decrypt secret.yml --output=decrypted.yml
```

Following is the output of the **`ansible-vault decrypt`** command, as shown in *Figure 3.10*:

```
Vault password: password

Decryption successful
```

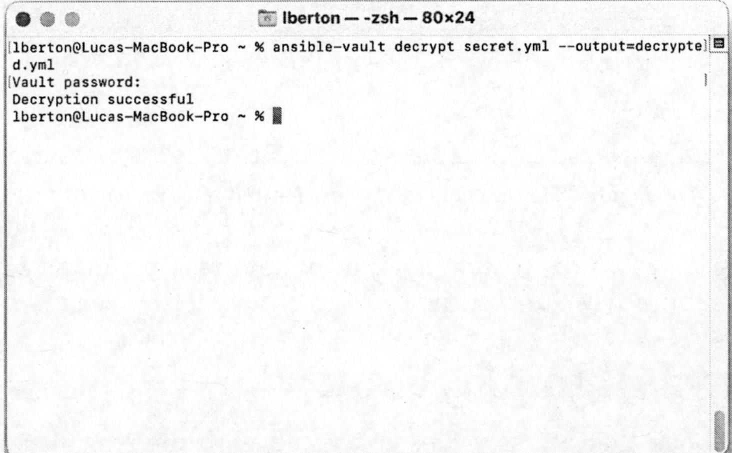


*Figure 3.10: The output of the ansible-vault decrypt command*

# Changing the password

We use the **rekey** parameter of the **ansible-vault** command to change the password of an encrypted file. This command can change the password of multiple data files at once. It prompts for the original password and then the new password.

For example, let us suppose we would like to change the password of the already encrypted **secret.yml** file using the following command:

```
ansible-vault rekey secret.yml
```

The **ansible-vault rekey** command asks for the current Ansible vault password and twice the new password, as shown in *Figure 3.11*:

```
Vault password:
New Vault password:
Confirm New Vault password:
Rekey successful
```

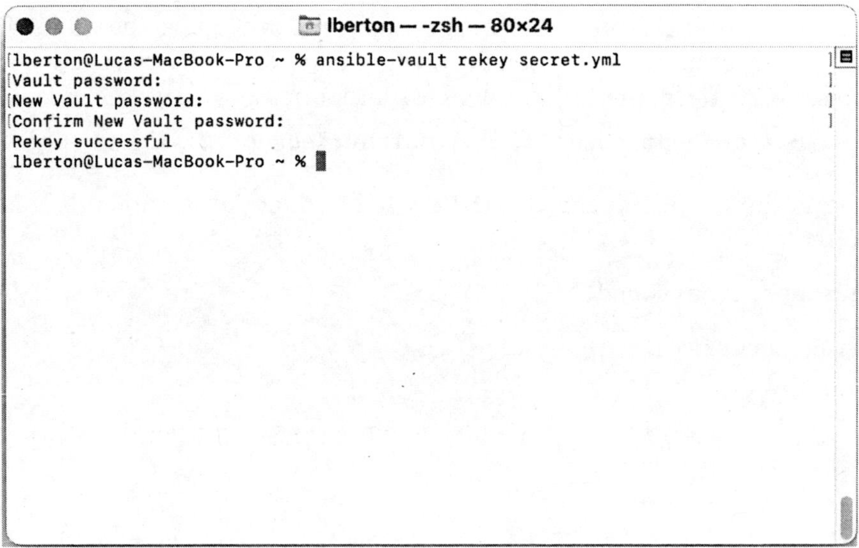


***Figure 3.11:*** *The output of the ansible-vault rekey command*

Implementing a password rotation is an important task for many IT departments nowadays as it improves our security.

# Include vault in playbook

To run a playbook that accesses files encrypted with the Ansible vault, we must provide the encryption password to the **ansible-playbook** command, as shown in

*Figure 3.3*. If we do not give the password, the playbook returns an error. To provide the vault password to the playbook, use the vault id option. For example, to provide the vault password interactively, use **`--vault-id @prompt`**, as illustrated.

The Ansible playbook **`playbook.yml`** contains a simple code to include our Ansible vault **`secret.yml`** and display the password variable on the screen:

```
---
- name: Vault print
  hosts: all
  tasks:
    - name: Include vars
      ansible.builtin.include_vars:
      file: secret.yml
    - name: Print variable
      ansible.builtin.debug:
        var: password
```

The following command executes the Ansible playbook **`playbook.yml`** and asks the user for the Ansible vault password:

```
ansible-playbook --vault-id @prompt playbook.yml
```

We can also specify the password via a password file using the following command:

```
ansible-playbook --vault-password-file=vault-password.txt playbook.yml
```

In this module, we explored the Ansible vault security storage to save secrets and confidential information inside Ansible. These tools are robust and wholly integrated into Ansible technology.

**Tip: Enterprise users can use an additional Ansible plugin to interact with secrets stored in CyberArk Application Identity Manager (AIM), CyberArk Conjur, HashiCorp Vault Key-Value Store (KV), HashiCorp Vault SSH Secrets Engine, Microsoft Azure Key Management System (KMS), Thycotic Secret Server, and so on.**

## Inline vault in playbook

Another alternative to store encrypted sensitive data in our Ansible playbook is using the Ansible vault inline. For example, let us suppose we would like to encrypt the variable named "**`password`**" with the value "**`mypassword`**" in our Ansible playbook.

We can generate the code using the following **`ansible-vault`** command:

```
ansible-vaultencrypt_string
```

First of all, the command requests to type in the password twice, in order to encrypt our sensitive data (in our case, we used the password "**password**"):

```
New Vault password:

Confirm New Vault password:
```

After the successful insertion of the password, the message on the screen invites us to insert the text and terminate with a *Ctrl* + *D* keystroke sequence:

```
Reading plaintext input from stdin. (ctrl-d to end input, twice if your content does not already have a newline)
```

For example, let us insert the following text in plaintext and terminate by the end of the text sequence (*Ctrl* + *D* keystroke):

```
mypassword
```

The command processes our inputs, the password, and the cleartext text and displays the following text, as shown in *Figure 3.12*:

```
Encryption successful
!vault |
          $ANSIBLE_VAULT;1.1;AES256
          33323438663430343838353432366533356432623234626463343464306139
343965653733626236
          37643137643136353538346332326265396265613766643320a356638343763
376266653465313563
          31616265616638363866623962316166623537356164363032323266623761
643931663732353034
          34653935333430633360a636461396139646335326463343666393062666430
386334383235666662
          6632%
```

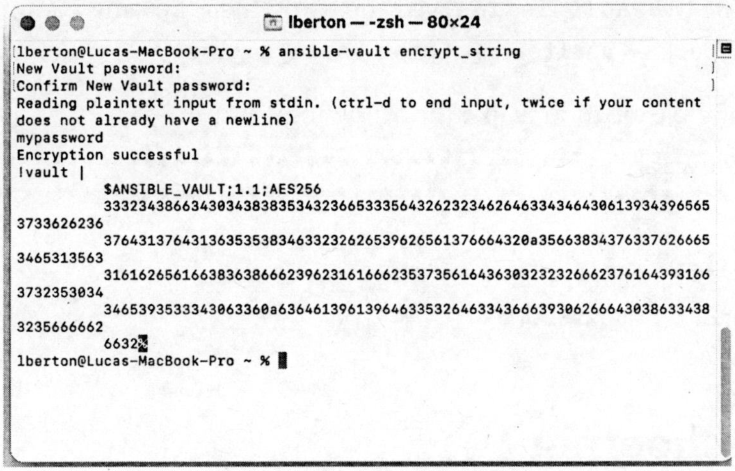

```
lberton — -zsh — 80×24
lberton@Lucas-MacBook-Pro ~ % ansible-vault encrypt_string
New Vault password:
Confirm New Vault password:
Reading plaintext input from stdin. (ctrl-d to end input, twice if your content
does not already have a newline)
mypassword
Encryption successful
!vault |
          $ANSIBLE_VAULT;1.1;AES256
          33323438663430343838353432366533356432623234626463343464306139343965653
3733626236
          37643137643136353538346332326265396265613766643200a3566383437633762666
53465313563
          31616265616638363866623962316166623537356164363032323266623761643931663
3732353034
          34653935333430633600a63646139613964633532646334366639306266643038633438
3235666662
          6632%
lberton@Lucas-MacBook-Pro ~ %
```

*Figure 3.12: Output of the ansible-vaultencrypt_string command*

We can now integrate our inline vault in our playbook like the following **vault_inline.yml** file:

```
---
- name: inline vault
  hosts: all
  vars:
    password: $ANSIBLE_VAULT;1.1;AES256
          33323438663430343838353432366533356432623234626463343464306139
343965653733626236
          37643137643136353538346332326265396265613766643200a356638343763
376266653465313563
          31616265616638363866623962316166623537356164363032323266623761
643931663732353034
          34653935333430633600a63646139613964633532646334366639306266643038633438
386334383235666662
          6632
  tasks:
    - name: Print variable
      ansible.builtin.debug:
        var: password
```

We can execute the **vault_inline.yml** file using the following command:

```
ansible-playbook --vault-id @prompt vault_inline.yml
```

The output of the execution is like the following:

```
TASK [Print variable] ***********************************************
**********************************************************************
*****
ok: [localhost] => {
    "password": "mypassword\n"
}
```

# Troubleshooting

Learn more about the common error, troubleshooting, and resolution in *Chapter 6, Ansible Troubleshooting*, in section *Ansible vault*.

# Ansible handler

The Ansible handler runs operations only when the first task reports a change in status. The Ansible idempotency property is significant when dealing with handlers' statements. Handlers allow the execution of some steps only if necessary, and save computer cycles when there is no need to be executed. Handlers execute only when the previous task reports a changed status. If the previous task report has an ok status, the handler is not executed at all. Handlers are very useful in implementing Ansible idempotence. The following **apache_update.yml** Ansible playbook executes the update of the **Apache** web server and performs the "**apache2**" service restart (in a Debian-like distribution) only when the package is updated:

```
---
- name: Rolling update
  hosts: all
  become: true
  tasks:
    - name: Latest apache2 package
      ansible.builtin.apt:
        name: apache2
        state: latest
       update_cache: true
      notify: Apache restart
  handlers:
```

```
- name: Apache restart
  ansible.builtin.service:
  name: apache2
  state: restarted
```

We can execute the Ansible playbook using the **ansible-playbook** command line utility included in all Ansible installations.

The full command is as follows:

```
ansible-playbookapache_update.yml
```

The **apache_update.yml** is the file name of our Ansible playbook. It produces the following output when the **apache2** package is updated with the handler executed:

```
TASK [Latest apache2 package] *****************************************
************************

changed: [server01.example.com]

RUNNING HANDLER [Apache restart] ***************************************
*************************

changed: [server01.example.com]
```

When no package update has required that the status of the Latest apache2 package task should be "ok", no handler is triggered without the update operation:

```
TASK [Latest apache2 package] *****************************************
************************

ok: [server01.example.com]
```

The **apache_update.yml** file is composed of one task and one handler. The handler code is executed only if necessary. Please note that the "**notify**" statement mentions the handler's name to run. This playbook checks the version of the Apache HTTP web server on all hosts; if an update is available, the **apt** module provides the upgrade process and displays the message on the screen. If an upgrade is not necessary, the handler code is not executed.

# Multiple handlers

In the real world, an Ansible playbook can sometimes trigger multiple handlers, and we can reference them by name. The following two playbooks show us two options for how we can trigger two messages with a single Ansible task, as shown in the **two-1.yml** playbook file:

```
---
- name: handler demo
```

```
  hosts: all
  tasks:
    - name: Uptime
      ansible.builtin.command: "uptime"
      notify: message
  handlers:
    - name: message 1
      ansible.builtin.debug:
         msg: message 1
      listen: message
    - name: message 2
      ansible.builtin.debug:
         msg: message 2
      listen: message
```

We can execute the code using the **ansible-playbook** command:

```
ansible-playbook two-1.yml
```

The execution of the **two-1.yml** playbook file produces the following output:

```
TASK [Uptime] *********************************************************
************

changed: [server01.example.com]

RUNNING HANDLER [message 1] *******************************************
**************************

ok: [server01.example.com] => {
    "msg": "message 1"
}

RUNNING HANDLER [message 2] *******************************************
**************************

ok: [server01.example.com] => {
    "msg": "message 2"
}
```

Instead, we can specify multiple Ansible handlers in the **notify** statement as a list as shown in the following **two-2.yml** playbook file:

```
---
- name: handler demo
```

```
hosts: all
tasks:
  - name: Uptime
    ansible.builtin.command: "uptime"
    notify:
      - message 1
      - message 2
handlers:
  - name: message 1
    ansible.builtin.debug:
      msg: message 1
  - name: message 2
    ansible.builtin.debug:
      msg: message 2
```

We can execute the code using the **ansible-playbook** command:

```
ansible-playbook two-2.yml
```

Handlers are useful to execute tasks only on the status "**changed**" in our Ansible playbook. The execution of the **two-2.yml** playbook file produces the following output:

```
TASK [Uptime] **************************************************************
************
changed: [server01.example.com]
RUNNING HANDLER [message 1] ************************************************
**************************
ok: [server01.example.com] => {
    "msg": "message 1"
}
RUNNING HANDLER [message 2] ************************************************
**************************
ok: [server01.example.com] => {
    "msg": "message 2"
}
```

# Code reuse

It is possible to speed up the code development process by taking advantage of code reuse as much as possible. They include an import statement that enables us to incorporate part of tasks or playbooks in a new playbook. When the amount of tasks is greater than a few, we can package our code as an Ansible role or collection, and distribute it to other creators worldwide. The Ansible Galaxy is a public web archive to simplify code collaboration and distribution.

## Include and import

It is possible to include code from other files in our automation scripts. We can import single tasks or handlers or an entire playbook file, as shown in *Table 3.1.* All the modules are part of the "**ansible.builtin**" collection.

| Static import | Dynamic include |
|---|---|
| **import** | **include** |
| **import_playbook** | **include_vars** |
| **import_role** | **include_playbook** |
| **import_tasks** | **include_role** |
| | **include_tasks** |

***Table 3.1:*** *The Static import and Dynamic include*

There are two possible ways:

- Static **import**
- Dynamic **include**

As the complexity arises, the Ansible team designs two statements for the inclusion of additional files in the current execution.

In the status import, any **import** statements (**import_playbook**, **import_tasks**, and so on.) are pre-processed at the time playbooks are parsed. For static imports, the parent task options will be copied to all child tasks contained within the **import**. On the other hand, the dynamic includes any **include** statements (**include_tasks**, **include_role**, and so on) that are processed as they are encountered during the execution of the playbook. The parent task options will only apply to the dynamic task as it is evaluated and will not be copied to child tasks.

The following code explains the different behavior when applying the **import** or **include** of a task combined with a loop statement:

```
- import_tasks: example.yml
with_items: [1,2]
```

This import statement imports the **example.yml** file one time, and every imported task executes the look loop over the elements of the sequence [1,2], so 1 and 2.

```
- include_tasks: example.yml
with_items: [1,2]
```

This **includes** the statement that imports the **example.yml** file two times and sets the '**item**' iteration variable to 1, 2 respectively of the sequence [1,2].

# Role and collection

Ansible role and collection are two standardized formats to package and share Ansible resources inside and outside our organization. They emphasize code reuse principles.

# Ansible role

The Ansible role enables code reusability in Ansible. Ansible roles are like functions in the traditional programming world. We can use Ansible roles to develop playbooks more quickly and reuse Ansible code. All the files related to the roles must be under our project's **roles** directory. Firstly, we are going to create an Ansible role and then use it in an Ansible playbook.

# Directories tree

Ansible role has a standard directory tree. Some directories are mandatory, but most of them are not. First of all, let us create the Ansible role named **role1** using the **ansible-galaxy** command included in every Ansible installation:

```
ansible-galaxy role init role1
```

The **ansible-galaxy** command requires the following parameters:

- **role** command interacts with the Ansible role.
- **init** command initializes a new role.
- **role1** is the name of the new role.

Successful execution of the previous command produces the creation of the **role1** inside the roles directory and the following output:

```
- Role role1 was created successfully
```

The following file system tree structure is created by the command execution shown in *Figure 3.13*:

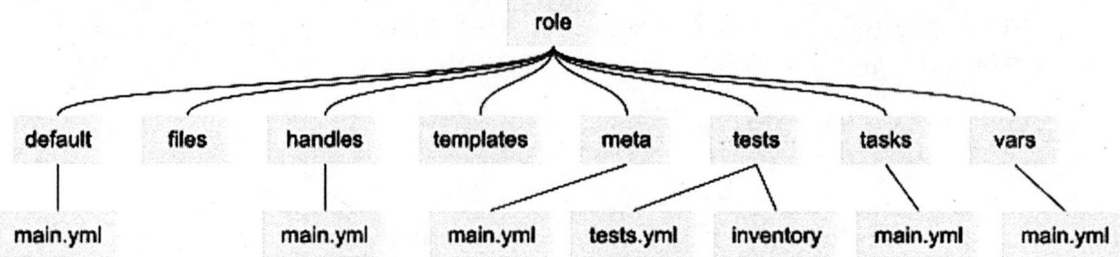


***Figure 3.13:** Ansible standard role directory tree.*

The description of the directory structure is as follows:

- **The `defaults` directory:** The **`main.yml`** file in this directory contains the default values of role variables that can be overwritten when the role is used. These variables have low precedence and are intended to be changed and customized in plays.
- **The `files` directory:** This directory stores static files for configuration. We reference this directory by role tasks.
- **The `handlers` directory:** The **`main.yml`** file in this directory contains the role's handler definitions.
- **The `meta` directory:** The **`main.yml`** file in this directory contains human-readable information about the role, including author, license, platforms, and optional role dependencies.
- **The `tasks` directory:** This is the most important directory. The **`main.yml`** file in this directory contains the main code to execute the role tasks.
- **The `templates` directory:** This directory contains Jinja2 templates used in any role tasks when needed.
- **The `tests` directory:** This directory can contain an **`inventory`** and **`test.yml`** playbook to test the role.
- **The `vars` directory:** The **`main.yml`** file in this directory defines the role's variable values. Often, these variables are used for internal purposes within the role. These variables have high precedence and are not intended to be changed when used in a playbook.

The only required directory is the **`tasks`** directory. Only some roles will have all of these directories. The most important file is the **`main.yml`** under the **`tasks`** directory. The content of this file is the content of the tasks of one of the Ansible playbooks. The content of the **`main.yml`** file under the tasks directory in the **`role1`** role:

```
---
name: role1 demo
ansible.builtin.debug:
  msg: "role1"
```

We could add some variables inside the Ansible role, specifying their name under the **defaults/main.yml** file. For example, let us define the **foo** with the value **foo**, as shown:

```
---
foo: foo
```

Once the **foo** variable is defined, we could use it in our **tasks/main.yml**, as shown:

```
---
- name: role1 demo
  ansible.builtin.debug:
    msg: "role1"
- name: role1 foo
  ansible.builtin.debug:
    var: foo
```

# Usage in playbook

We can include our roles in an Ansible playbook under the roles statement. The following example shows us how to include the **role1** Ansible role in our Ansible playbook.

```
---
- name: role example
  hosts: all
  roles:
    - role1
```

When Ansible is not able to find the **role1**, we obtain the following error:

```
ERROR! the role 'role1' was not found in /home/devops/roles/roles:/
root/.ansible/roles:/usr/share/ansible/roles:/etc/ansible/roles:/home/
devops/roles
```

As further explained in *Chapter 6, Ansible Troubleshooting*, it simply communicates to us that **role1** is not found in the directory listed after by Ansible. The solution is to verify to be in the correct directory for the execution or customize the role path in **ansible.cfg** file. Learn more about the **ansible.cfg** file in *Chapter 7, Ansible Enterprise,* section *Ansible configuration settings.*

The output of the execution is the following. As we can see, the result shows the two tasks defined in the **role1** role:

```
PLAY [role example] ****************************************************
******************

TASK [Gathering Facts] *************************************************
*********************

ok: [server01.example.com]

TASK [role1 : role1 demo] **********************************************
************************

ok: [server01.example.com] => {
    "msg": "role1"
}

TASK [role1 : role1 foo] ***********************************************
***********************

ok: [server01.example.com] => {
    "foo": "foo"
}

PLAY RECAP *************************************************************
**********

server01.example.com: ok=3    changed=0    unreachable=0    failed=0
skipped=0    rescued=0    ignored=0
```

Execution of the **role_simple.yml** playbook

The following example applies the "**role1**" Ansible role setting, on the "**foo**" with the value "**value**". The "**roles/role_vars.yml**" file looks like the following:

```
---
- name: role example
  hosts: all
  roles:
  - role: role1
    foo: value
```

The output of the execution is similar to the previous one but shows the value for the **foo** variable (instead of **foo**) in the **role_simple.yml** playbook:

```
PLAY [role example] ****************************************************
******************
```

```
TASK [Gathering Facts] *******************************************
*********************

ok: [server01.example.com]
TASK [role1 : role1 demo] ****************************************
************************

ok: [server01.example.com] => {
    "msg": "role1"
}
TASK [role1 : role1 foo] *****************************************
***********************

ok: [server01.example.com] => {
    "foo": "value"
}
PLAY RECAP *******************************************************
**********

server01.example.com: ok=3    changed=0    unreachable=0    failed=0
skipped=0    rescued=0    ignored=0
```

# Order of execution

For each play in a playbook, tasks execute as ordered in the tasks list. After all, tasks execute, and any notified handlers are executed. Ansible executes a playbook in the order of execution shown in *Figure 3.14*. Please note that the role can self-contain some tasks and handlers in the relative directory. We can specify some Ansible handlers in a role, like in a traditional Ansible play. When a role is added to a play, role tasks are added to the beginning of the tasks list. If a second role is included in a play, its tasks list is added after the first role. Please refer to the following figure:

*Figure 3.14: The Ansible playbook order of execution*

Executing some play tasks in specific scenarios may be necessary before the roles. To support such scenarios, the Ansible plays can specify a **`pre_tasks`** section.

Any task listed in this section executes before any roles are executed. If any of these tasks notify a handler, those handler tasks execute before the roles or regular tasks.

Plays also support a **`post_tasks`** keyword that executes some **`tasks`** after the usual play **`tasks`** but before any **`handlers`** section.

The following example shows the order of execution of an Ansible playbook specifying all the possible statements: **`pre_tasks`**, **`role`**, **`task`**, **`post_tasks`**, **`handlers`**:

```
---
- name: Order of execution
  hosts: all
  pre_tasks:
    - debug:
        msg: 'pre-task'
      notify: my handler
  roles:
    - role1
  tasks:
    - debug:
        msg: 'first task'
      notify: my handler
  post_tasks:
    - debug:
        msg: 'post-task'
      notify: my handler
  handlers:
    - name: my handler
      debug:
        msg: Running my handler
```

The output of the execution verifies the expected order of execution of the Ansible **`role_order.yml`** playbook:

```
PLAY [Order of execution] *********************************************
****************

TASK [Gathering Facts] ************************************************
*********************

ok: [server01.example.com]

TASK [debug] **********************************************************
******************

ok: [server01.example.com] => {
    "msg": "pre-task"
}
```

```
TASK [role1 : role1 demo] **********************************************
***********************

ok: [server01.example.com] => {
    "msg": "role1"
}
TASK [role1 : role1 foo] ***********************************************
***********************

ok: [server01.example.com] => {
    "foo": "foo"
}
TASK [debug] ***********************************************************
************

ok: [server01.example.com] => {
    "msg": "first task"
}
TASK [debug] ***********************************************************
************

ok: [server01.example.com] => {
    "msg": "post-task"
```

# Ansible Galaxy for roles

Ansible Galaxy is either a command line utility for managing roles in our Ansible controller or a public website directory to find any available Ansible resources. On the website, there is a search engine that quickly finds the proper Ansible role or collection. Every resource shows the author as well as the download count, the supported operating system, and much information about usage or internal variables.

## Manual installation

We can interact with the Ansible Galaxy website via browser or via the **ansible-galaxy** command line utility, that is included in every Ansible installation. It simplifies the interaction with Ansible Galaxy and enables the installation of roles and collection via the command line. For example, let us suppose we would like to install the **redis** role created by the **geerlingguy** author (**geerlingguy.redis**). The entire **ansible-galaxy** command is:

```
ansible-galaxy install geerlingguy.redis -p roles/
```

The parameters for the command are:

- **install parameter**: Installs role from file.
- **geerlingguy.redis**: Specifies the name of the galaxy role.
- **-p** or **--roles-path** lets us specify the path to a directory where we can save our roles files

Alternatively to the **-p** or **--roles-path** options, we can specify the path directory for our roles via **ansible.cfg** configuration file. See *Chapter 7, Ansible Enterprise,* section *Ansible Configuration Settings* for more details.

The output of the command looks like the following:

```
- downloading role 'redis', owned by geerlingguy
- downloading role from https://github.com/geerlingguy/ansible-role-redis/archive/1.8.0.tar.gz
- extracting geerlingguy.redis to /home/devops/roles/geerlingguy.redis
- geerlingguy.redis (1.8.0) was installed successfully
```

## Automated installation

When we need to install more than one Ansible role or when we would like to execute it automatically, we prefer to use a **requirements.yml** file.

The syntax is easily understandable because it lists all the roles under the src name. Optionally, we could specify a specific version. If the version is omitted, Ansible installs the latest available.

A simple **requirements.yml** file looks like this:

```
---
roles:
  - src: geerlingguy.redis
    version: "1.8.0"
```

We can execute our **requirements.yml** role file using the **ansible-galaxy** command:

```
ansible-galaxy install -r roles/requirements.yml -p roles
```

The parameters for the command are:

- **install** parameter installs role from file.
- **-r** parameter specifies the usage of the **requirements.yml** file.

- `-p` parameter shows the path to a directory where we can save our roles files.

The output of the `ansible-galaxy install -r` command is like the following:

```
Starting galaxy role install process
- downloading role 'redis', owned by geerlingguy
- downloading role from https://github.com/geerlingguy/ansible-role-redis/archive/1.8.0.tar.gz
- extracting geerlingguy.redis to /home/devops/roles/geerlingguy.redis
- geerlingguy.redis (1.8.0) was installed successfully
```

The expected outcome of the command will download our content for the Ansible Galaxy website, and save it in the specified roles directory.

Ansible roles are extremely helpful for code reuse and can save tons of time and human error. Always search for a role in Ansible Galaxy before writing your own.

## Configuration

We can customize the behavior of the `ansible-galaxy` command line tool specifying a configuration file, for example, for retrieving roles content from the public Ansible Galaxy website and a private archive inside our organization or Ansible automation hub (part of Ansible automation platform). For each server, we can specify authentication credentials or authentication tokens.

# Ansible collection

An Ansible collection is the most modern and complete way to distribute Ansible code between multiple platforms. It allows us to distribute Ansible roles, modules, and plugins in a standard way. The collection is often published in the public Ansible Galaxy website archive. An Ansible collection is a distribution format for Ansible content.

It solves one problem and contains all the relevant packages, and distributes playbooks, roles, modules, and plugins. For users, the Ansible collection is easy to download and share via Ansible Galaxy without actually knowing what is happening under the hood. It simply performs the expected task. For developers, the Ansible collection is easy to upload and share via Ansible galaxy. All the files related to the collections must be under our project's `collections` directory.

## Ansible Galaxy for collections

The Ansible Galaxy is a website that stores roles and collections for Ansible. The search engine, tags, and platform make it easy to find any content inside. We must carefully evaluate content quality before using it in our system. A quality indicator is usually the quality assurance of code, the supported operating systems and platforms, the documentation, the release numbers, the presence of changelog, the number of downloads, and the author or creator. Please notice that the website also contains Ansible roles beside Ansible collections.

# The community.general collection

The most comprehensive collection archive is the **community.general**. It has a lot of valuable Ansible resources. The archive is distributed with a community license. Hence, it means that the Ansible community is doing its best to support the product, but there is no specific time for a bug fix or new feature implementation.

Suppose we would like to use the **iso_create** Ansible module from the Ansible Galaxy collection **community.general** in our system. The **iso_create** module creates an ISO image from a list of files in our system. It is useful for backup purposes. In order to use the **iso_create** module, we need to specify the entire Ansible namespace in our task: **community.general.iso_create**.

For example, the following **collection.yml** Ansible playbook creates the **test.iso** file from a list of files:

```
---
- name: iso_create module demo
  hosts: all
  tasks:
    - name: Create an ISO file
      community.general.iso_create:
         src_files:
           - /home/devops/helloworld.yml
         dest_iso: /home/devops/devops.iso
         interchange_level: 3
```

We can execute our code in the terminal with the **ansible-playbook** command line tool included in every Ansible installation. The parameter is only the file name. In our case, it is the path for the **collection.yml** file, that is, **collections/collection.yml**.

The full command is:

```
ansible-playbook collections/collection.yml
```

The expected execution of the **collection.yml** file when the collection is installed, is with **ok** and **changed** status:

```
TASK [Create an ISO file] ***********************************************
************************

changed: [server01.example.com]

PLAY RECAP **************************************************************
*********

server01.example.com: ok=2    changed=1    unreachable=0    failed=0
skipped=0    rescued=0    ignored=0
```

The output of the execution is the **devops.iso** ISO file in the directory **/home/devops** containing the **helloworld.yml** file seen in the previous chapter. Feel free to adapt the Ansible playbook as needed with real files and directories.

The following Ansible fatal error means that the collection is not currently installed in the Ansible controller:

```
ERROR! couldn't resolve module/action 'community.general.iso_create'.
```

We can read about the full error in *Chapter 6, Ansible Troubleshooting,* section *Ansible Collection.* We can easily install or update an Ansible collection using the **ansible-galaxy** command line utility.

# Installing Ansible collection

There are two different methods for installing Ansible collections using the **ansible-galaxy** command line utility:

- Manual installation
- Automated installation

Any collections or roles we download using the **ansible-galaxy** command line utility are installed under a directory called **.ansible** underneath our home directory if not customized via the **ansible.cfg** file. Learn more about the **ansible.cfg** file in *Chapter 7, Ansible Enterprise,* section *Ansible Configuration Settings.*

## Manual installation

We could manually install the desired collection using the **ansible-galaxy** command line utility. This utility is included in every Ansible installation and allows us to simplify the management of Ansible roles and collections.

The command is:

```
ansible-galaxy collection install community.general
```

The command to install a collection requires two parameters:

- **`collection install`** specifies a collection installation activity.
- **`community.general`** is the name of the collection.

We obtain the following message when the collection is already installed in our system:

```
Starting galaxy collection install process

Nothing to do. All requested collections are already installed. If you want to reinstall them, consider using `--force`.
```

As suggested by the output, we can download the collection again adding the –**`force`** parameter.

**Tip: It is also possible to install content from a tarball archive. This feature is useful for disconnected or "airgap" environments. We can manually download content from the Ansible Galaxy website in a tarball. It is also possible to install downloaded collections using the following command:**

```
ansible-galaxy collection install ~/Downloads/ansible-windows-1.13.0.tar.gz
```

## Automated installation

We can perform an automated Ansible collection installation using the **`ansible-galaxy`** command line utility and a **`requirements.yml`** file.

The following **`requirements.yml`** file downloads the **`community.general`** collection from the Ansible Galaxy archive:

```
---
collections:
  - name: community.general
    source: https://galaxy.ansible.com
```

We could execute our **`requirement.yml`** file using the command line **`ansible-galaxy`** command, as shown:

```
ansible-galaxy install -r collections/requirements.yml
```

The preceding command has the following parameters:

- **`install`** parameter specifies the installation operation.
- **`-r`** specifies that we would like to use the **`requirement.yml`** file.

This produces the following output:

```
Starting galaxy collection install process
Process install dependency map
Starting collection install process
Downloading https://galaxy.ansible.com/download/community-general-6.1.0.tar.gz to /home/devops/.ansible/tmp/ansible-local-257gjb377e/tmp3h2ee5fy/community-general-6.1.0-po7d9tp6
Installing 'community.general:6.1.0' to '/home/devops/.ansible/collections/ansible_collections/community/general'
community.general:6.1.0 was installed successfully
```

As we can see, the **ansible-galaxy** tools connects to the Ansible Galaxy website, finds the collection and downloads the latest release version (6.1.0 at the time of writing this book) in our target system. It also confirms to the user the path on the local file system, where the files are available. Advanced users could also specify the "**signatures**" parameter for each collection listed in the file to verify the genuine copy of the software between the distribution server and our systems. At the moment of writing this book, a limited selection of distribution server supports this feature.

# Python dependencies

Please note that some Ansible modules require more Python library dependencies to operate. The requirements are specified in the manual and must be installed before the Ansible execution.

The following Ansible fatal error means that the **pycdlib** Python library is required by the **community.general.iso_create** Ansible module, and is not installed in the Ansible controller Python system-wide or in the current Python virtual environment:

```
The error was: ModuleNotFoundError: No module named 'pycdlib'.
```

We can read about the full error in *Chapter 6, Ansible Troubleshooting,* section *Ansible Collection.*

# List collections

The same **ansible-galaxy** utility could be used to list the installed collection.

```
ansible-galaxy collection list community.general
```

The parameters for the command are:

- **collection** specifies that we would like to interact with collections.

- **list** specifies that we would like to list the installed collections.
- **community.general** is the name of the collection.

The output shows the directory path of the local Ansible collection, the name, and the installed version.

In this case, the output looks like this:

```
# /usr/local/lib/python3.8/dist-packages/ansible_collections
Collection         Version
------------------ -------
community.general 5.4.0
# /home/devops/.ansible/collections/ansible_collections
Collection         Version
------------------ -------
community.general 6.1.0
```

Once the Ansible collection **community.general** is successfully installed in our system, we can execute our Ansible playbook code **collection.yml**.

Ansible collections are extremely helpful for code reuse and can save tons of time and human errors.

## Configuration

We can customize the behavior of the **ansible-galaxy** command line tool specifying a configuration file, for example, for retrieving collections content from the public Ansible Galaxy website and a private archive inside our organization or Ansible automation hub (part of Ansible Automation Platform). For each server, we can specify authentication credentials or authentication tokens.

# Ansible filters

We can perform some alterations of variable or configuration files using the Ansible native support for Jinja2 filters. They are parts that extend the functionality of the Ansible control node. Ansible filters manipulate data at a variable level.

The following three filters are most used:

- **default**: Provides a default value for a variable if it is undefined,
- **join**: Makes a single string out of a list,
- **map**: Applies a filter to every item in a list or dictionary,

- **`selectattr`**, **`filter`**, and **`rejectattr`**: Filter dictionary and select the matching items.

The Ansible **`default`** filter is useful when we would like to provide the default value for a variable that might be overridden by a user (using an interactive input or extra variable). We can concatenate the elements of a list in a string using the Ansible **`join`** filter that relies on the Python **`join()`** built-in function. Moreover, the Ansible **`map`** filter relies on the Python **`map()`** built-in function that process and transforms all the items in an iterable, without using an explicit loop, a technique commonly known as mapping. The **`map()`** apply a transformation function to each item and transform them into a new iterable. The Ansible **`selectattr`** filter is inherited from Jinja, and it returns matching objects from an input sequence by applying a test across all the objects in a sequence (usually a dictionary). The **`selectattr`** filter has parameters based on the type of test that we would like to perform in the object: "**`equalto`**", "**`match`**", and "**`search`**". We can use the Jinja2 comparison operators **`"==","!=",">","<",`** and the Jinja2 tests "**`eq`**", "**`ne`**", "**`ge`**", "**`gt`**", "**`in`**", "**`not`**". If no test is specified, the attribute value is evaluated as a boolean. The **`selectattr`** filter applies the test also to the nested objects, whereas the select Ansible **`"filter"`** only filters a sequence of objects by applying a test to each object. The opposite of the **`selectattr`** Ansible filter is the **`rejectattr`** Ansible filter. The **`rejectattr`** Ansible filter removes any items from the specified iterable which do not satisfy the provided test.

Some commons use cases for Ansible filters are summarized in the following *Table 3.2*, applying a filter to the user-defined **`"myvariable"`** variable.

| Filter | Expression | Result |
|---|---|---|
| Assign default mandatory values | `{{ myvariable \| default(10) }}` | `10` |
| Making variables optional | `{{ myvariable \| default(omit) }}` | `(NDR: nothing)` |
| Assign ternary value | `{{ status \| ternary('start', 'restart') }}` | `start or restart` |
| Managing data types | `{{ myvariable \| items2dict }}` | `Dictionary data structure` |
| Formatting data to JSON and YAML | `{{ myvariable \| to_json }}` or `{{ myvariable \| to_nice_yaml }}` | `JSON`<br>`YAML` |
| Working with regex | `{{ "ansible" \| regex_replace('^.', 'A') }}` | `Ansible` |

*Table 3.2: The most common Ansible filters*

**Tip: When the filter has a dictionary as an input parameter, only the keys are transferred by default. We can use the ".values()" method for the dictionary values to the filter or the ".items()" method for both key and value.**

The following **filter_map.yml** file Ansible playbook showcases the usage of the **map**, **join**, and **selectattr** filters in a simple list of **servers**:

```
---
- hosts: all
  vars:
    servers:
      host01:
          ip: 192.168.1.11
          type: large
      host02:
          ip: 192.168.1.12
          type: small
  tasks:
    - name: Map IP addresses
      ansible.builtin.debug:
        msg: "{{ servers.values() | map(attribute='ip') }}"

    - name: List IP addresses
      ansible.builtin.debug:
        msg: "{{ servers.values() | map(attribute='ip') | join(',') }}"

    - name: Only large machines
      ansible.builtin.debug:
        msg: "{{ servers.values() | selectattr('type', 'eq', 'large') |
map(attribute='ip') | join(',') }}"
```

The full command is as the following:

```
ansible-playbookfilter_map.yml
```

The output of the command is the following:

```
TASK [Map IP addresses] *************************************************
*********************
ok: [server01.example.com] => {
```

```
    "msg": [
        "192.168.1.11",
        "192.168.1.12"
    ]
}

TASK [List IP addresses] ************************************************
*********************
ok: [server01.example.com] => {
    "msg": "192.168.1.11,192.168.1.12"
}

TASK [Only large machines] **********************************************
***********************
ok: [server01.example.com] => {
    "msg": "192.168.1.11"
}
```

There are also more Ansible filters that apply string modification. Let us apply the **upper** filter to the Ansible string "**Automate Everything with Ansible**". The **upper** filter applies uppercase to the variable and returns on the screen. The expected output of the modification is from "**Automate Everything with Ansible**" to "**AUTOMATE EVERYTHING WITH ANSIBLE**". We demonstrate the behavior using the "**debug**" module in the **filter_upper.yml** playbook file:

```
---
- name: Upper filter
  hosts: all
  tasks:
  - name: Apply a filter
    ansible.builtin.debug:
      msg: '{{ "Automate Everything with Ansible" | upper }}'
```

We can execute our Ansible playbook using the **ansible-playbook** command included in every Ansible installation, specifying the filename as a parameter.

The full command is as the following:

```
ansible-playbookfilter_upper.yml
```

The output of the execution of the `filter_upper.yml` playbook is the following:

```
TASK [apply a filter] ***************************************************
***********************

ok: [server01.example.com] => {
    "msg": "AUTOMATE EVERYTHING WITH ANSIBLE"
}
```

As we can see, the output is "`AUTOMATE EVERYTHING WITH ANSIBLE`" which is the capitalization of the input text "`Automate Everything with Ansible`" using an `upper` Ansible filter. Ansible filters are useful to perform variable alternations for on-screen purposes or reuse the output of one task for another.

**Tip: The opposite of the upper Ansible filter is the lower Ansible filter that transforms the input text "Automate Everything with Ansible" to "automate everything with Ansible"**

To manipulate JSON format files or variables, the `json_query` filter is useful for extracting fields from a data structure and flattening complex structures.

Refer to the section "*Temporary Facts*" in the Ansible facts, to save the result of the manipulation in an Ansible fact.

**Tip: Use the "version" filter for comparing versions of the software to increase consistency, save time in comparison, and improves accuracy. For example, the statement "is version('2.15', '>=')" checks for at least version 2.15 of your software.**

# Ansible template

An Ansible template generates an entire file dynamically using a mix of static content, variable data, and control logic. The `ansible.builtin.template` module is a flexible and powerful way to generate configuration content. Templates are regular files with embedded controls and variable references.

Templates use the Jinja2 template language. Jinja2 is a full-featured template engine language written in Python, created by Armin Ronacher in 2008 and licensed under a BSD License. Jinja2 template language became popular, combined with the Flask web framework written in Python. Jinja2 supports simple substitution and conditionals, loops, and other control structures. We store our Jinjia2 template files under the "`templates`" directory in Ansible projects and roles. We can add variable references using the `{{ variable }}` syntax in the template to make the content dynamic. The files are stored in the Ansible control node. The Ansible template is handy for the service configuration file. The Ansible templates help apply some variable values to configuration files. Ansible template works by taking advantage of the Jinja2 programming language, the Ansible built-in template module.

The following example explores how to create and use templates in Ansible playbooks using a variable defined in our playbook. In the following example, we apply a Jinja template and fill a variable with some text using the template Ansible module.

The **template_helloworld.yml** Ansible playbook applies the template module that replaces part of the target template with a custom text.

```
---
- name: template module
  hosts: all
  vars:
    file_content: |
      Automate Everything with Ansible example.
      Multiline.
  tasks:
    - name: Apply template
      ansible.builtin.template:
        src: templates/helloworld.txt.j2
        dest: /home/devops/helloworld.txt
```

The **templates/helloworld.txt.j2** template file is a simple Jinja2 document where we could use double curly brackets to specify the value of the Ansible variable **file_content**, as shown:

```
{{ file_content }}
This line will not change.
```

We can execute our Ansible playbook with the **ansible-playbook** command line tool included in every Ansible installation using the command:

```
ansible-playbooktemplate_helloworld.yml
```

The command produces the following output:

```
TASK [Apply page template] *********************************************
************************

changed: [server01.example.com]
```

After successful execution, the content of the output **/home/devops/helloworld.txt** contains three lines and looks like the following. We can, for example, visualize using the VI command line text editor **vi /home/devops/helloworld.txt**.

```
Automate Everything with Ansible example.
Multiline.
This line will not change.
```

As we can see, the variable **file_content** is substituted in the destination file with the variable's value. In this case, the variable **file_content** is a long multi-line text spread across multiple lines. We can apply the Ansible template to modify any configuration file for any service in our system.

Ansible templates are a fundamental tool for performing configuration management in our IT infrastructure fleet and implementing **Configuration as Code** (**CaC**).

# Control statement

The control statements in an Ansible template use a different syntax than Ansible syntax, **{% statement %}**. Jinja2 supports the conditional statement beginning with **{% if … %}** and ending with **{% endif %}** statements. Most of the usual Python tests are supported: math expressions like "==", "!=", "<=", and "in" for checking the list membership. We can use **{% elif … %}** and **{% else %}** for branches.

When we use control statements, everything between the **{% … %}** brackets is excluded from the output. However, any whitespace we include around these brackets is included by default. We can use a minus sign to tell Jinja 2 to absorb whitespace:

- "{%-" absorbs whitespace from before the control statement.
- "-%}" absorbs whitespace from after the control statement.

The **template_group1.yml** Ansible playbook applies the template module that creates a **group1.txt** file in the target node with a custom text.

```
---
- name: template module
  hosts: all
  tasks:
    - name: Apply template
      ansible.builtin.template:
          src: templates/group1.txt.j2
          dest: group1.txt
```

The "**group1.txt.j2**" file inside the "**templates**" directory is testing if the server is in the "**group1**" group in the inventory:

```
{% if 'group1' in group_names %}
This server is in group1
{%- else %}
This server is NOT in group1
{% endif -%}
```

Let us suppose we have the following **inventory_group.ini** YAML inventory file with **server01.example.com** in the **group1** group, and **server02.example.com** in the **group2** group.

```
---
[group1]
server01.example.com
[group2]
server02.example.com
```

We execute the **template_group1.yml** playbook file with the **inventory.ini** file using the following command:

```
ansible-playbook -i inventory_group.ini template_group1.yml
```

The command produces the following output:

```
TASK [Apply template] *****************************************************
********************
changed: [server01.example.com]
changed: [server02.example.com]
```

In each target node, the playbook creates the text file **group1.txt**:

- The content of the **group1.txt** file in the **server01.example.com**:

  ```
  This server is in group1
  ```

- The content of the **group1.txt** file in the **server01.example.com**:

  ```
  This server is in NOT in group1
  ```

As we can see in the control, operation is completely executed inside the template level using the Jinja2 language and not in the Ansible playbook.

# Loop statement

Jinja2 has only one kind of loop: the **for** loop. The **for** loop starts with **{% for … %}** and ends with **{% endfor %}**. A **for** loop always iterates over some Python sequence: **{% for x in sequence %}**. To run a loop a certain number of times, we can use a **range** statement like "**range(10)**" to create a sequence of ten iterations.

If we need access to a value in a dictionary, the best way to loop over is using the "**.items()**" method and return a couple of keys and values.

# Nested control statement

We can also nest control statements in Jinja2, and so we can have **{% if … %}** inside a **{% for … %}**. An advanced way is to combine the loop and conditional like in the following expression:

```
{% for x in myvariable if x > 2 %}
```

This statement is going to filter the **myvariable** user-defined variable ahead of looping over it. We can also use "**else**" with "**for**" to provide separate content if the **myvariable** is empty.

The **template_type.yml** Ansible playbook applies the **template** module that creates a **type.txt** file in the target node with a custom text.

```
---
- name: template module
  hosts: all
  tasks:
    - name: Apply template
      ansible.builtin.template:
          src: templates/type.txt.j2
          dest: type.txt
```

The "**type.txt.j2**" file inside the "**templates**" directory is testing if the server is in the "**group1**" group in the inventory:

```
{% for key, value in servers.items() if value.type == 'large' %}
{{ key }} is large
{% else %}
{{ key }} is {{ value.type }}.
{% endfor %}
```

We execute the **template_type.yml** playbook file with the **inventory.ini** file using the following command:

```
ansible-playbooktemplate_type.yml
```

The command produces the following output:

```
TASK [Apply template] ***************************************************
********************

changed: [server01.example.com]
```

The execution of the **template_type.yml** playbook creates a **type.txt** file in the target host with the following content:

```
host01 is large
```

# Template filters

Ansible template filters are used when we need to perform some data transformation on the data structure. Usually, we need a template filter when the data structure is more complex than just extracting a value from a list or dictionary. In the same way, as Ansible filters in playbook, we can apply filters also in templates using Jinja2 filters. See the "*Ansible Filter*" section for more information.

# Template extension

The template extension is useful when we need to use templates to generate similar content across multiple files. In this way, we could avoid duplication in our templates. Jinja2 supports two ways to extend templates:

- **include**
- **inheritance**

The "**include**" statement reads the content from another template file and renders it. Ansible searches for the included template in the included search path. The included template has the same facts and variables available to it, as well as any loop variables.

On the other hand, the "**inheritance**" statement is more complex and powerful and creates a parent/child relationship between templates. The "parent" template can be rendered differently by different "child" templates.

The "parent" template is a normal template file that includes one or more **{% block … %}** control statements. The "child" templates use an **{% extends … %}** control statement to inherit from the parent. The "child" templates just have to override whatever blocks need unique content.

# Ansible plugin

The Ansible plugins are some extra Python script that helps extend Ansible. Ansible plugins enable the creation of pieces of code to extend the Ansible base functionality and achieve more interesting applications. Ansible plugins are classified by the function that they have. The complete list of plugin types is listed in *Table 3.3*.

| Plugin type | Plugin description |
|---|---|
| `action` | It executes the actions required by playbook tasks. |
| `cache` | It stores gathered facts or inventory source data. |
| `callback` | It adds new behaviors to Ansible when responding to events. |
| `connection` | It connects to the target hosts so that it can execute tasks on them. |
| `filter` | It extracts a particular value, transforms data types and formats, and makes much more. |
| `inventory` | It points to additional inventory data sources. |
| `lookup` | It accesses data from outside sources (files, databases, key/value stores, APIs, and other services). |
| `test` | It evaluates template expressions and returns True or False. |
| `vars` | It injects additional variable data into Ansible runs that did not come from an inventory source. |

***Table 3.3:** Ansible plugin types*

# Lookup plugin

The most used Ansible plugins are the lookup plugins that enable us to extend Jinja2 to access data from outside sources within our playbooks. They execute and are evaluated on the Ansible control node. Important Ansible lookup plugin use cases are summarized in the following *Table 3.4*:

| Plugin name | Description |
|---|---|
| `file` | It reads file contents. |
| `ini` | It reads from Windows INI-style files. |
| `csvfile` | It reads from CSV files. |
| `fileglob` | It listens to files matching shell expressions. |
| `lines` | It reads lines from stdout. |
| `password` | It generates a random password. |
| `pipe` | It reads from a Unix pipe. |
| `url` | It returns content from a URL via HTTP or HTTPS. |

***Table 3.4:** Popular lookup Ansible plugins*

## Copy multiple files to remote hosts

Often, we need to copy a list of files that matches a pattern from local to remote. Let us suppose we would like to copy all the files with the **.txt** extension inside the examples directory. We need to use the Ansible lookup plugin **fileglob**. The Ansible lookup plugin will act like an Ansible loop statement allowing us to loop on the found files one by one. We can refer to every single filename using the **{{ item }}** variable inside our Ansible module, as in a loop statement. The full Ansible playbook looks like the following **plugin_fileglob.yml** file:

```
---
- name: Copy multiple files to remote hosts
  hosts: all
  become: false
  tasks:
    - name: copy multiple file(s)
      ansible.builtin.copy:
        src: "{{ item }}"
        dest: "/home/devops/"
        mode: '0644'
      with_fileglob:
        - "examples/*.txt"
```

We can execute our Ansible playbook with the **ansible-playbook** command-line tool included in every Ansible installation using the command:

```
ansible-playbookplugin_fileglob.yml
```

The output of the previous **ansible-playbook** command looks like the following:

```
TASK [Copy multiple file(s)] *******************************************
**********************
changed: [server01.example.com] => (item=/home/devops/examples/example.
txt)
```

As expected, the Ansible code loop for each file is found in the examples directory. In this case, only one file matching the criteria was found (**examples/example.txt**). The full path is displayed on the screen. For each file found, Ansible executes the **ansible.builtin.copy** module to copy the file from the Ansible controller to the target host. The expected result is when the Ansible playbook runs against **server01.example.com** in a copy of the file from **/home/devops/examples/example.txt** to **/home/devops/example.txt**.

Ansible plugin extends every Ansible functionality and enables an excellent level of customization in our Ansible environment.

Learn more about the Ansible callback plugins in *Chapter 8, Ansible Advanced,* section *Callback plugin.*

# Conclusion

Ansible has some unique features due to the nature of an infrastructure automation tool for storing sensitive information (Ansible vault), executing tasks only when really needed (handler), applying text manipulation (filters), and configuration management (template).

The best part is that the Ansible engine is completely extensible using some Ansible plugins. When adopted in an organization, we can be benefitted from code reuse standard packages (role and collection) from the public Ansible Galaxy archive.

In the following chapters, we are going to simplify some Linux and Windows administration tasks using this knowledge. In the next chapter, we are going to learn how to configure a Linux target for Ansible and automate the configuration management, file system, install packages, rolling update, and user management.

# Points to remember

- We can extend all the Ansible functions using Ansible plugin.
- Sensitive information could be saved in an Ansible vault and managed using the **`ansible-vault`** command line utility.
- We can concatenate tasks only when a changed status occurs, using Ansible handlers.
- We can automate configuration management using the Ansible template module.
- The Ansible Galaxy is the largest archive of Ansible resources packaged as Ansible roles and collections.

# Key terms

- **Vault:** A password-protected encrypted format to store sensitive data.
- **Handler:** A special task in our Ansible playbook executed only when a changed status happens.
- **Role:** A standard Ansible format to share Ansible playbook code within and outside the organization.

- **Collection:** A standard Ansible format to share modules, plugins, and additional Ansible resources within and outside the organization.

# Multiple choice questions

1. **What is the command to change the password of the Ansible vault?**
   a. `ansible-vault create`
   b. `ansible-vault edit`
   c. `ansible-vault encrypt`
   d. `ansible-vault rekey`
2. **How can we trigger an Ansible handler in an Ansible playbook?**
   a. `notify` statement
   b. `listen` statement
   c. `loop` statement
   d. `when` statement
3. **What utility is used to install Ansible roles?**
   a. `ansible-playbook` command
   b. `ansible-galaxy` command
   c. `ansible-inventory` command
   d. `ansible` command
4. **How can we specify a control statement in an Ansible template?**
   a. `% statement %`
   b. `{{ statement }}`
   c. `{% statement %}`
   d. `statement`

## Answers

1. d
2. a
3. b
4. c

## Questions

1. When is useful to package our code as a role?
2. Why do we need the "`community.general`" collection?
3. How data can be manipulated using "`selectattr`" filter?
4. Why do we need the nested control statement?

## Join our book's Discord space

Join the book's Discord Workspace for Latest updates, Offers, Tech happenings around the world, New Release and Sessions with the Authors:

**https://discord.bpbonline.com**

# CHAPTER 4

# Managing Linux Systems with Ansible

## Introduction

Automating Linux tasks with Ansible is incredibly easy and useful using native Ansible modules. We are going to begin with the host configuration, and then we can move forward with the automation part. There are Ansible native modules for the file system, user management, and many of the daily system administration tasks. Take advantage of the Ansible technology to save time and reduce human errors.

In this chapter, we are going to learn about how to configure a Linux target system and how to perform files and directories operations, and update the software on the most common Linux distributions.

## Structure

In this chapter, we shall cover the following topics:

- Configuring Linux target
- Testing host availability
- Printing text during execution
- Configuration management

- File system
- Installing packages and rolling update
- Linux system roles
- User management
- Executing commands

# Objectives

By the end of this chapter, the reader will know/be able to understand how to apply Ansible technology to automate some Linux daily tasks and operations.

# Configuring Linux target

Linux is the first citizen of Ansible automation. The good news is that we have nothing to configure for most modern operating systems. We only need to enable the OpenSSH service during the setup of the machine. The requirements are only OpenSSH service running and the Python interpreter successfully installed on the target system, as will subsequently be shown in *Figure 4.1*. Nowadays, there is already part of the Linux base installation for the most common modern distribution. The OpenSSH configuration for connecting to the target host is the same in any Linux distribution.

First of all, let us perform the Ansible SSH configuration for the target host, which could be:

- Password authentication
- SSH key authentication

Password authentication is simpler, but we prefer to use the SSH key authentication because it is the strongest mechanism. The SSH key authentication relies on the public and private key pairs, that are often generated using elliptic curves and more complex techniques.

Please note that the initial SSH connection saves the fingerprint of the target system in the **`~/.ssh/known_hosts`** file in order to guarantee more security and verify that the target host was not tampered with or altered.

# OpenSSH configuration

The general OpenSSH configuration of the "**`sshd`**" service is performed in the **`/etc/ssh/sshd_config`** configuration file. However, for each authentication user, we can change the behavior of the service just by creating or modifying a simple text configuration file.

The **.ssh** directory is a hidden configuration folder for each local account under the user's home directory. It determines the behavior of an SSH connection for the current user. The following is the content of a typical **~/.ssh** directory in a standard Linux system for the **devops** user.

```
/home/devops/.ssh
├── authorized_keys
├── id_rsa
├── id_rsa.pub
└── known_hosts

1 directory, 4 files
```

The **~/.ssh/authorized_keys** authentication file determines what keys are enabled to authenticate in the current system.

To implement the SSH key authentication, first of all, we need a pair of public and private keys generated by the **ssh-keygen** terminal utility. By default, the public key is stored in the **~/.ssh/id_rsa.pub** file, whereas the private key is stored in the **~/.ssh/id_rsa** file. Some system administrators use it to customize this path. Using customized path, we can store multiple keys to access different systems. Consequently, multiple key files might be stored or be present in our systems.

We need to verify that the username account exists on the target host and specify the SSH key file in our inventory file. We can copy the public key (supposedly stored in the **~/.ssh/id_rsa.pub** file) to the target host using the **ssh-copy-id** command line utility.

```
ssh-copy-id -i ~/.ssh/id_rsa.pub devops@server01.example.com
```

Under the hood, the preceding command connects to the target system and creates or appends the public key to the target system under the connection user **~/.ssh/authorized_keys** authentication file and to the current system **~/.ssh/known_hosts** file.

The initial message for host key checking, is as follows:

```
ssh devops@server01.example.com
The authenticity of host 'server01.example.com
(192.168.0.20)' can't be established. RSA key fingerprint is
SHA256:42JErOjO9fKNNBapEEyhpfTNn+rt8SPNob00uRlmqRs. This key is not
known by any other names Are you sure you want to continue connecting
(yes/no/[fingerprint])?
```

Host keys are normally generated automatically when OpenSSH is first installed or when the computer is first booted. After verifying and accepting, the SSH fingerprint is added to the **~/.ssh/known_hosts** file. This host verification is called the host key checking mechanism. In a fast-paced infrastructure with very frequent, or sometimes multiple, changes per day, hostname and IP reuse are the normality. We can disable the host key checking to set the appropriate parameter in the **ansible.cfg** configuration file as shown in the file in *Chapter 8, Ansible Advanced,* section *Ansible configuration settings.*

# Host variables

In inventory, it is possible to store variable values related to a specific host or group. The most common usage of host variables is to specify authentication credentials for the target node. For example, defining different connection credentials or methods between different hosts is common. Let us say, for example, we use the **local** connection for the **server01.example.com** and **ssh**, the default connection type, for all the other hosts. We could customize each host's login user **devops** for **server01.example.com** and **Ansible** for **server02.example.com** as in the following **hostinventory.ini** file:

```
[web]
server01.example.com ansible_connection=local
server01.example.com ansible_connection=sshansible_user=devops
server02.example.com ansible_connection=sshansible_user=ansible
```

We can verify the list view using the following Ansible command:

```
ansible-inventory -i hostinventory.ini --list
```

The command produces the following output for the **hostinventory.ini** inventory:

```
"server01.example.com": {
    "ansible_connection": "local"
},
"server01.example.com": {
    "ansible_connection": "ssh",
    "ansible_user": "devops"
},
"server02.example.com": {
    "ansible_connection": "ssh",
    "ansible_user": "ansible"
}
```

```
        }
    },
    "all": {
        "children": [
            "ungrouped",
            "web"
        ]
    },
    "web": {
        "hosts": [
            "server01.example.com",
            "server01.example.com",
            "server02.example.com"
        ]
    }
}
```

## Group variables

We can also use a single host to define group variables. In these two inventory files in the example (INI and YAML format), the variables **ntp_server** has assigned the value **europe.pool.ntp.org** for all the group hosts.

In the following inventory, we set the group variable **ntp_server** for a shared NTP server for all the hosts inside the **web** group as shown in the **groupsvariables_inventory.ini** file:

```
[web]
server01.example.com
server02.example.com
[web:vars]
ntp_server=europe.pool.ntp.org
```

We can have a list view result using the **ansible-inventory** command:

```
ansible-inventory -i groupsvariables_inventory.ini --list
```

The command produces the following output for the **groupsvariables_inventory.ini** inventory:

```
{
  "_meta": {
      "hostvar": {
          "server01.example.com": {
              "ntp_server": "europe.pool.ntp.org"
           },
          "server02.example.com": {
              "ntp_server": "europe.pool.ntp.org"
           }
      }
   },
  "all": {
      "children": [
          "ungrouped",
          "web"
      ]
   },
  "web": {
      "hosts": [
          "server01.example.com",
          "server02.example.com"
      ]
   }
}
```

As we learned in the previous section, we can obtain the same result with a YAML inventory. This is the same example as before in a YAML format in the **groupsvariables_inventory.yml** file:

```
---
web:
  hosts:
    server01.example.com:
    server02.example.com:
  vars:
ntp_server: europe.pool.ntp.org
```

We could obtain the list view using the following **ansible-inventory** command:

```
ansible-inventory -igroupsvariables_inventory.yml --list
```

This is the list view output of the **groupsvariables_inventory.yml** inventory:

```
{
    "_meta": {
        "hostvars": {
            "server01.example.com": {
                "ntp_server": "europe.pool.ntp.org"
            },
            "server02.example.com": {
                "ntp_server": "europe.pool.ntp.org"
            }
        }
    },
    "all": {
        "children": [
            "ungrouped",
            "web"
        ]
    },
    "web": {
        "hosts": [
            "server01.example.com",
            "server02.example.com"
        ]
    }
}
```

For the full code on how to configure an NTP server refer to the *Linux System Roles* section.

# Inheriting variable values

The hosts and groups variable could be combined. In this example, the group **web** has two members, **asia** and **europe**. These two variables have the definition in the single host, **server01.example.com** and **server02.example.com**, respectively, but could also contain more hosts. The **ntp_server** variables have the definition at the **web** level. So, in the end, the **ntp_server** variable is available for the **web**, **asia**, and **europe** groups. The **ntp_server** variable is also available in **server01.example.com** and **server02.example.com** hosts.

This **variableinheriting_inventory.ini** file is the final inventory with inheriting variables inside:

```
[web:children]
asia
europe
[asia]
server01.example.com
[europe]
server02.example.com
[web:vars]
ntp_server=europe.pool.ntp.org
```

We can obtain the list view of the inventory using the **ansible-inventory** command:

```
ansible-inventory -i variableinheriting_inventory.ini --list
```

This command produces the output for the **variableinheriting_inventory.ini** inventory:

```
{
    "_meta": {
        "hostvars": {
            "server01.example.com": {
                "ntp_server": "europe.pool.ntp.org"
            },
            "server02.example.com": {
                "ntp_server": "europe.pool.ntp.org"
            }
        }
    },
    "all": {
        "children": [
            "ungrouped",
```

```
                "web"
            ]
        },
        "asia": {
            "hosts": [
                "server01.example.com"
            ]
        },
        "europe": {
            "hosts": [
                "server02.example.com"
            ]
        }
[...]
```

We could obtain the same Ansible inventory result as the INI format using the YAML format using the **variableinheriting_inventory.yml** file:

```
---
children:
  hosts:
    web:
asia:
        hosts:
          host1.example.com:
europe:
        hosts:
          host2.example.com:
      vars:
ntp_server: europe.pool.ntp.org
```

We can check the list view result using the **ansible-inventory** command:

```
ansible-inventory -ivariableinheriting_inventory.yml --list
```

The output is long but not as complex as it seems. It reports the configuration as expected for the **variableinheriting_inventory.yml** file:

```
{
    "_meta": {
        "hostvars": {
            "web": {
                "asia": {
                    "hosts": {
                        "host1.example.com": null
                    }
                },
                "europe": {
                    "hosts": {
                        "host2.example.com": null
                    }
                },
                "vars": {
                    "ntp_server": "europe.pool.ntp.org"
                }
            }
        }
    }
```

## Password authentication

To implement the SSH password authentication, we need to verify that the username account exists on the target host and specify the credentials (username and password) in our inventory file. Alternatively, we can store this sensitive data in an Ansible vault (see *Chapter 3, Ansible Language Extended*, section *Ansible Vault*). We can apply the configuration to a single host or group in our Ansible inventory specifying host or group variables. Please note that password authentication must be enabled for the target Linux system before starting the configuration.

The configuration usually requires adding the following line in the service SSH configuration file **`/etc/ssh/sshd_config`** and restarting the **`sshd`** service:

```
PasswordAuthentication yes
```

It is also possible to automate the editing of the configuration file as shown with a playbook in the "*Edit single-line text*" section of this chapter; see "*Edit OpenSSH configuration*" code.

The following **ssh_password_inventory.ini** file uses password authentication for connection to the **server01.example.com**:

```
server01.example.com ansible_connection=sshansible_user=devopsansible_
password=mypasswordansible_host=192.168.0.20
```

With:

- **ansible_connection**, the protocol of the connection - **"ssh"** in this case.
- **ansible_user**, the username for the initial authentication - **"devops"** in this case.
- **ansible_password**, the password for the authentication - **"mypassword"** in this case.
- **ansible_host**, the customized IP address of the host - **"192.168.0.20"** in this case

Every time we specify the Ansible inventory in our execution, the connection with the target node is established using the username and password specified in the file. If the credentials for the connection change, simply edit the file otherwise, the connection ends with a credential error.

Password authentication is heavily discouraged for security reasons in a production environment. However, it might be useful for laboratory or development purposes. Sometimes, we can have issues when the "**sshpass**" program is not installed in the Ansible controller (see *Chapter 6, Ansible Troubleshooting*, section *Ansible Connection*).

# SSH key authentication

We can specify the connection credentials in an Ansible inventory using host variables or group variables. The easiest way to is to specify the SSH key for our connection per host.

The **ssh_password_inventory.ini** file uses SSH key based authentication for connection to the **server01.example.com:**

```
server01.example.com ansible_connection=sshansible_user=devopsansible_
ssh_private_key_file=~/.ssh/id_rsaansible_host=192.168.0.20
```

With:

- **ansible_connection**, the protocol of the connection - "**ssh**" in this case.
- **ansible_user**, the username for the initial authentication - "**devops**" in this case.
- **ansible_ssh_private_key_file**, the private SSH key for the authentication - "**~/.ssh/id_rsa**" in this case.

- **ansible_host**, the customized IP address of the host - **"192.168.0.20"** in this case.

Every time we specify the Ansible inventory in our execution, the connection with the target node is established using the SSH key specified in the file. If the credentials for the connection change, simply edit the file otherwise, the connection ends with a credential error (see *Chapter 6, Ansible Troubleshooting*, section *Ansible Connection*).

# Testing host availability

Successfully testing when the target host is available, is the foundation for executing any further automation to our target host. It is useful to move forward in our automation journey and verify that the target host is able to execute our Ansible code.

## Ansible ping module

We can test the host availability using the Ansible module "**ping**", the full name of which is "**ansible.builtin.ping**". It is used to test the availability of target hosts. The module is part of the collection of modules "**builtin**" with Ansible and shipped with it. It is a pretty sound module that has been out for years. It verifies the ability of Ansible to log in to the managed host and that a Python interpreter can execute our code. So it is pretty different for the ping in the network context. Make sure not to be confused about it. When our target system is Windows, we need to use the **win_ping** module instead, as shown in *Chapter 5, Ansible For Windows*.

It is possible not to specify any parameters, and neither use a return value. The default parameter of the ping module is already good enough. Therefore, it is possible to execute the module without specifying any parameters. In the same way, managing the return value is not mandatory. There is only one input parameter named "**data**":

- **pong**: default behavior
- **data**: specify a custom text
- **crash**: generate an exception

By using the **pong** option of the **data** parameter, the default behavior of the **ping** module tests the connection and returns pong when the connection is successful. In the **crash** option of the **data** parameter, the ping module always returns an exception. This behavior helps simulate a problem on the host and verify the halting of our play execution.

The return value for the Ansible "**ping**" module, when the execution is successful, is the **"ping": "pong"** string, but we could customize the text with the data parameter.

# Data parameter - ping

The following **ping.yml** playbook shows how to use the Ansible **ping** module with the default **ping** parameter.

```
---
- name: Ping Test
  hosts: all
  tasks:
    - name: Test Connection
      ansible.builtin.ping:
```

We can execute the code using the **ansible-playbook** command. The full command for executing the **ping.yml** playbook:

```
ansible-playbookping.yml
```

The execution of the **ping.yml** Ansible playbook produces the following output:

```
PLAY [Ping Test] ******************************************************
*****************

TASK [Gathering Facts] ************************************************
************************

ok: [server01.example.com]
TASK [Test Connection] ************************************************
************************

ok: [server01.example.com]
PLAY RECAP ************************************************************
****************

server01.example.com: ok=2    changed=0    unreachable=0    failed=0
skipped=0    rescued=0    ignored=0
```

The previous execution shows the "**ok**" status for the host **server01.example.com**.

We can see the **"ping": "pong"** message adding the verbose execution parameter **-v** for level one verbosity in the **ansible-playbook** command:

```
ansible-playbook -v ping.yml
```

The output of the verbose execution shows us the **"ping": "pong"** message on the screen:

```
PLAY [Ping Test] ******************************************************
**************
```

```
TASK [Gathering Facts] ************************************************
*********************

ok: [server01.example.com]

TASK [Test Connection] ************************************************
*********************

ok: [server01.example.com] => {"changed": false, "ping": "pong"}

PLAY RECAP ************************************************************
****************

server01.example.com                    : ok=2    changed=0
unreachable=0    failed=0    skipped=0    rescued=0    ignored=0
```

With the verbose execution, we revealed the **"ping": "pong"** message on the screen in the "**Test Connection**" task.

# Data parameter - custom

We can customize the output of the "**pong**" by passing value in the "**data**" parameter of the Ansible ping. Suppose we would like to obtain "**ready for connections**" instead of the pong result in the output message the **"ping": "pong"** message. By customizing the data value, we can obtain the output **"ping": "ready for connections"**. We need to just change the value of the data parameter to "**ready for connections**". The full Ansible playbook **ping2.yml** looks like the following:

```
---
- name: Ping Test
  hosts: all
  tasks:
    - name: Test Connection
      ansible.builtin.ping:
        data: "ready for connections"
```

We can see the **"ping": "ready for connections"** message executing the previous playbook with the verbose execution parameter **-v** for verbosity level one of the **ansible-playbook** command:

```
ansible-playbook -v ping2.yml
```

The output of the verbose execution shows us the "**"ping": "ready for connections**" message:

```
PLAY [Ping Test] ******************************************************
**************

TASK [Gathering Facts] ************************************************
```

```
*********************

ok: [server01.example.com]

TASK [Test Connection] *************************************************
*********************

ok: [server01.example.com] => {"changed": false, "ping": "ready for connections"}

PLAY RECAP *************************************************************
***************

server01.example.com           : ok=2    changed=0
unreachable=0    failed=0    skipped=0    rescued=0    ignored=0
```

As expected, the "**ready for connections**" value of the data parameter displays the output "**ping": "ready for connections**" message.

# Data parameter - crash

We can test the usage of the "**crash**" value of the "**data**" parameter. The following **ping3.yml** Ansible playbook is similar to the previous **ping2.yml** with the data parameter with the crash value at the end:

```
data: crash
```

The whole **ping3.yml** playbook is the following:

```
---
- name: Ping Test
  hosts: all
  tasks:
    - name: Test Connection
      ansible.builtin.ping:
        data: crash
```

We can execute the code **ping3.yml** using the full command:

```
ansible-playbook ping3.yml
```

The **ansible-playbook** command produces the following output:

```
PLAY [Ping Test] *******************************************************
**************

TASK [Gathering Facts] *************************************************
*********************

ok: [server01.example.com]

TASK [Test Connection] *************************************************
```

```
*********************

An exception occurred during task execution. To see the full traceback, use
-vvv. The error was: Exception: boom

fatal: [server01.example.com]: FAILED! => {"changed": false, "module_
stderr": "Traceback (most recent call last):\n  File \"/home/devops/.
ansible/tmp/ansible-tmp-1675972209.0283306-517-3057200066775/AnsiballZ_ping.
py\", line 107, in <module>\n    _ansiballz_main()\n  File \"/home/devops/.
ansible/tmp/ansible-tmp-1675972209.0283306-517-3057200066775/AnsiballZ_
ping.py\", line 99, in _ansiballz_main\n    invoke_module(zipped_mod,
temp_path, ANSIBALLZ_PARAMS)\n  File \"/home/devops/.ansible/tmp/ansible-
tmp-1675972209.0283306-517-3057200066775/AnsiballZ_ping.py\", line 47,
in invoke_module\n    runpy.run_module(mod_name='ansible.modules.ping',
init_globals=dict(_module_fqn='ansible.modules.ping', _modlib_path=modlib_
path),\n  File \"/usr/lib/python3.8/runpy.py\", line 207, in run_module\n
return _run_module_code(code, init_globals, run_name, mod_spec)\n  File
\"/usr/lib/python3.8/runpy.py\", line 97, in _run_module_code\n    _run_
code(code, mod_globals, init_globals,\n  File \"/usr/lib/python3.8/runpy.
py\", line 87, in _run_code\n    exec(code, run_globals)\n  File \"/tmp/
ansible_ansible.builtin.ping_payload_hqari_b8/ansible_ansible.builtin.ping_
payload.zip/ansible/modules/ping.py\", line 89, in <module>\n  File \"/tmp/
ansible_ansible.builtin.ping_payload_hqari_b8/ansible_ansible.builtin.ping_
payload.zip/ansible/modules/ping.py\", line 79, in main\nException: boom\n",
"module_stdout": "", "msg": "MODULE FAILURE\nSeestdout/stderr for the exact
error", "rc": 1}

PLAY RECAP ****************************************************************
****************

server01.example.com                  : ok=1    changed=0
unreachable=0    failed=1    skipped=0    rescued=0    ignored=0
```

As expected, the "**crash**" value of the "**data**" parameter is the runtime exception as we can see by failed status and the message "**An exception occurred during task execution**". As we learned in this section, the Ansible module **ping** is a convenient test for our target host availability.

# Printing text during execution

We often need to print messages or the variable's value in Ansible. The statements could be text, Ansible variables, magic variables, facts, and so on, or combinations of these together.

# Ansible debug module

We use the Ansible module "**debug**" included in the "**ansible.builtin**" collection to display text or variables on the screen. The "**ansible.builtin**" modules are shipped with any Ansible installation. We perform this task using the Ansible module "**`debug`**", part of the "**`ansible.builtin`**" collection. We already introduced this module to print debugging information, as shown in *Chapter 2, Ansible Language Core,* section *Ansible Playbook.*

The Ansible "**`debug`**" module has three parameters:

- "**`msg`**" parameter
- "**`var`**" parameter
- "**`verbosity`**" parameter.

When we execute the module without any parameter, the default text "**`Hello world!`**" (with an exclamation mark) is used. We can customize the text using the "**`msg`**" parameter. It could be a static string, a variable, a fact, a magic variable, or a combination of them. The "**`var`**" parameter prints a variable.

Please note that double brackets are used whenever we want the variable value, not the name in the "**`msg`**" parameter. On the other hand, only the variable name is present in the "**`var`**" parameter. For example, the **`"{{ ansible_version }}"`** is an internal variable, Ansible magic variable, that contains the current Ansible version in the Ansible controller machine.

# The verbosity parameter

As anticipated in *Chapter 2, Ansible Language Core,* section *Ansible Playbook,* the "**`verbosity`**" parameter is used when we want to hide our debug code in normal execution but keep it in the playbook if we need it in debug mode. The value of the "**`verbosity`**" parameter could be from zero to four specified in digits. Specifying the "**`verbosity`**" parameter, the text is printed on the screen only when our code is executed with the same verbosity level or a higher one. There are five verbosity levels in Ansible. We can specify the running verbosity level using the **`-v`** parameter of the **`ansible-playbook`** command as shown in the following *Table 4.1*:

| Levels | ansible-playbook parameter |
|---|---|
| `0 (zero)` | no parameter |
| `1 (one)` | -v |
| `2 (two)` | -vv |
| `3 (three)` | -vvv |
| `4 (four)` | -vvvv |

***Table 4.1:*** *Ansible verbosity levels*

We can specify the verbosity **level 1 (one)** using the **-v** parameter, **level 2 (two)** using the **-vv** parameter and so on. The amount of the "**v**" character determines the verbosity level.

The message with some level of verbosity is displayed only when the same verbosity level. If not marched at the same verbosity level, we obtain a skipping state on the task. The following code prints the value of the "**ansible_version**" Ansible magic variable when executing with the **ansible-playbook** command using the verbosity **level 1**.

See *Chapter 8, Ansible Advanced,* section *Ansible configuration settings,* for more information about how to customize the default verbosity level for the **ansible-playbook** command.

# Show Ansible version

The following **debug.yml** Ansible playbook shows a message on the screen only when running with the verbosity **level 1**:

```
---
- name: Ansible version
  hosts: all
  tasks:
    - name: Display version
      ansible.builtin.debug:
        msg: "{{ ansible_version }}"
        verbosity: 1
```

# Execution verbosity level 0

This is when we execute our Ansible Playbook without specifying any verbosity level. The verbosity **level 0** is assumed using the **ansible-playbook** command without any additional arguments:

```
ansible-playbookdebug.yml
```

The message is only visible when the verbosity level is at least one. Because the current verbosity level is zero, we are not reaching **level 1**, we obtained a skipping status on the task **"Display version"**.

```
TASK [Display version] *************************************************
**************************

skipping: [server01.example.com]
```

```
PLAY RECAP ******************************************
********************************server01.example.com                :
ok=1    changed=0    unreachable=0    failed=0    skipped=1    rescued=0
ignored=0
```

We can customize the default verbosity level using the next level.

## Execution verbosity level 1

When executing the Ansible Playbook with verbosity **`level 1`**, please notice the "**`-v`**" parameter compared to the previous execution. Here, we obtain a different result:

```
ansible-playbook -v debug.yml
```

The full output is like the following. Please note that the Ansible playbook output is more verbose than in normal execution with verbosity **`level 1`**:

```
TASK [Display version] *****************************************
********************************

ok: [server01.example.com] => {

    "ansible_version": {

        "full": "2.14.4",

        "major": 2,

        "minor": 14,

        "revision": 4,

        "string": "2.14.4"

    }

}
PLAY RECAP ****************************************
* **********************************server01.example.
com                    : ok=2    changed=0    unreachable=0    failed=0
skipped=0    rescued=0    ignored=0
```

As expected, executing the playbook with verbosity **`level 1`**, we are able to see our debug message with the full value of the **`ansible_version`** variable.

The Ansible "**`debug`**" module is a convenient way to print messages for internal use or testing the code. We can easily hide them in normal execution by specifying the verbosity level and printing only when needed.

# Configuration management

Ansible is very powerful for editing a text file. This ability is handy when handling configuration files for services in Linux. We are going to learn about the Ansible "**lineinfile**" module and a special use case of the Ansible "**copy**" module. We can control the behavior of the Linux system with a text configuration file, since "Everything is a file" concept is the foundation of the Unix operating system. Editing text configuration files is a day-to-day task of every System Administrator, IT Ops Engineer, and SRE. It could be a service configuration file, enabling options, or Unix parameters. **Configuration Management** (CM) is also a method of ensuring that systems perform in a manner consistent with expectations over time. Due to the nature of Ansible being a declarative programming language, it is easy to implement configuration management audit in our system using the "**check**" option. Refer to *Chapter 2, Ansible Language Core*, section *Ansible Playbook* for more details. All of these use cases require the editing of a text file. Security automation, infrastructure, provisioning, and application deployment use cases usually rely on this ability. Please remember that Ansible uses the declarative model compared to the sequential approach of many script languages (such as Perl, Bash, and Python), and so the following modules are focused on the result than the steps to achieve the result.

# Single-line edit

Editing a single line of text in a file usually requires some manual effort to connect to the target machine and avoid any typo mistakes. When the number of servers to manage grows, we need an automated way to perform these types of changes on our fleet.

## Ansible lineinfile module

We can edit any text files using the Ansible module "**lineinfile**". The module's full name is "**ansible.builtin.lineinfile**". The module is part of the collection of modules "**builtin**" with any Ansible installation. This module has support for many Unix-like operating systems. We can insert, update and remove a single line of text in a file using this module.

The "**lineinfile**" Ansible module has many parameters, but the only mandatory parameter is "**path**" which specifies the filesystem path of the file to edit. The following *Table 4.2* summarizes the most important six optional parameters of the "**lineinfile**" Ansible module:

| Parameter | Description |
|---|---|
| **`line`** | The line of text |
| **`insertafter and insertbefore`** | Specify a text position |
| **`regex`** | Specify the regular expression for matching |
| **`create`** | It creates the file if it does not exist |
| **`state`** | Is the line "**`present`**" or "**`absent`**"? |

***Table 4.2:*** *The lineinfile module optional parameters*

As expected, the parameter "**`line`**" specifies the line of text we would like to insert into the file. By default, the text will be inserted at the end of the file, but we could personalize it in a specific position with "**`insertafter`**" or "**`insertbefore`**" parameters. Alternatively, it is even better to use a regular expression to search for a specific pattern in the file. We can specify the regular expression in the regex parameter.

If there is any tool to validate the file, we could specify the command line in the "**`validate`**" parameter, which is very useful for configuration files. In this case, we can use the special **`"%s"`** for the temporary file path to validate. If the file does not exist, we could create it using the create parameter. It is also possible to remove a line of text specifying the value "**`absent`**" of the parameter "**`state`**". The default value of the "**`state`**" parameter is "**`present`**" which means to add or verify the presence of the line in the text file. The following optional parameters summarized in *Table 4.3* specify the file system permissions for the "**`lineinfile`**" Ansible module:

| Parameter | Description |
|---|---|
| **`owner`** | Specifies the filesystem `username` |
| **`group`** | Specifies the filesystem `group` |
| **`mode`** | Specifies the filesystem permission in octal mode (`0644`) or symbolic mode (`u=rw,g=r,o=r`) |

***Table 4.3:*** *File System Permissions*

# Edit OpenSSH configuration

Suppose we would like to enable password authentication in our OpenSSH service. We need to manually edit the SSH configuration **`/etc/ssh/sshd_config`** file and change the line "**`PasswordAuthentication yes`**" or add it, if it is not present. We can take advantage of the regular expression to match all lines that begin with "**PasswordAuthentication**" and substitute with a "**PasswordAuthentication yes**". We also add the "**validate**" parameter to test the result configuration file in order or not, ending with a syntax error. In this case, the SSH service, like many Linux services, has its inherent configuration file check that we can execute with the "**sshd -t -f %s**" command. Refer to the SSH manual page for deep dive into this command. The "**%s**" part is going to be substituted at runtime by Ansible with the path of the edited temporary file. The interesting part is that when the playbook is going to fail if the validation test is unsuccessful. We take advantage of the Ansible handler to restart the service only when any configuration file is performed. If no changes are made, no restart will occur. The whole Ansible Playbook is the following:

```
---
- name: Edit OpenSSH Configuration
  hosts: all
  become: true
  tasks:
    - name: Allow Password Authentication
      ansible.builtin.lineinfile:
        state: present
        dest: /etc/ssh/sshd_config
        regexp: "^PasswordAuthentication"
        line: "PasswordAuthentication yes"
        validate: 'sshd -t -f %s'
      notify: Restart service

  handlers:
    - name: Restart service
      ansible.builtin.service:
        name: sshd
        state: restarted
```

We can execute the Ansible Playbook using the **ansible-playbook** command. The full command is like the following:

```
ansible-playbooklineinfile.yml
```

We executed the code against the target node "**localhost**" with the "**localhost_inventory.ini**" local inventory shown in the *Chapter 2, Ansible Language Core*. The output of the **ansible-playbook** command is the following:

```
TASK [Allow Password Authentication] ***********************************
**********************

changed: [localhost]

PLAY RECAP *************************************************************
**************

localhost: ok=2    changed=1    unreachable=0    failed=0    skipped=0
rescued=0    ignored=0
```

As we can see, the allow password authentication task is in a changed state, which means that some modifications were performed on the target host.

The Ansible module "**lineinfile**" allows us to modify any text file on the filesystem. This module is very powerful, especially when combined with a regular expression, as shown in the example.

When dealing with more lines in a file, we can use the Ansible module "**blockinfile**" with similar parameters and options as the Ansible module "**lineinfile**". However, when editing Linux configuration files, the Ansible template module is preferred. See *Chapter 3 Ansible Language Extended*, section *Ansible template* for more information.

# Create text file

Creating a configuration file is a day-to-day task of every System Administrator, IT Operation Engineer, and SRE. This is because in Linux, everything is a file. It could be a service configuration file, enabling options, or Unix parameters. All of these use cases require the creation of a text file.

The Ansible module "**copy**" is commonly used to copy files to remote locations, as we can learn in the "*Copy Local Files to Remote Hosts*" section. The copy operation is performed from the Ansible controller to the target node. However, the copy module can also create simple text files from scratch. The full name of the Ansible "**copy**" module is "**ansible.builtin.copy**", which means that it is part of the collection of modules of Ansible core installation. The purpose is to copy files to remote locations, but it can also create some simple text files. If we need a more complex configuration, it is recommended to use the Ansible "**template**" module (see *Chapter 3, Ansible Language Extended*, section *Ansible template*).

The Ansible "**copy**" module has many parameters, but the only mandatory parameter is "**dest**". The "**dest**" parameter specifies the remote absolute path destination. The following four optional parameters could become handy summarized in *Table 4.4*:

| Parameter | Description |
|---|---|
| `content` | The contents of a file. |
| `owner` | Specifies the filesystem username. |
| `group` | Specifies the filesystem group. |
| `mode` | Specifies the filesystem in octal mode (`0644`) or symbolic mode (`u=rw,g=r,o=r`) |

***Table 4.4:** Module copy optional parameters*

The content parameter sets the contents of a file directly to the specified value. It works only when the "**`dest`**" is a file. Please note that using a variable in the content parameter will result in unpredictable output. For advanced formatting or if the content contains a variable, use the "**`ansible.builtin.template`**" module (see *Chapter 3, Ansible Language Extended,* section *Ansible template*). We can also specify the file system permissions (mode, owner, and group).

# Create example.txt file

The following Ansible playbook creates a file "**`report.txt`**" with three lines of text inside:

```
1. Automate
2. Everything
3. with Ansible
```

The whole Ansible playbook is the following:

```
---
- name: Create example.txt file
  hosts: all
  vars:
     myfile: "report.txt"
  tasks:
  - name: Create a text file
    ansible.builtin.copy:
      dest: "{{ myfile }}"
      content: |
        1 Automate
```

```
2 Everything
3 with Ansible
```

We can execute our code using the **ansible-playbook** command included in every Ansible installation. The full command is the following:

```
ansible-playbookcopy.yml
```

The output of the execution of the "**copy.yml**" Ansible playbook is the following:

```
TASK [create a text file] ********************************************
***********************
changed: [server01.example.com]
PLAY RECAP ***********************************************************
****************
server01.example.com: ok=2    changed=1    unreachable=0    failed=0
skipped=0    rescued=0    ignored=0
```

As expected, the file **example.txt** was created. We can print the content of the file using the **cat** command:

```
cat report.txt
```

The output of the cat command is the following "**report.txt**" file:

```
1. Automate
2. Everything
3. with Ansible
```

The Ansible module "**copy**" is commonly used to copy files between Ansible Controller and the target node. But we discovered how we could use it to create text files. When we would like to use Ansible variables, facts, or magic variables in the generated file, use the Ansible "**template**" module to avoid some weird fatal error or unexpected behavior. See *Chapter 3, Ansible Language Extended,* section *Ansible Template*.

# File system

Ansible automates many file system operations, as well as handling files and directories. These abilities are very useful when dealing with infrastructure provisioning and application deployment use cases. We are now going to explore the Ansible "**stat**" and "**file**" modules. Please note that there is a common standard about the important files and directories as specified below.

**Tip: All the Linux distributions adhere to the Filesystem Hierarchy Standard (FHS) and Linux Standard Base (LSB), maintained by the Linux Foundation, convection to describe the layout of a UNIX system.**

# Check file exists

The Ansible "**stat**" module, part of the "**ansible.builtin**", retrieves a file entry or a file system status. For Windows target, use the "**ansible.windows.win_stat**" module instead, as described in *Chapter 5, Ansible For Windows*, section *File system*.

The parameter of the Ansible "**stat**" module is **path string**.

The only mandatory parameter is the "**path**" parameter which is the full path on the filesystem of the object to check. The module returns a complex object. The property that is interesting for us is the "**exists**". When this attribute is "**true**", it means that the object exists. This module has the following optional parameter to define some file or directories proprieties described in *Table 4.5*:

| Parameter | Description |
|---|---|
| Owner | It specifies the filesystem username. |
| Group | It specifies the filesystem group. |
| Mode | It specifies the filesystem in octal mode (0644) or symbolic mode (u=rw,g=r,o=r) |

***Table 4.5:*** *File systems modules optional parameters*

Additionally, we can define the SELinux filesystem object context using the "**selevel**", "**serole**", "**setype**", and "**seuser**" parameters.

The following "**check_file.yml**" Ansible playbook displays a message if the file exists or not in the **/home/devops/example.txt** path:

```
---
- name: Check file exists
  hosts: all
  vars:
    myfile: /home/devops/example.txt
  tasks:
    - name: Check if a file exists
      ansible.builtin.stat:
        path: "{{ myfile }}"
```

```
    register: path_data

  - name: Report file exists
    ansible.builtin.debug:
      msg: "The file {{ myfile }} exist"
    when: path_data.stat.exists

  - name: Report file not exists
    ansible.builtin.debug:
      msg: "The file {{ myfile }} doesn't exist"
    when: not path_data.stat.exists
```

In the same way, we can test if the destination path is a directory by checking the "**isdir**" property. The following code shows how to use the condition applied to the "**path_data**" registered variable of the previous code:

```
path_data.stat.isdir is defined and path_data.stat.isdir
```

# Creating an empty file

The Ansible "**file**" module, part of the "**ansible.builtin**" collection, manages files and file properties. For Windows targets, use the "**ansible.windows.win_file**" module instead.

The main parameter of the Ansible "**file**" module are:

- **path string**
- **state string: (file/absent/directory/hard/link/touch)**

The only required parameter is "**path**", which is used to specify the filesystem path of the file or directory. The "**state**" defines the type of object we are modifying. The default is "**file**", but for our use case, we need the "**touch**" option.

This module has the following optional parameter to define some file or directories properties described in *Table 4.6*:

| Parameter | Description |
|---|---|
| `owner` | It specifies the filesystem username. |
| `group` | It specifies the filesystem group. |
| `mode` | It specifies the filesystem in octal mode (`0644`) or symbolic mode (`u=rw,g=r,o=r`) |

***Table 4.6:** File systems modules optional parameters*

Additionally we can define the SELinux filesystem object context using the "**selevel**", "**serole**", "**setype**", and "**seuser**" parameters.

The following "**file.yml**" Ansible playbook creates the "**example.txt**" file in the current user home directory:

```
---
- name: File module
  hosts: all
  vars:
     myfile: "~/example.txt"
  tasks:
    - name: Creating an empty file
      ansible.builtin.file:
        path: "{{ myfile }}"
        state: touch
```

We can execute using the following **ansible-playbook** command:

```
ansible-playbookfile.yml
```

At the end of the execution, we are going to see the **example.txt** file in the current user home directory.

# Creating a directory

In the same way we created a file, we can create a directory using the "**directory**" parameter of the Ansible "**file**" module. The following "**directory.yml**" Ansible playbook creates an "**example**" directory in the current home directory:

```
---
- name: Create directory
  hosts: all
  vars:
    mydir: "~/example"
  tasks:
    - name: Creating a directory
      ansible.builtin.file:
        path: "{{ mydir }}"
        state: directory
        owner: devops
```

```
      group: users
      mode: '0644'
```

We can execute using the following **ansible-playbook** command:

```
ansible-playbookdirectory.yml
```

At the end of the execution, we are going to see the **example** directory in the current user home directory.

```
[devops@server01.example.com ~]$ ls -al
drw-r--r--. 2 devops users    6 Apr 15 13:45 example
```

# Soft and hard link

The Ansible "**file**" module enables us also to create a soft (symbolic link or symlink) and hard link to a file or directory. We just need to specify in the "**state**" parameter, the value "link" for the soft link and "hard" for a hard link and define the file system path using the parameters:

- "**src**" string - link path
- "**dest**" string - destination file path

The following "**link.yml**" Ansible playbook creates a symlink named "**link**" pointing to the **/proc/cpuinfo**" file:

```
---
- name: File module
  hosts: all
  vars:
     mylink: "~/link"
     mysrc: "/proc/cpuinfo"
  tasks:
    - name: Creating a symlink
      ansible.builtin.file:
         src: "{{ mysrc }}"
         dest: "{{ mylink }}"
         state: link
```

We can execute using the following **ansible-playbook** command:

```
ansible-playbooklink.yml
```

At the end of the execution, we are going to see the "**link**" symlink in the current user home directory.

```
[devops@server01.example.com ~]$ ls -al
lrwxrwxrwx. 1 devops wheel   13 Nov 14 14:29 link -> /proc/cpuinfo
```

# Deleting a file

We can delete a file or directory using the Ansible "**file**" module. We need to specify the value "**absent**" of the parameter "**state**".

The following "**delete.yml**" Ansible playbook deletes the "**deleteme**" file or directory in the "**devops**" user home directory:

```
---
- name: File module
  hosts: all
  vars:
    mypath: "/home/devops/deleteme"
  become: false
  tasks:
    - name: "{{ mypath }}" not present
      ansible.builtin.file:
        path: "{{ mypath }}"
        state: "absent"
```

We can execute using the following **ansible-playbook** command:

```
ansible-playbookdelete.yml
```

At the end of the execution, the expected file or directory "**deleteme**" was deleted in the "**devops**" user home directory.

# Copying local files to remote hosts

The Ansible "**copy**" module is part of the "**ansible.builtin**" collection, which copies files to remote locations. Please note that the opposite is done by the Ansible "**fetch**" module. The main parameters of the Ansible "**copy**" module are as follows:

- `dest path`
- `src string`
- `backup boolean`

- `validate string`
- `checksum string`
- `owner/group/mode string - permission`
- `setype/seuser/selevel - SELinux`

The "**dest**" required parameter specifies the remote absolute path destination. The "**src**" specifies the source file in the controller host. It could be a relative or absolute path. The "**backup**" boolean parameter allows you to create a backup if the utility overwrites any file. We can specify how to validate the validation command, in order to run before copying the updated file into the final destination, using the "**validate**" parameter. We can also specify the file system parameters as shown in *Table 4.7*:

| Parameter | Description |
|---|---|
| `Owner` | It specifies the filesystem username |
| `Group` | It specifies the filesystem group |
| `Mode` | It specifies the filesystem in octal mode (`0644`) or symbolic mode (`u=rw,g=r,o=r`) |

*Table 4.7: Copy module optional parameters*

The following "**copy.yml**" Ansible playbook copies the local file "**report.txt**" from the "**devops**" user home directory to the remote host:

```
---
- name: Copy file
  hosts: all
  tasks:
    - name: Copy report.txt
      ansible.builtin.copy:
        src: report.txt
        dest: /home/devops/report.txt
        owner: devops
        mode: '0644'
```

We can execute using the following **ansible-playbook** command:

```
ansible-playbookcopy.yml
```

At the end of the execution, the "**report.txt**" file is copied into the remote path **/home/devops/report.txt** owned by the "**devops**" user.

## Copying remote files to local

We can copy files from remote hosts to local ones using the Ansible "**fetch**" module. It is part of the "**ansible.builtin**" collection. The purpose of the module is to copy files from remote locations. Please note that the opposite is done by the Ansible "**copy**" module.

The main parameters of the Ansible "**fetch**" module are:

- **dest** path
- **src** string
- **fail_on_missing boolean**
- **validate_checksum boolean**
- **flat boolean**

The only required parameter is "**dest**" which specifies a directory to save the file into, and the "**src**" specifies the source files in the remote hosts. It must be a file, not a directory. The "**fail_on_missing**" boolean is set to true, and so the task is going to fail if the file does not exist. The file is going to be transferred and validated in the source and the destination with a checksum. If we do not want this behavior, we could override with the value "**false**" in the "**validate_checksum**" option (default "**true**"). The "**flat**" option allows us to override the default behavior of appending the "**hostname/path/to/file**" directory structure to the destination. A typical use case is to fetch log files from remote servers.

The following "**fetch.yml**" Ansible playbook copies the remote file **/var/log/messages** to the local Ansible controller:

```
---
- name: Fetch log
  hosts: all
  become: true
  vars:
     log_file: "/var/log/messages"
     save_dir: "logs"
  tasks:
    - name: Fetch log
      ansible.builtin.fetch:
          src: "{{ log_file }}"
          dest: "{{ save_dir }}"
```

We can execute the "**fetch.yml**" playbook using the following **ansible-playbook** command:

**ansible-playbookfetch.yml**

At the end of the execution, the **/var/log/messages** file is copied from the remote server to the local "**logs**" directory of the Ansible controller. Learn more about another usage of the Ansible "**copy**" module in the "**Create Text File**" section.

# File download

We can download some files from a remote server using the Ansible "**get_url**" module, which is part of the "**ansible.builtin**" collection. It downloads files from HTTP, HTTPS, or FTP to the node for Windows targets, using the "**ansible.windows.win_get_url**" module.

The main parameters of the Ansible "**get**" module are as follows:

- **url** string: URL
- **dest** string: path
- **force** string: no/yes
- **checksum** string : <algorithm>:<checksum | url>
- **force_basic_auth/url_username/url_password/use_gssapi** authentications
- **headers** dictionary: custom HTTP headers
- **http_agent** string
- **owner/group/mode** string: permission
- **setype/seuser/selevel**: SELinux

The two required parameters are "**url**" and "**dest**". The "**url**" parameter specifies the URL of the resource you are going to download. The "**dest**" parameter specifies the filesystem path where the resource is going to be saved on the target node. When the destination ("**dest**" parameter) is a file, Ansible is going to download the file every time. When the destination ("**dest**" parameter) is a directory, the default behavior is not to replace a file until we enable the "**force**" parameter. The parameter "**checksum**" is very useful for validating the consistency of the downloaded file. You could specify the algorithm, usually with **sha1** or **sha256** hashing libraries, and directly the checksum or a URL for the checksum. We might need the third-party "**hashlib**" library installed as a package in the system for access to additional algorithms. Another interesting parameter is "**headers**" which allows us to specify some custom HTTP headers. Ansible presents itself as "**ansible-httpget**" in the web server logs, but we customize it in the "**http_agent**" parameter. There are some additional parameters for authentication, for example, to handle HTTP basic authentication with username and password or for more complex GSSAPI-Kerberos scenarios, Ansible uses the additional "**httplib2**" Python library. Let us also highlight that we can also specify the file system permission with the same parameter of *Table 4.5* and SELinux filesystem object context using the "**selevel**", "**serole**", "**setype**", and "**seuser**" parameters.

The following "**download.yml**" Ansible playbook downloads a file from an HTTPS website, verifies the SHA checksum, and saves it in the home directory of the "**devops**" user:

```
---
- name: File download
  hosts: all
  vars:
       myurl: "https://releases.ansible.com/ansible/ansible-2.9.27.tar.gz"
       mycrc: "sha256:https://releases.ansible.com/ansible/
ansible-2.9.27.tar.gz.sha"
       mydest: "/home/devops"
  tasks:
     - name: File Download
       ansible.builtin.get_url:
          url: "{{ myurl }}"
          dest: "{{ mydest }}"
          checksum: "{{ mycrc }}"
          mode: '0644'
          owner: devops
          group: users
```

**Tip: Latest releases of Ansible are not hosted on the https://releases.ansible.com website but on the PyPI website. See Chapter 1, Getting Started, section Ansible Installation.**

We can execute the "**download.yml**" playbook using the following **ansible-playbook** command:

```
ansible-playbookdownload.yml
```

At the end of the execution, the "**ansible-2.9.27.tar.gz**" file is downloaded, the checksum is verified, and saved on the path "**ansible-2.9.27.tar.gz**" owned by the "**devops**" user. We can interact with an API service using the "**ansible.**

**builtin.uri**" module as described in *Chapter 8, Ansible Advanced,* section *Third-Party Integrations, Fragility, Agility.*

# Backup with rsync

To back up with **rsync** using Ansible, we can use the "**synchronize**" Ansible module, which allows us to synchronize files between two directories. The "**synchronize**" Ansible module is part of the "**ansible.builtin**" collection. Here are the steps to backup with **rsync**:

1. Define the source and destination directories in our playbook.
2. Use the "**synchronize**" module to synchronize the directories. We can set the `**mode**` parameter to "**backup**" in order to create a backup of the destination directory before copying any files.
3. Run the playbook to synchronize the directories.

Here is an example playbook that backs up files from a remote server to a local backup directory using rsync:

```
---
- name: Backup
  hosts: all
  vars:
       source_dir: /var/www
       dest_dir: /backups
  tasks:
     - name: Backup files with rsync
       ansible.builtin.synchronize:
         src: "{{ source_dir }}"
         dest: "{{ dest_dir }}"
         mode: backup
```

This will create a backup of the destination directory in the format "**dest_dir.TIMESTAMP**" before copying any files.

# Checkout a Git repository

When we need to deploy an application, we often need to download "**checkout**" a Git repository. This is useful for deploying an application or single file using Ansible. We can use the Ansible "**git**" module, which is a part of the "**ansible.builtin**" collection. The easiest way is to "**checkout**" a repository is using the HTTPS method.

The main parameters of the Ansible "**git**" module are as follows:

- **repo** path
- **dest** string
- **update** boolean
- **key_file** path: SSH private key

The only required parameters are "**repo**" and "**dest**". As probably expected by the name, the "**repo**" parameter specifies the source repository URL. The "**dest**" parameter specifies the destination path. The "**update**" retrieves new revisions from the already synched origin repository. When the SSH protocol is used instead of the HTTPS protocol, the "**key_file**" parameter specifies the path in the filesystem where to store the SSH private key. Please note that the SSH private key is a path on the target host. Please also note that the SSH public key needs to be already shared in our Git server. On the return values, the "**after**" value contains the last commit after the update process.

The following "**git.yml**" Ansible playbook first verifies that the "**git**" package is present in the target hosts and then checkout the specified repository via HTTPS protocol.

```
---
- name: Deploy Application
  hosts: all
  tasks:
    - name: Git installed
      ansible.builtin.package:
      become: true
        name: git
        state: present

    - name: Checkout git repo
      ansible.builtin.git:
        repo: https://github.com/ansible/ansible.git
        dest: /home/devops/automate-everything-with-ansible
```

We can execute the "**git.yml**" playbook using the following **ansible-playbook** command:

```
ansible-playbookgit.yml
```

At the end of the execution, the content of the Git repository is saved on the path **/home/devops/automate-everything-with-ansible** owned by the "**devops**" user in the target host.

# Installing packages and rolling update

Installing software as packages and rolling updates are great Ansible use cases for package and patch management in our fleet. When we need to modify the software on the target machine, we need to classify the Linux distributions by the package format used. This is a simple classification used from now onward:

- "Red Hat"-like,
- "Debian"-like,
- "SUSE"-like,
- Other types.

The "Red Hat-like" operating systems are based on the RPM package format, using the **yum** or **DNF** package manager. The list of Linux distribution is **Red Hat Enterprise Linux** (**RHEL**), CentOS, CentOS Stream, AlmaLinux, Rocky Linux, Fedora, ClearOS, Oracle Linux, Amazon Linux, EuroLinux, Fermi Linux, EulerOS, ROSA Linux, Springdale Linux, and Asianux. Since RHEL version 8 adopted the DNF package manage stands for Dandified YUM and is basically an improved version of the YUM package manager. The "Debian-like" operating systems are based on the DEB package format, using the APT package manager. The list of Linux distributions is Debian, Ubuntu, Linux Mint, MX Linux, Deepin, antiX, PureOS, Kali Linux, Parrot OS, Devuan, Knoppix, and AV Linux. The "SUSE-like" operating systems are based on the RPM package format, using the Zypper package manager. The list of Linux distributions is limited to the SUSE Linux Enterprise Server and openSUSE. The package format and the package manager are relevant only when we need to modify the software on the target system to determine the relevant Ansible module for the target system:

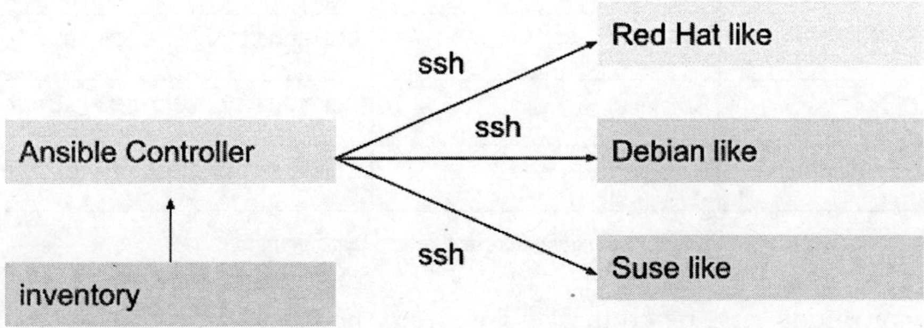


*Figure 4.1: Ansible Linux target architecture*

The full list of the operating system package manager and Ansible modules is summarized in *Table 4.7*:

| Distribution | Package Manager | Ansible module |
|---|---|---|
| "Red Hat"-like | YUM | **`ansible.builtin.yum`** |
| | DNF | **`ansible.builtin.dnf`** |
| AIX | installp | **`community.general.installp`** |
| Alpine Linux | Alpine Package Keeper | **`community.general.apk`** |
| | Local Backup Utility | **`community.general.lbu`** |
| Arch Linux | pacman | **`community.general.pacman`** |
| ClearLinux | swupd | **`community.general.swupd`** |
| Debian-like | APT | **`ansible.builtin.apt`** |
| FreeBSD | pkgng | **`community.general.pkgng`** |
| Gentoo Linux | Portage | **`community.general.portage`** |
| | Layman | **`community.general.layman`** |
| HP-UX | swdepot | **`community.general.swdepot`** |
| macOS | MacPorts | **`community.general.macports`** |
| | Homebrew | **`community.general.homebrew`** |
| OpenBSD | pkg | **`community.general.openbsd_pkg`** |
| Openembedded/Yocto | opkg | **`community.general.opkg`** |
| Slackware | slackpkg | **`community.general.slackpkg`** |
| SmartOS, NetBSD | pkgsrc | **`community.general.pkgin`** |
| Solaris 11 | Image Packaging System | **`community.general.pkg5`** |
| Solaris SVR4 | svr4pkg | **`community.general.svr4pkg`** |
| Source Mage | Sorcery | **`community.general.sorcery`** |
| SUSE and openSUSE | Zypper | **`community.general.zypper`** |

***Table 4.7:*** *Ansible modules for OS package manager*

The rolling update and patch management are the typical use case of Ansible. We can use it in the provisioning or maintenance of our server infrastructure fleet. Ansible installed modules work by automating existing package management tools.

In a "Red Hat"-like Linux distribution target, we are going to use the YUM or DNF package management, whereas in the "Debian"-like Linux distribution target, we are going to use the APT package manager. To implement a full rolling update process complement with the "**`fork`**" and "**`serial`**" statement in our playbook. Learn more about in the *Chapter 8, Ansible Advanced,* section *Ansible Orchestration.*

# Ansible package module

There is a "**`package`**" module, part of the "**`ansible.builtin`**" collection, which can install packages using different tools. It detects which package management tool to use for each target machine. There are the following limitations for the "**`package`**" Ansible module:

- Package names are often different.
- Package versions are often different.
- Different package tools support different options.

It is virtually impossible to map all the package name differences between the different distributions. Some simple examples are the following packages names in *Table 4.8*:

| "Red Hat"-like | "Debian"-like |
|---|---|
| **`httpd`** | **`apache2`** |
| **`sqlite`** | **`sqlite3`** |
| **`bzip2-devel`** | **`libbz2-dev`** |
| **`xorg-x11-server`** | **`xorg`** |

***Table 4.8:*** *Common package names differences*

# Ansible yum module

We can update a "Red Hat"-like Linux distribution using the "**`yum`**" Ansible module or the "**`dnf`**" Ansible module, and furthermore, both are part of the "**`ansible.builtin`**" collection. Since Ansible Core 2.15, there is also the newest "**`dnf5`**" Ansible module to work with, which is the version 5 of the DNF package manager included in the Fedora 39 release. The Ansible "**`yum`**", "**`dnf`**" and "**`dnf5`**" modules required "**`root`**" privileges to execute any actions on the target host. The parameter list is pretty wide, and the following four options are relevant to our use case.

The main parameters of the Ansible "**`yum`**", "**`dnf`**" and "**`dnf5`**" modules are as follows:

- **`name`** string
- **`state`** string

- **update_cache** boolean
- **bugfix** boolean
- **security** boolean

The "**name**" parameter specifies a single package or all the packages of the system with the "*" star symbol. The state for this case needs to be "**latest**" so that we target the latest version for every package. The "**update_cache**" is useful to force the update of repository metadata before the installation, default "**no**". Other very interesting options are "**bugfix**" and "**security**" which allow us to update only packages marked as a bugfix or security-related update.

The following "**yum.yml**" playbook updates all the Red Hat Enterprise Linux distributions and derivates:

```
---
- name: Rolling update
  hosts: all
  become: true
  tasks:
    - name: System update
      ansible.builtin.yum:
        name: "*"
        state: latest
        update_cache: true
```

We can execute the "**yum.yml**" playbook using the following **ansible-playbook** command:

```
ansible-playbookyum.yml
```

# Ansible apt module

We can update a Debian-like Linux distribution using the "**apt**" Ansible module, which is part of the "**ansible.builtin**" collection. The module "**apt**" required "**root**" privileges to execute any actions on the target host.

The main parameters of the Ansible "**apt**" module are as follows:

- **name** string
- **state** string
- **update_cache** boolean
- upgradeno/safe/full/dist

The "**name**" parameter specifies a single package or we could select all the packages of the system with the "*****" star symbol. The state for this case needs to be "**latest**" so that we target the latest version for every package. The "**update_cache**" is useful to force the update of repository metadata before the installation.

Another useful option is the "**upgrade**" when performing a distribution upgrade with four alternatives:

- the default value is a "**no**" (disabled)
- **safe**: performs an **aptitude safe-upgrade**
- **full**: performs an **aptitude full-upgrade**
- **dist**: performs an **apt-get dist-upgrade**

The following "**apt.yml**" Ansible playbook is useful for updating all the packages in the current system, to the latest version, before it updates the repository cache. Therefore, we are going to download the latest version of each package, as shown:

```
---
- name: Rolling update
  hosts: all
  become: true
  tasks:
    - name: System update
      ansible.builtin.apt:
        name: "*"
        state: latest
        update_cache: true
```

We can execute the "**apt.yml**" playbook using the following **ansible-playbook** command:

```
ansible-playbookapt.yml
```

# Ansible zypper module

We can update a SUSE-like Linux distribution using the "**zypper**" Ansible module, which is part of the "**community.general**" collection. Please ensure the "**community.general**" collection is installed in the Ansible controller before executing the following "**suse.yml**" playbook. The parameter list is similar to the previous modules. See *Chapter 3, Ansible Language Extended,* section *Ansible Collection* for more information. The "**suse.yml**" Ansible playbook looks like the following:

```
---
- name: Rolling update
  hosts: all
  become: true
  tasks:
    - name: System update
      community.general.zypper:
        name: "*"
        state: latest
       update_cache: true
```

We can execute the "**suse.yml**" playbook using the following **ansible-playbook** command:

```
ansible-playbooksuse.yml
```

The time of execution of the "**yum.yml**", "**apt.yml**" and "**suse.yml**," depends on the connection speed, the number of packages to update, and the performance of the target machine. The result of the execution is a system up-to-date with the latest packages available in the distribution repository.

# Linux System Roles

The Linux System Roles are a set of Ansible roles and collections to manage and configure common GNU/Linux operating system components. Do not reinvent the wheel for most command tasks in our everyday work with Linux systems. The supported target operating systems are Fedora, **Red Hat Enterprise Linux** (**RHEL 6+**), and derivatives such as CentOS 6+. At the moment of writing this book, the following subsystems are supported:

- email (postfix)
- kdump (kernel crash dump)
- network
- SELinux
- TimeSync
- storage
- TLOG (terminal logging, session recording)
- logging

- metrics
- nbde_server
- nbde_client
- certificate
- kernel_settings (sysctl, sysfs, and so on.)
- SSH server (used in the collection) ansible-sshd
- SSH client
- VPN (IPSec - libreswan)
- Crypto policies
- Cluster HA (pacemaker/corosync)
- Cockpit
- firewall
- Systemd-journald
- Active Directory join
- podman
- Red Hat Subscription Management and Insights

The first step is to install the selected Linux System Roles. Let us suppose we would like to set up an NTP service in our fleet to keep the time in sync with the atomic clocks via the Internet. We can manually download the latest role from the Ansible Galaxy archive using the **`ansible-galaxy`** command:

```
ansible-galaxy install linux-system-roles.timesync
```

As always, we can create a **`requirements.yml`** file to automate the installation of the role from the Ansible Galaxy archive. See *Chapter 3, Ansible Language Extended,* section *Ansible role.* In Red Hat Enterprise Linux 9 and 8.6 and later, it is possible to install RHEL System Roles ("**`rhel-system-roles`**" package) from the Application Streams repository:

```
dnf install rhel-system-roles ansible-core
```

The following **`ntp.yml`** Ansible playbook sets up the NTP client service (usually the **`chrony`** service):

```
---
- hosts: all
  vars:
```

```
    timesync_ntp_servers:
      - hostname: europe.pool.ntp.org
        iburst: true
  roles:
    - linux-system-roles.timesync
```

The **ntp.yml** Ansible Playbook sets up the configuration file to use the **europe.pool.ntp.org** server and execute an initial synchronization with the target server (**iburst: true**), adjusting the time straightaway if necessary. The output of the execution via the command **ansible-playbook** is long and verbose, and at the end, we obtain a configured NTP service on the target server.

In the same way, we can use other Ansible Roles and collections to install and configure other services in our workflow.

# User management

Using the Ansible "**user**" module, we can manage users in our target nodes, that are part of the "**ansible.builtin**" collection. It is a module stable and out for years. It manages user accounts. It supports a huge variety of Linux distributions, SunOS and MacOS, and FreeBSD. This module uses the Linux distribution "**useradd**" tool for user creation. On FreeBSD, it uses **pw useradd**, and on MacOS, this module uses "**dscl create**". For Windows, use the "**ansible.windows.win_user**" module of *Chapter 5, Ansible for Windows*, section "*User Management*". The main parameters of the Ansible "**user**" module are as follows:

- **name** string: username
- **state** string: present / absent
- **password** string
- **uid** string
- **comment** string
- **shell** string
- **expires** string
- **password_expire_min** string
- **password_expire_max** string
- **group/groups** string: primary / membership group(s)
- **create_home** boolean: yes / no
- **generate_ssh_key** string

- **ssh_key_bits** string
- **ssh_key_file** string
- **ssh_key_type** string
- **ssh_key_passphrase** string

The only required parameter of the module is "**name**", which is the local user username. The "**state**" parameter allows us to create or delete a user. In our use case, the default is already set to "**present**" to create a user. We need to use the "**password**" parameter in conjunction with the "**passhword_hash**" filter to generate a SHA512 password hash. Please note that we could specify the encryption algorithm as well as the salt to make our password more robust. We could specify all the usual Unix properties such as "**uid**", "**comment**", "**shell**", "**expires**", "**password_expire_min**", and "**password_expire_max**".

Other important parameters are "**group**" and "**groups**". The first (without the "s" suffix) indicates the primary group of the user, and the second (with the "s" suffix) sets the other group members. So be very careful with the "s" suffix. It could end up in a very different setup. Usually, we would like to create a user home directory so that the "**create_home**" parameter defaults to yes, but we could override it if we do not need a home directory. Let us also highlight that we could also generate an SSH key with a lot of options. The fingerprint and the public key are available in the long list of returned values. The full "**user.yml**" Ansible playbook creates a user "**example**" in the target system with the following characteristics:

```
---
- name: Create a user account
  hosts: all
  become: true
  tasks:
    - name: User example exist
      ansible.builtin.user:
        name: example
        password: "{{ 'password' | password_hash('sha512', 'mysecretsalt') }}"
        groups:
          - wheel
          - adm
        state: "present"
        shell: "/bin/bash"
        system: false
```

```
create_home: true
home: "/home/example"
comment: "Automate Everything with Ansible"
generate_ssh_key: true
```

We can execute the "**user.yml**" playbook using the following **ansible-playbook** command:

```
ansible-playbookuser.yml
```

At the end of the execution, the local user "**example**" is created with the options specified in the Ansible playbook.

# Linux aging policy

Another common use case of Ansible is to configure the Linux password expiration for local users. We use the "**password_expire_min**" and "**password_expire_max**" parameters of the Ansible "**user**" module. Please note that these parameters are Linux only.

Refer to *Figure 4.2:*

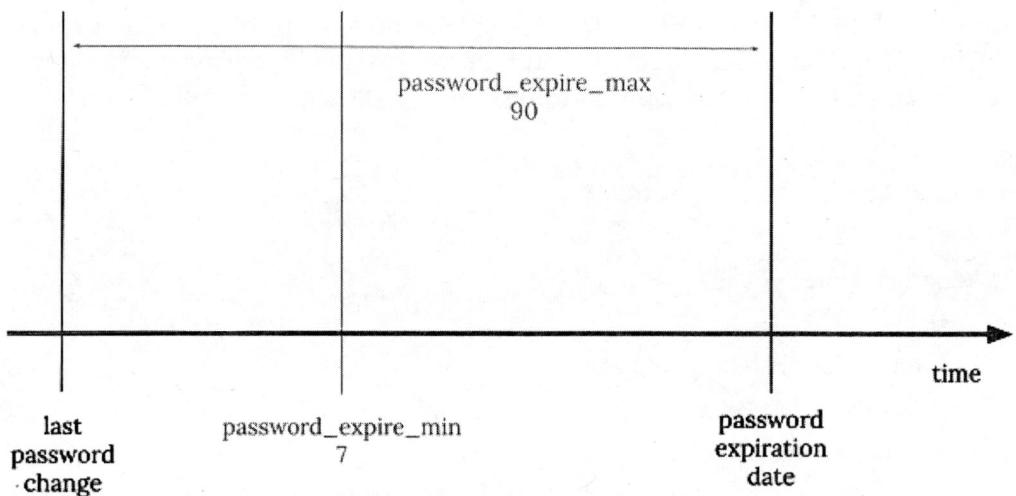


***Figure 4.2:*** *The Linux password aging policy.*

The schema in *Figure 4.2* represents the Linux password aging policy. We can set the Linux minimum days validity with the "**password_expire_min**", whereas we set the Linux maximum days validity with the "**password_expire_max**". To disable password aging, specify the value of 99999.

The following "**expiration.yml**" Ansible playbook specifies that the user named "example" must wait for a minimum of 7 days to change their password, and the password will expire in 90 days.

```
---
- name: Password expiration
  hosts: all
  become: true
  vars:
      myuser: "example"
  tasks:
    - name: Set password expiration
      ansible.builtin.user:
        name: "{{ myuser }}"
        password_expire_min: 7
        password_expire_max: 90
```

We can execute the "**expiration.yml**" playbook using the following **ansible-playbook** command:

```
ansible-playbook expiration.yml
```

At the end of the execution, the local user "**example**" has 7 days of minimum password expiration days and 90 days of password maximum expiration days.

We can check these parameters using the "**change**" command line with the "**-l**" parameter with the name of the user.

```
chage -l example
```

The output shows the last password change, the expiration date, and the password aging policies in place at the moment for the user.

```
Last password change     : Apr 17, 2023
Password expires     : Jul 16, 2023
Password inactive     : never
Account expires     : never
Minimum number of days between password change  : 0
Maximum number of days between password change  : 90
Number of days of warning before password expires : 7
```

# Group management

In the same way as the Ansible "**user**" module, the "**group**" module manages the local group(s) in the target Linux system. The main parameters of the Ansible "**group**" module:

- **name** string: group name
- **state** string - present/absent
- **system boolean**: yes/no
- **gid** integer: GID to set for the group
- **local** string: "local" command alternatives

The only required parameter is "**name**", which is the group name. The "**state**" parameter allows us to create or delete a group. In our use case, the default is already set to "**present**" to create a group. The "**system**" parameter allows for the creation of a system group. By default, it's not. We could specify the GID, the group identifier, by using the "**gid**" parameter. The "**local**" parameter allows using the "**local**" command alternatives on platforms that implement it if we have a central authentication system. The following "**group.yml**" Ansible playbook creates a local group "**accounting**" in the target system:

```
---
- name: Group management
  hosts: all
  become: true
  vars:
      mygroup: 'accounting'
  tasks:
    - name: Create group
      ansible.builtin.group:
        name: "{{ mygroup }}"
        state: present
```

We can execute the "**group.yml**" playbook using the following **ansible-playbook** command:

```
ansible-playbook group.yml
```

At the end of the execution, the local group "**accounting**" is created in the target Linux system.

# Executing commands

As a general rule, always prefer a dedicated module for a task. When there is not any Ansible module, we can still execute direct terminal commands on the target nodes using the command and shell Ansible modules. From the top point of view, they look similar, but underneath, they have different behavior. Using an Ansible module to execute a task is always a good practice, but sometimes, there isn't any Ansible module for our use case. In such a case, we can use the **`command`** and **`shell`** Ansible modules to execute commands on the target nodes.

In these circumstances, we can use the command and shell Ansible modules to execute commands on the target nodes. This is a suboptimal solution because we effectively execute a terminal command via the command and shell Ansible modules.

Let us clarify the differences between "**`command`**" vs. "**`shell`**" Ansible modules. Both allow us to execute commands on Linux target hosts. Most people confuse these two Ansible modules, but they are fundamentally different. Both modules allow us to execute commands on a target host but in slightly different ways. We should avoid using the **`command`** or **`shell`** Ansible module as much as possible and instead, use an Ansible-specific module. Both of these modules return a changed status on execution, as Ansible cannot analyze the execution of these modules and detect if they have or have not altered the target system.

# Ansible command module

The Ansible "**`command`**" module executes commands against the target Unix-based hosts bypassing the target node shell. It always returns the changed status. The "**`command`**" Ansible module executes commands on the target machine without using any target shell; it simply executes the command. The "**`command`**" Ansible module is the default module in Ansible Ad-hoc mode. The **`command`** module can execute only the binaries on remote hosts. Local shell variables will not impact the **`command`** module because it bypasses the shell. At the same time, it may not be able to run "**`shell`**" built-in features and redirections. From the security point of view, the **`command`** module is more robust and has a more predictable outcome because it bypasses the shell.

# Ansible shell module

The Ansible "**`shell`**" module executes shell commands against the target Unix-based hosts using the target node shell for redirection and inbuilt functionality. It always returns the changed status. The target shell is, for example, the famous "**`bash`**", "**`zsh`**", or "**`sh`**". As a side effect user environment, variable expansions, output redirections, stringing two commands together, and other shell features are unavailable. On the other side, every command executed using the **`shell`** module has all shell features so that it can be expanded in runtime. The **"shell"** Ansible module is potentially more dangerous than the **command** module and should only be used when we need the shell functionality. So we don't need the shell module if we are not stringing two commands together (using pipes or even just "**&&**" or "**;**" operators). Similarly, expanding shell variables or files globally requires the shell module. Use the Ansible **shell** module only when strictly needed.

# Uptime playbook

Let me demonstrate the difference between the "**command**" and "**shell**" Ansible modules in an Ansible Playbook.

```
uptime
```

```
13:10:16 up 45 min,  0 users,  load average: 0.12, 0.08, 0.07
```

Suppose we would like to check the "**uptime**" time of a server. It is an overall operation that does not require full shell capabilities. Hence, the full Ansible "**command.yml**" file:

```
---
- name: Check uptime
  hosts: all
  tasks:
    - name: Check uptime
      ansible.builtin.command: uptime
      register: command_output

    - name: Command output
      ansible.builtin.debug:
        var: command_output.stdout_lines
```

We can execute our code using the **ansible-playbook** command included in every Ansible installation.

```
ansible-playbook command.yml
```

The execution of the **ansible-playbook** command results in output as follows:

```
TASK [Check uptime] *****************************************************
***********************

changed: [server01.example.com]

TASK [Command output] ***************************************************
***********************
```

```
ok: [server01.example.com] => {
    "command_output.stdout_lines": [
        "13:10:16 up 45 min,  0 users,  load average: 0.12, 0.08, 0.07"
    ]
}
PLAY RECAP ***********************************************************
****************
server01.example.com: ok=3    changed=1    unreachable=0    failed=0
skipped=0    rescued=0    ignored=0
```

## Listing files

Listing files is a typical operation requiring full "**shell**" capabilities displayed in the following "**shell.yml**" playbook file:

```
---
- name: Listing files
  hosts: all
  tasks:
    - name: List file(s) and folder(s)
      ansible.builtin.shell: 'ls -l *'
      register: command_output

    - name: Command output
      ansible.builtin.debug:
        var: command_output.stdout_lines
```

We can execute the "**shell.yml**" Ansible playbook using the **ansible-playbook** command in every Ansible installation. The full command is the following:

```
ansible-playbook shell.yml
```

The output of the execution of the Ansible playbook **shell.yml** is the following:

```
TASK [List file(s) and folder(s)] ***********************************
***********************
changed: [server01.example.com]
TASK [Command output] ***********************************************
************************
ok: [server01.example.com] => {
```

```
    "command_output.stdout_lines": [
        "-rwxrwxrwx1  devops users  245 Apr 14 11:04 command.yml",
        "-rwxrwxrwx1  devops users  258 Apr 14 11:04 shell.yml",
    ]
}
PLAY RECAP ************************************************************
****************

server01.example.com: ok=3    changed=1    unreachable=0    failed=0
skipped=0    rescued=0    ignored=0
```

# Wrong module

When we use the wrong module between the "**command**" and "**shell**" modules, we obtain a fatal error. Refer to *Chapter 6, Ansible Troubleshooting,* section *Ansible Modules,* for further troubleshooting. For example, when we execute the listing of the files of the previous "**shell.yml**" playbook using the "**command**" module instead of the "**shell**" module:

```
"stderr": "ls: cannot access '*': No such file or directory", "stderr_
lines":
["ls: cannot access '*': No such file or directory"], "stdout": "",
"stdout_lines": []
```

The "**command**" and "**shell**" Ansible modules are the jolly module to use when there is not a specific Ansible module for our task. Use them wisely! The command module is more limited, whereas the shell is more powerful and potentially harmful.

# Conclusion

We learned how we could save time by automating some tasks in our Linux infrastructure. As we learned, automation is simple, and we can easily extend it for our everyday use cases. In the next chapter, we are learning how to automate the Windows target system in a similar way to the Linux infrastructure.

# Points to remember

- Most of the recent Linux distributions are already ready to use Ansible. Just set up an SSH password or key authentication and use the Python interpreter.
- The simplest Ansible module is "**ping**" which tests the authentication and execution of a Python code on a Linux target host

- Configuration management could be performed using the Ansible "**`lineinfile`**" module, Ansible "**`blockinfile`**" module, and Ansible "**`template`**" module.
- Many modules simplify file system management: check the existence of files and directories with the Ansible "**`stat`**" module, create files, directories, soft and hard links with the Ansible "**`file`**" module, download contents with the Ansible "**`get_url`**" module and checkout a Git repository using the Ansible "**`git`**" module.
- The Ansible "**`user`**" and "**`group`**" modules simplify the local user and group management
- We can categorize the Linux distributions via the package format and use an Ansible module to automate the interaction between the package managers. There is a wide support of operating systems and tools.

# Key terms

- **Verbosity:** We can execute our Ansible playbook specifying the verbosity level from 0 to 4, increasing the printing of debugging information.
- **Configuration Management (CM):** Refers to the process of maintaining computer software in a desired state. Configuration Management is also a method of ensuring that systems perform in a manner consistent with expectations over time.
- **File system:** Refers to the method and data structures (files and directories) used by the operating system uses to store and retrieve data from storage.
- **User Management:** Refers to the activities to create, update, delete, and maintain local users and groups in a system.
- **Rolling update:** Refers to a strategy to update a system in place with zero downtime.

# Multiple choice questions

1. **What are the requirements to configure a Linux target?**
    a. OpenSSH service running and Python interpreter
    b. WinRM service running and Python interpreter
    c. WinRM service running and PowerShell interpreter
    d. OpenSSH service running and PowerShell interpreter

2. **What is the best way to install an NTP client in a Red Hat Enterprise Linux?**
    a. Ansible apt module
    b. Linux System Roles
    c. Ansible package module
    d. Ansible file module
3. **How can we execute the command "`cat /proc/cpuinfo | grep 'model'`" on a Linux target?**
    a. Ansible **`command`** module
    b. Ansible **`shell`** module
    c. Ansible **`cpuinfo`** module
    d. It is not possible
4. **What is the easiest way to install the "`git`" package in different Linux distributions?**
    a. Use multiple Ansible modules with the **`when`** statement
    b. Ansible **`apt`** module
    c. Ansible **`package`** module
    d. Ansible **`yum`** module

## Answers

**1. a** **2. b** **3. b** **4. c**

# Questions

1. Why is SSH key authentication preferred instead of SSH password authentication?
2. What is the effect of the usage of the "**`verbosity`**" parameter of the Ansible "**`debug`**" module?
3. What is another usage of the Ansible "**`copy`**" module apart from copying files to the target node?
4. How can we check if a file or directory exists on the target node?
5. Why is it discouraged from using the Ansible "**`package`**" module?
6. When is it necessary to use the Ansible "**`command`**" and "**`shell`**" modules?

CHAPTER 5

# Automating Windows Infrastructure with Ansible

## Introduction

Automating Windows using Ansible is very convenient, especially for a large fleet. We are going to begin with the host configuration, and then we can move forward with the automation part. We are going to explore the same use case of the Linux operating system in a Windows environment with different Ansible modules for the file system, user management, and many of the daily system administration tasks. We are going to capitalize on all the lessons we have learned so far about Ansible technology. In this chapter, we are learning about how to configure a Windows target system and how to perform files and directories operations and update the software on Windows and Windows Server.

## Structure

In this chapter, we shall cover the following topics:

- Configuring Windows target
- Testing the host availability
- Configuration management
- File system

- Installing packages
- Rolling update
- User management
- Windows registry
- Executing commands

# Objectives

By the end of this chapter, the reader will know/be able to understand how to save time by automating tasks and operations in the Windows operating system with Ansible technology.

# Configuring Windows target

It is incredible the amount of time that can be saved by using Ansible, especially in a hybrid cloud environment in configuration management administration and patch management. We can manage desktop operating systems, including Windows 10 and 11, and server operating systems, including Windows Server 2012, 2012 R2, 2016, Version 1803, Version 1809, 2019, and 2022. The first step is to configure our Windows target machine to use Ansible. Even if the SSH connection has been supported since Ansible 2.8, it might lead to unforeseen scenarios. The stable and recommended way to connect to Windows and Windows server systems is using the **Windows Remote Management** (**WinRM**) native library. WinRM is created by Microsoft for WS-Management in Windows operating systems. WinRM enables us to access systems and share management information via the network.

The steps to successfully getting started with a Windows target host:

1. Create the Ansible user
2. Verify PowerShell & .NET
3. Setup WinRM
4. Windows Collections
5. Create inventory and playbook

On the Ansible Controller, the requirements are easy to fulfill. We simply need the inventory, and we can use many Ansible modules to automate our tasks inside the "`ansible.windows`" and "`community.windows`" Ansible collections. The difference is that the first collection is directly maintained by the Ansible Engineering Team, whereas the second is managed by the Ansible community.

# Creating the Ansible user

Ansible requires a user in the target host to execute our automation. The easiest way is to create a local user using the "Computer Management" tool. We can also use an Active Directory user, but it requires more configurations. Feel free to customize the name of the user as you wish.

The following steps enable us to create an "`ansible`" local user on a Windows system:

1. Open "**Computer Management**". We can open the "**Computer Management**" tool using the **Start** menu or with a right-click on **This PC | Manage**. The interface looks like the following *Figure 5.1*:

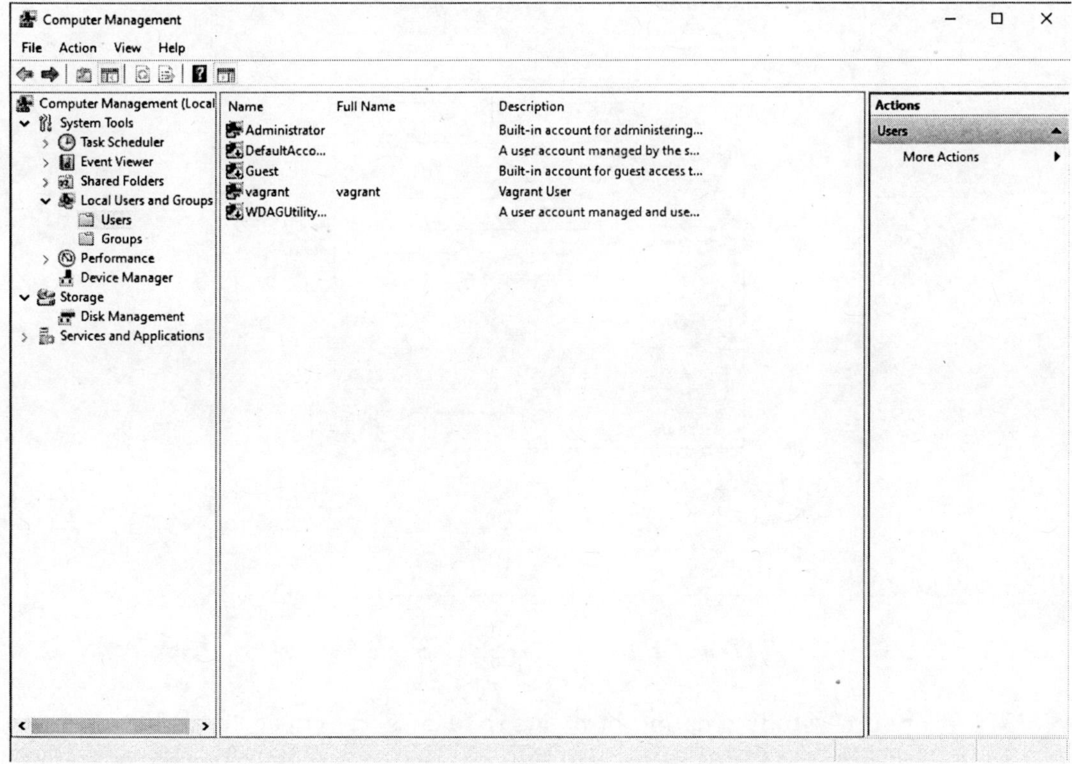


***Figure 5.1:*** *Computer Management main interface*

2. Create the new "`ansible`" user. Create a new user by right-clicking on **Users | New User**. Fill up the pop-up form using the following details (the interface looks like *Figure 5.2*):

   User name: `ansible`

   Full name: `ansible`

Description: **`ansible user`**

Password and Confirm Password: (specify a password for our "**`ansible`**" user). For example, let us suppose to use "**`MyPassword123@`**" as the password. This value should match our inventory.

It is extremely important to enable the option **Password never expires** and disable the option **User must change password at next logon**. Please refer to the following figure:

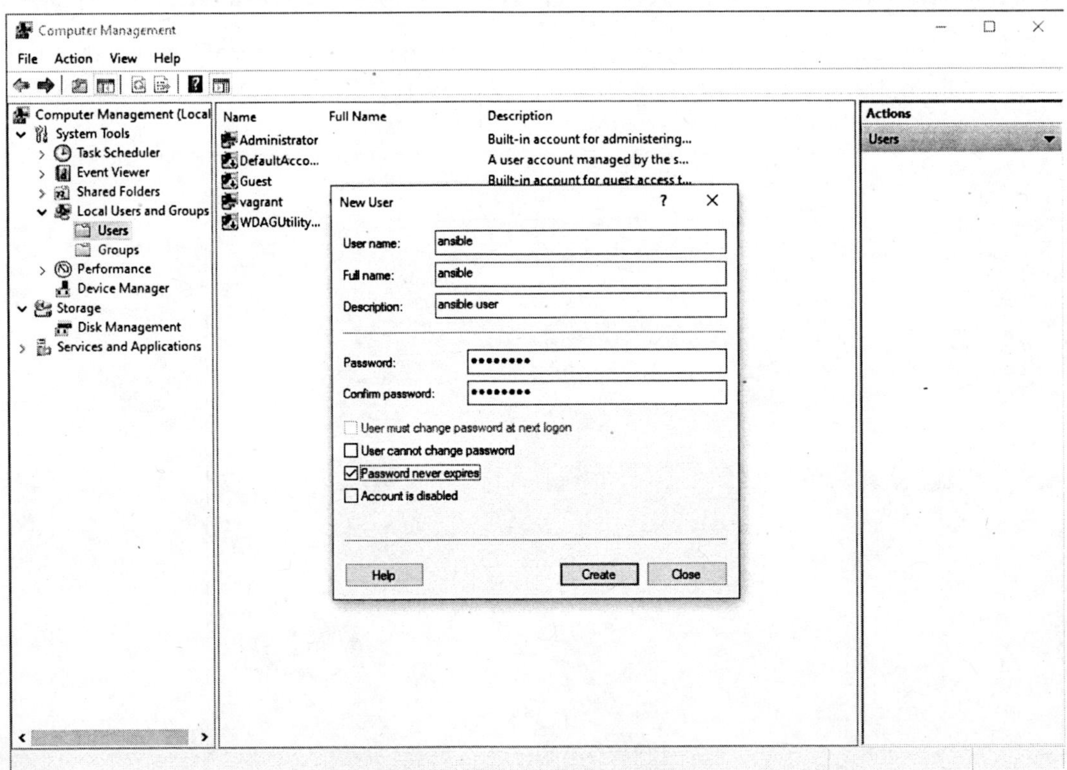


*Figure 5.2: The new "ansible" user interface*

3. After successfully creating our "**`ansible`**" user, we need to add the user to the "**`administrators`**" group. In this way, we are going to be able to execute any type of command to our Windows target. If we did not perform this step, some code might fail for permission reasons. Refer to the following *Figure 5.3:*

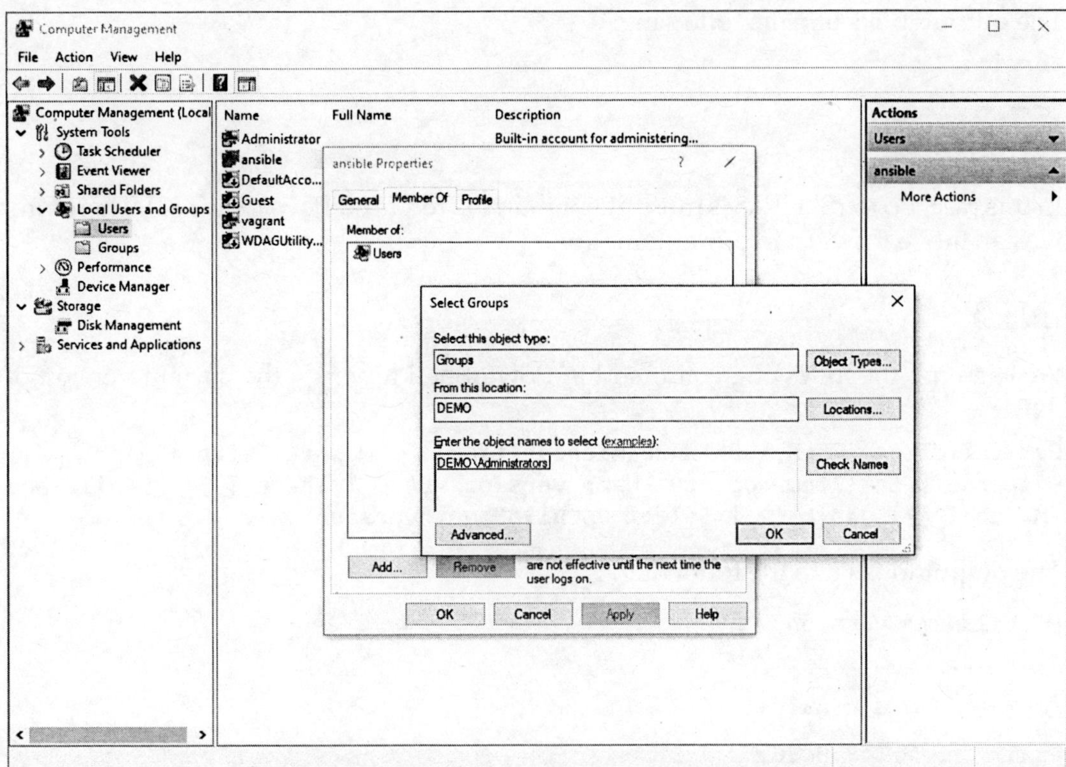


*Figure 5.3: Add "ansible" user to "administrators" group*

# Verifying PowerShell, .NET and setting up WinRM

Once the local user is successfully created in our Windows system, we can verify that the PowerShell and .NET libraries are up-to-date before installing the WinRM component. Ansible requirements are PowerShell 3.0 or newer, and .NET 4.0 or newer on the Windows host. In the modern operating system, these requirements are already fulfilled. If not, we simply need to use Windows Update before proceeding to install the WinRM component. Let us verify the current version of PowerShell and .NET in our system.

## PowerShell

We can type the following command in PowerShell to verify the current version of PowerShell:

```
Get-Host | Select-Object Version
```

The output looks like the following:

```
Version
-------
7.3.0.0
```

In this case, PowerShell 7.3 is more major than the required PowerShell 3.0. Therefore, we can move forward in our automation.

## .NET

We can type the following command in PowerShell to verify the current version of .NET:

```
Get-ChildItem 'HKLM:\SOFTWARE\Microsoft\NET Framework Setup\NDP'
-Recurse | Get-ItemProperty -Name version -EA 0 | Where { $_.PSChildName
-Match '^(?!S)\p{L}'} | Select PSChildName, version
```

The output looks like the following:

```
PSChildName Version
----------- -------
Client      4.8.04161
Full        4.8.04161
Client      4.0.0.0
```

In this case, .NET 4.8 is installed, which is more major than the required .NET 4.0. As such, we can move forward in our automation.

# Installing WinRM

The first step is to actually verify if the WinRM service is already enabled in our target. We can verify if WinRM is enabled in our system with the following PowerShell commands:

```
winrm get winrm/config/Service
winrm get winrm/config/Winrs
winrm enumerate winrm/config/Listener
```

In a freshly installed machine, we expect to receive an error message for each command, as shown:

```
WSManFault
Message = The client cannot connect to the destination specified in the
request. [...]
Error number:  -2144108526 0x80338012
```

An initial configuration for the WinRM service for a novice user could be difficult. The good news is that the Ansible Engineer Team releases a "**ConfigureRemotingForAnsible.ps1**" PowerShell script for easy configuration of our target host. The following command downloads and executes the latest version of the PowerShell configuration script directly from the GitHub repository of Ansible:

```
[Net.ServicePointManager]::SecurityProtocol = [Net.
SecurityProtocolType]::Tls12
>> $url = "https://raw.githubusercontent.com/ansible/ansible/devel/
examples/scripts/ConfigureRemotingForAnsible.ps1"
>> $file = "$env:temp\ConfigureRemotingForAnsible.ps1"
>>
>> (New-Object -TypeName System.Net.WebClient).DownloadFile($url, $file)
>>
>> powershell.exe -ExecutionPolicy ByPass -File $file
```

The execution is going to take a while and show us more messages on the screen. We can verify if WinRM is enabled in our system with the following PowerShell commands:

```
winrm get winrm/config/Service
winrm get winrm/config/Winrs
winrm enumerate winrm/config/Listener
```

The output message is going to show us more detail about the network service, the maximum number of connected users, and more technical details:

```
Service
    RootSDDL = O:NSG:BAD:P(A;;GA;;;BA)(A;;GR;;;IU)S:P(AU;FA;GA;;;WD)
(AU;SA;GXGW;;;WD)
    MaxConcurrentOperations = 4294967295
    MaxConcurrentOperationsPerUser = 1500
    EnumerationTimeoutms = 240000
    MaxConnections = 300
    MaxPacketRetrievalTimeSeconds = 120
    AllowUnencrypted = true
    Auth
        Basic = true
        Kerberos = true
        Negotiate = true
        Certificate = false
```

```
        CredSSP = false
        CbtHardeningLevel = Relaxed
    DefaultPorts
        HTTP = 5985
        HTTPS = 5986
    IPv4Filter = *
    IPv6Filter = *
    EnableCompatibilityHttpListener = false
    EnableCompatibilityHttpsListener = false
    CertificateThumbprint
    AllowRemoteAccess = true
```

The important part is that the WinRM is now active and accepts connection via HTTP port **5985** and HTTPS port **5986**. Many organizations choose to enable the WinRM service in some "template image", "baseline image," or "gold image" in order to speed up the deployment of infrastructure.

From now on, we just need to configure our Ansible controller to connect to the Windows target.

# Windows collections

First of all, we need to ensure that the Ansible collections are installed in our Ansible Controller. As we learned in *Chapter 3, Ansible Language Extended,* section *Ansible collection,* we can use the "**ansible-galaxy**" command line tool to install or verify the installed version of the collections in our system. Let us verify if the Ansible collection is successfully installed in our system using the following commands:

- The "**ansible.windows**" Ansible collection

  ```
  ansible-galaxy collection list ansible.windows
  ```

  The following output is displayed when the "**ansible.windows**" collection is successfully installed:

  ```
  # /usr/share/ansible/collections/ansible_collections
  Collection      Version
  --------------- -------
  ansible.windows 1.13.0
  ```

The output shows the version installed, "**1.13.0**," and the installation path "**/usr/share/ansible/collections/ansible_collections**". As we probably noted, the path is system-wide. It is possible to receive a multiple-line output specifying all the alternative versions in different file system paths. When we receive no line output, it means that the package is not installed in our system.

- The "**community.windows**" Ansible collection

  ```
  ansible-galaxy collection list community.windows
  ```

  The following output is displayed when the "**community.windows**" collection is successfully installed:

  ```
  # /usr/share/ansible/collections/ansible_collections
  Collection        Version
  ----------------- -------
  community.windows 1.12.0
  ```

  The output shows the version installed, "**1.12.0,**" and the installation path "**/usr/share/ansible/collections/ansible_collections**". As in the previous collection, the path is system-wide. It is possible to receive a multiple-line output specifying all the alternative versions in different file system paths. When we receive no line output, it means that the package is not installed in our system.

When the collections are not installed in our system, we can install them manually or in an automated way.

# Manual

We can manually install the Ansible Windows collections specifying the name via the "**ansible-galaxy**" command line tool. The tool is going to connect to the Ansible Galaxy distribution server, download, and install it in the current system. Repeat the command twice to install both Ansible collections.

```
ansible-galaxy collection install ansible.windows
ansible-galaxy collection install community.windows
```

The command shows output like the following:

```
Starting galaxy collection install process
Process install dependency map
Starting collection install process
```

```
Downloading https://galaxy.ansible.com/download/ansible-windows-1.13.0.tar.gz to /home/devops/.ansible/tmp/ansible-local-26442bn4cixq4/tmp8hxd6zuo/ansible-windows-1.13.0-r6p9u1uq
Installing 'ansible.windows:1.13.0' to '/home/devops/.ansible/collections/ansible_collections/ansible/windows'
ansible.windows:1.13.0 was installed successfully
```

At the end of the execution, our Ansible Windows collections are successfully installed in our system.

## Automated

To automate the installation of the Windows Ansible collections, we need to create a **requirements.yml** file with the desired collections. When we do not specify any distribution server, Ansible Galaxy is used. The full **requirements.yml** file looks like the following:

```
---
collections:
  - name: ansible.windows
  - name: community.windows
```

We can execute the automated installation of the code using the following command:

```
ansible-galaxy install -r requirements.yml
```

The output of the command is similar to the following:

```
Starting galaxy collection install process
Process install dependency map
Starting collection install process
Downloading https://galaxy.ansible.com/download/community-windows-1.12.0.tar.gz to /home/devops/.ansible/tmp/ansible-local-26397ml0anda6/tmpl5a7igpa/community-windows-1.12.0-nrnbikbk
Installing 'community.windows:1.12.0' to '/home/devops/.ansible/collections/ansible_collections/community/windows'
Downloading https://galaxy.ansible.com/download/ansible-windows-1.13.0.tar.gz to /home/devops/.ansible/tmp/ansible-local-26397ml0anda6/tmpl5a7igpa/ansible-windows-1.13.0-r4kpb230
community.windows:1.12.0 was installed successfully
Installing 'ansible.windows:1.13.0' to '/home/devops/.ansible/collections/ansible_collections/ansible/windows'
ansible.windows:1.13.0 was installed successfully
```

At the end of the execution, both Ansible Windows collections are successfully installed in our system.

# Inventory

When we need to specify some Windows targets, we need a specific Ansible inventory with WinRM parameters. We are going to use WinRM as a connection method to the target with basic authentication. Since Ansible version is 2.8, it is also possible to use the experimental SSH connection for Windows-managed nodes (Windows 10+ and Windows Server 2019+).

*Table 5.1* summarizes the possible authentication methods: Basic, Certificate, NTLM, Kerberos, and CredSSP, for a local user account, Active Directory account, credential delegation, and HTTP encryption:

| Authentication | Local Accounts | Active Directory Accounts | Credential Delegation | HTTP Encryption |
|---|---|---|---|---|
| Basic | Yes | No | No | No |
| Certificate | Yes | No | No | No |
| Kerberos | No | Yes | Yes | Yes |
| NTLM | Yes | Yes | No | Yes |
| CredSSP | Yes | Yes | Yes | Yes |

***Table 5.1:*** *WinRM authentication methods*

Please note that the basic authentication, which is the simplest option, is also insecure because it transmits the password with Base64 encoding.

The following example shows the WinRM host variables for basic authentication in the Ansible inventory. The following **`winrm_basic.ini`** file showcases the usage of WinRM certificate authentication:

```
ansible_connection: winrm
ansible_winrm_transport: basic
ansible_user: LocalUsername
ansible_password: Password
```

As we can see, we use the WinRM host variables for specifying the authentication parameters in the Ansible Inventory. WinRM certificate authentication uses a pair of public and private certificates encoded in the PEM format. These certificates are usually provided by the System Administrator. The following **`winrm_certificate.ini`** file showcases the usage of WinRM certificate authentication:

```
ansible_connection: winrm
ansible_winrm_transport: certificate
ansible_winrm_cert_pem: /path/to/certificate/public/key.pem
ansible_winrm_cert_key_pem: /path/to/certificate/private/key.pem
```

For all the other installation scenarios and the comprehensive WinRM configuration details, refer to the documentation on the official Ansible website.

The following **win10.ini** Ansible inventory is a full inventory for a Windows 10 target system. Please note that the password should match the one specified in the Windows local account.

```
[windows]
WindowsServer ansible_host=192.168.0.129
[windows:vars]
ansible_user=ansible
ansible_password=MyPassword123@
ansible_port=5986
ansible_connection=winrm
ansible_winrm_transport=basic
ansible_winrm_server_cert_validation=ignore
```

The **win10.ini** Ansible inventory specifies a Windows host on IP "**192.168.0.129**" with the name "**WindowsServer**" with basic authentication using the credentials username "**ansible**" and password "**MyPassword123@**". The connection will be executed on the HTTPS port 5986 ignoring self-signed certificates.

This Ansible inventory fulfills all the configurations from the Ansible controller's point of view.

# Testing the host availability

As seen in the previous chapter, the ability to test when the target host, is the first step of a successful automation journey. As in Linux, we have the Ansible "**ping**" module; as in Windows, we have the Ansible "**win_ping**" module. It verifies the ability of Ansible to login to the managed host, and that there is a shell, usually PowerShell, that is able to execute our code. It is possible to also configure the "cmd.exe" shell instead. The Ansible "**win_ping**" module is completely different from the network ping, as we learned in *Chapter 4, Ansible for Linux*, section *Test host availability*. The default behavior is to connect to the target host and execute a simple script that returns the text "**ping: pong**" when successful.

The module has an optional parameter "**data**" string to customize the testing message. It is possible to specify the parameter value "**crash**" to generate an exception for every execution.

**Tip: For Network targets, use the Ansible "net_ping" module instead, which is part of the "ansible.netcommon" collection.**

The following "**win_ping.yml**" Ansible playbook tests the connection of the Windows target host:

```
---
- name: Testing the host availability
  hosts: all
  tasks:
    - name: Test connection
      ansible.windows.win_ping:
```

Please note that we need to disable the facts gathering because they are not supported in the Windows target ("**gather_facts: false**").

We can execute our "**win_ping.yml**" Ansible playbook using the **ansible-playbook** command:

```
ansible-playbook win_ping.yml
```

The output of the execution is the following:

```
PLAY [Testing the host availability] ***********************************
***********************************

TASK [Test connection] ***************************************************
***************************

ok: [WindowsServer]

PLAY RECAP ***************************************************************

WindowsServer: ok=1    changed=0    unreachable=0    failed=0
skipped=0    rescued=0    ignored=0
```

As we can see, the result is an "**ok**" status when the connection to the target host is successful. We can move forward in our automation journey.

# Configuration management

We can automate the Windows system configuration using Ansible. Sometimes we need to edit a single line of text, especially for the Unix-like services, such as the HTTPD webserver.

# Editing single-line test

We can edit a single line in a configuration file using the "**win_lineinfile**", part of the "**community.windows**" collection. The following "**win_lineinfile.yml**" playbook file edits a line in the Apache web server configuration file, as shown:

```
- community.windows.win_lineinfile:
    path: C:\apache\httpd.conf
    regex: '^Listen '
    insertafter: '^#Listen '
    line: Listen 8080
```

We can execute our "**win_lineinfile.yml**" Ansible playbook using the **ansible-playbook** command:

```
ansible-playbook win_lineinfile.yml
```

At the moment of writing this book, there does not exist any Ansible module to edit a full block of configuration in a text file (like the "**blockinfile**" module for Linux) for a Windows target host. We can use the Ansible "template" module, that we discussed in *Chapter 3, Ansible Language Extended*, section *Ansible template*, for more information.

# Creating text file

Creating a text file is useful to automate the **Configuration as Code** (**CaC**). We can accomplish the text file creation with content using the Ansible "**win_copy**" module. For creating an empty file, refer to the next section, *File System*, under the *Creating an empty file* use case. The Ansible module "**win_copy**" is commonly used to copy files to remote locations, as we can learn in the "*Copying local files to remote hosts*" section. The copy operation is performed from the Ansible controller to the target host. However, the "**win_copy**" module can also create simple text files with content. The full name of the Ansible "**win_copy**" module is "**ansible.windows.win_copy**", which means that it is part of the collection of modules maintained by the Ansible Team for automating Windows. If we need a more complex configuration or include the value of some variables, it is recommended to use the Ansible "**template**" module (refer to *Chapter 3, Ansible Language Extended*, section *Ansible Template*).

The Ansible "**win_copy**" module has many parameters, but the only mandatory parameter is the "**dest**" alias of "**path**". The "**dest**" parameter specifies the remote absolute path destination.

The content parameter sets the contents of a file directly to the specified value. It works only when the "**dest**" is a file. Please note that using a variable in the content parameter will result in an unpredictable output. For advanced formatting or if the content contains a variable, use the "**ansible.builtin.template**" module (refer to *Chapter 3, Ansible Language Extended,* section *Ansible Template*). The created file will have the same permission as the creating user, in this case, our "**ansible**" user. The following Ansible Playbook creates a file "**report.txt**" with three lines of text inside the Desktop of the "**ansible**" user:

```
1 Automate

2 Everything

3 with Ansible
```

The whole "**win_file_create.yml**" Ansible Playbook is the following:

```
---

- name: Create a text file

  hosts: all

  vars:

    myfile: 'C:\Users\ansible\Desktop\example.txt'

  tasks:

  - name: Create a text file

    ansible.windows.win_copy:

      dest: "{{ myfile }}"

      content: |

        1 Automate

        2 Everything

        3 with Ansible
```

We can execute our code using the **ansible-playbook** command included in every Ansible installation. The full command is the following:

```
ansible-playbook win_file_create.yml
```

The output of the execution of the "**win_file_create.yml**" Ansible playbook is the following:

```
TASK [Create a text file] ***********************************************
***********************

changed: [WindowsServer]
```

Refer to the following *Figure 5.4:*

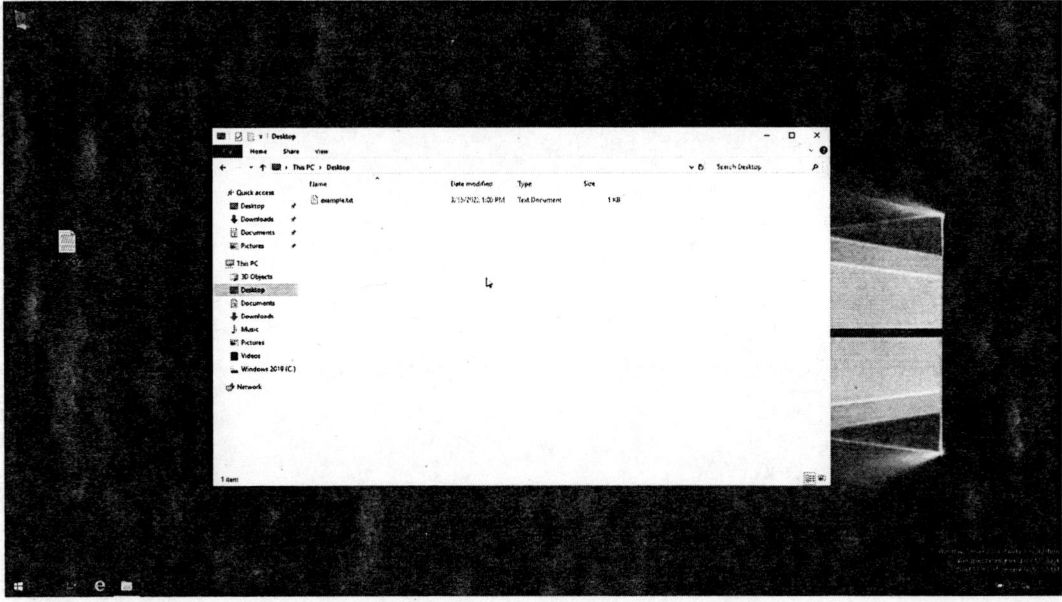

***Figure 5.4:*** *File example.txt in the Ansible user desktop*

As expected, the file "**`example.txt`**" was created on the Desktop of the "**`ansible`**" user, as shown in *Figure 5.4*. We can open the text file with a Notepad application to see the content:

```
1 Automate

2 Everything

3 with Ansible
```

The Ansible module "**`win_copy`**" is commonly used to copy files from the Ansible controller to the Windows target host. However, we discovered how we could use it to create text files. When we would like to use Ansible variables, facts, or magic variables in the generated file, use the Ansible "**`template`**" module to avoid some weird fatal error or unexpected behavior. Refer to *Chapter 3, Ansible Language Extended,* section *Ansible Template.*

# Checkout a Git repository

We can download "checkout" a Git repository using the same "**`git`**" Ansible module used in a Linux target. Refer to *Chapter 4, Ansible for Linux,* section *Configuration management,* for further information. We can automate the installation of the **`git`** package on Windows using the "**`win_chocolatey`**" module described in the section *Install Packages.*

# File system

Managing file system files and directories with Ansible is very convenient to speed up creation, management, and deletion. It is very similar to the use case of *Chapter 4, Ansible for Linux*, section *File System*, for Linux target machines.

> **Tip: At the moment of writing this book, is not possible to create a file system symbolic link for a file with the native Ansible module. It is possible to use the: "cmd.exe /k mklink" command via the "ansible.windows.win_command" Ansible module.**

## Check file exists

The Ansible "**win_stat**" module is instrumental in verifying if files and directories exist on the Windows target host. The module is part of the "**ansible.windows**" collection for Windows target hosts. The module retrieves information from the file system about Windows files and directories. It is the Windows version of the Linux "**ansible.builtin.stat**" module. There is only one "**path**" mandatory parameter for the module. The "**path**" parameter contains the path in the file system of the object to check. The module also calculates the checksum of the file system object in the most popular hash algorithms. The module returns a complex object. In our use case, to check the existence of the file, we need to check the "**exists**" attribute. The value of the attribute is "**true**" when the object exists. The following "**win_check_file.yml**" Ansible playbook displays a message when the file "**example.txt**" exists on the desktop of the local "**ansible**" user:

```
---
- name: Check file exists
  hosts: all
  vars:
    myfile: 'C:\Users\ansible\Desktop\example.txt'
  tasks:
    - name: Check if a file exists
      ansible.windows.win_stat:
        path: "{{ myfile }}"
      register: path_data

    - name: Report file exist
      ansible.builtin.debug:
        msg: "The file {{ myfile }} exist"
```

```
    when: path_data.stat.exists

  - name: Report file does not exist
    ansible.builtin.debug:
      msg: "The file {{ myfile }} doesn't exist"
    when: not path_data.stat.exists
```

The Ansible playbook registers the output of the "**win_stat**" module on the "**path_data**" variable. The following tasks have two conditionals to evaluate the "**path_data.stat.exists**" boolean. When the value of the **.stat.exists** attribute is "**true**" it means that the file exists. On the other hand, whereas when the value is "**false**," it means that the file does not exist. We can execute the "**win_check_file.yml**" code using the **ansible-playbook** command:

```
ansible-playbook win_check_file.yml
```

When the "**example.txt**" file exists on the desktop of the local "**ansible**" user, as shown in *Figure 5.4*, we obtain the following result:

```
TASK [Check if a file exists] *******************************************
****************************

ok: [WindowsServer]
TASK [Report file exist] ************************************************
***************************

ok: [WindowsServer] => {
    "msg": "The file C:\\Users\\vagrant\\Desktop\\example.txt exist"
}
TASK [Report file not exist] ********************************************
***************************

skipping: [WindowsServer]
```

When the "example.txt" file exists on the desktop of the local "ansible" user, as shown in *Figure 5.5*, we obtain the following result:

```
TASK [Check if a file exist] ********************************************
***************************

ok: [WindowsServer]
TASK [Report file exist] ************************************************
***************************

skipping: [WindowsServer]
TASK [Report file not exist] ********************************************
***************************
```

```
ok: [WindowsServer] => {
    "msg": "The file C:\\Users\\ansible\\Desktop\\example.txt doesn't
exist"
}
```

Refer to the following figure:

*Figure 5.5: File example.txt doesn't exist in the ansible user desktop*

In the same way, we can test if the destination path is a directory by checking the "**isdir**" attribute. The following code shows how to use the condition applied to the "**path_data**" registered variable of the previous code:

```
path_data.stat.isdir is defined and path_data.stat.isdir
```

# Creating an empty file

Ansible is able to create an empty file in Windows using the Ansible "**win_file**" module. It is included in the "**ansible.windows**" collection. The module enables us to touch, create, or remove files or directories. For Linux targets, use the "**ansible.builtin.file**" module instead. For creating a file with content, refer to the *Create a text file* section. The parameters list resembles the Linux "file" module:

- **path**
- **state** string (touch, file, absent, and directory)

The "**path**" parameter is mandatory and specifies the path in the file system. The "**state**" parameter defines the desired state of the path we specified. For our use case, creating an empty file, we need the "**touch**" option for creating a new file when not present. Just for context, the default value for "state" is "file" to verify that a file exists. The following Ansible playbook creates a file on the Desktop of the local "**ansible**" user. The full "**win_file.yml**" playbook looks like the following:

```
---
- name: Creating an empty file
  hosts: all
  vars:
    myfile: 'C:\Users\ansible\Desktop\example.txt'
  tasks:
    - name: Creating an empty file
      ansible.windows.win_file:
        path: "{{ myfile }}"
        state: touch
```

We can execute our "**win_file.yml**" Ansible playbook using the **ansible-playbook** command:

```
ansible-playbook win_file.yml
```

The output of the "**win_file.yml**" Ansible playbook command is like the following:

```
TASK [Creating an empty file] *******************************************
**************************
changed: [WindowsServer]
```

The empty file "**example.txt**" is created on our Windows target host.

# Creating a directory

The Ansible "**win_file**" module can also create a directory in a target Windows host. It is part of the "**ansible.windows**" collection. This module has some parameters to perform different tasks. The only required parameter is "**path**", where you specify the filesystem path of the file you are going to edit. The "**state**" parameter defines the type of object we are modifying. The default value of the "**state**" parameter is "**file**," but in this use case, we need to set the "**directory**" option. The following Ansible "**win_dir_create.yml**" playbook creates the "**example**" directory in the Desktop of the user "**ansible**":

```
---
- name: Create a directory
  hosts: all
  vars:
    mydir: 'C:\Users\ansible\Desktop\example'
  tasks:
    - name: Create a directory
      ansible.windows.win_file:
        path: "{{ mydir }}"
        state: directory
```

We can execute our "**`win_dir_create.yml`**" Ansible playbook using the **`ansible-playbook`** command:

```
ansible-playbook win_dir_create.yml
```

The output of the execution of the "**`win_dir_create.yml`**" Ansible playbook command is like the following:

```
TASK [Create a directory] ******************************************
***************************

changed: [WindowsServer]
```

The empty directory "**`example`**" is created on the Desktop of the "**`ansible`**" user of our Windows target host. We can see the host before the execution in *Figure 5.6* without the "**`example`**" directory on the Desktop.

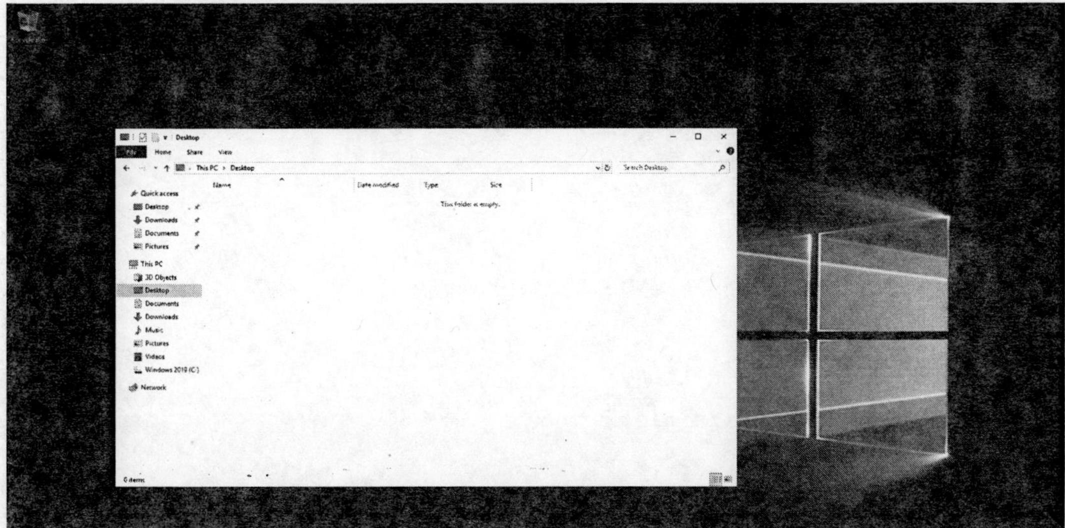

*Figure 5.6: The empty Desktop of the ansible user before the execution*

The result of the execution is shown in *Figure 5.7* with the "**example**" directory on the Desktop:

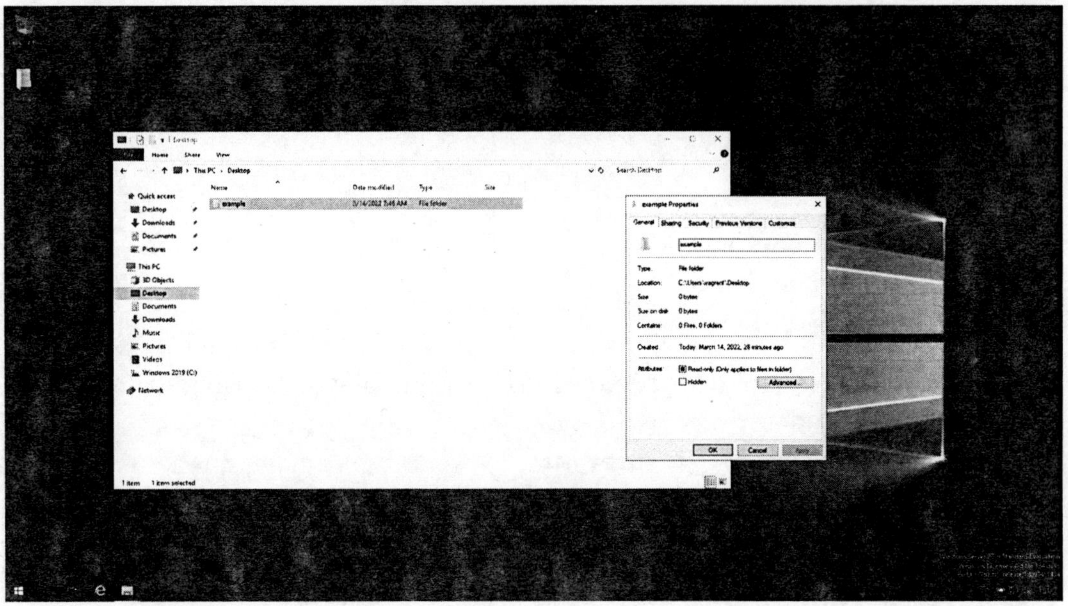

*Figure 5.7: The example folder on the Desktop of the ansible user after the execution*

# Deleting a file

We can delete a file or directory using the Ansible "**win_file**" module for a Windows target. We need to specify the value "**absent**" of the parameter "**state**". The following "**win_delete_dir.yml**" Ansible playbook deletes the "**example**" file or directory in the "**ansible**" user Desktop:

```
---
- name: Delete a directory
  hosts: all
  vars:
    mydir: 'C:\Users\ansible\Desktop\example'
  tasks:
    - name: Delete a directory
      ansible.windows.win_file:
        path: "{{ mydir }}"
        state: absent
```

We can execute the "**win_delete_dir.yml**" using the following **ansible-playbook** command:

**ansible-playbook win_delete_dir.yml**

At the end of the execution, the expected file or directory "**example**" was deleted in the Desktop folder of the "**ansible**" user.

# Copying local files to remote hosts

In the same way as using the "**copy**" Ansible module for Linux target, we can use the "**win_copy**" Ansible module. The "**win_copy**" Ansible module is included in the "**ansible.windows**" collection. The module enables us to copy files from the local Ansible controller machine to a remote Windows target. Please note that the file transfer runs over the WinRM connection. Unfortunately, the WinRM is not the most efficient transfer mechanism. For transferring large files, please consider hosting files on a web service and retrieving them using the "**ansible.windows.win_get_url**" instead. The following five are useful parameters of the "**win_copy**" Ansible module:

- **dest** path
- **src** string
- **remote_src** string
- **backup** boolean
- **force** string

The only mandatory parameter is "**dest**". The "**dest**" parameter specifies the remote destination path on the file system. When we specify the string with a single quote, we could specify the file system path in the Windows way, using a backslash as a directory separator. Also verify that the Ansible connection authentication used has permission to access and write in the specified path. The "**src**" specifies the source of the file in the Ansible Controller host. It could be a local relative, or absolute local path, or a remote path. When a remote path is specified, we also need to enable the "**remote_src**" boolean. If we specify a directory as a source, Ansible is going to copy all the content. Please be more careful when you put a "/" (slash) at the end. When the slash ("/") in the end is present, only the content of the directory is copied, whereas when omitted, all the folder and content are copied. The "**backup**" boolean parameter allows us to create a copy of the file as a backup including the timestamp information, so that you can get the original file back if you somehow clobbered it incorrectly. Ansible is going to transfer only the files not present or that differ in the target host by default. Each file is verified with a checksum created by Ansible on the source and target host automatically. We can force to transfer all the files and directories, enabling the "**force**" parameter. Please note that disabling the "**force**" parameter also disables the checksum feature, that speed up the process but potentially, we might end up with some corrupt file. The following "**win_copy.yml**"

Ansible playbook copies a source "**report.txt**" file to the desktop of the Windows target:

```
---
- name: Copy report.txt
  hosts: all
  vars:
    source: "report.txt"
    destination: "Desktop/report.txt"
  tasks:
    - name: Copy report.txt
      ansible.windows.win_copy:
        src: "{{ source }}"
        dest: "{{ destination }}"
```

We can execute the "**win_copy.yml**" using the following **ansible-playbook** command:

```
ansible-playbook win_copy.yml
```

At the end of the execution, the expected file "**report.txt**" was copied in the Desktop folder of the "**ansible**" user.

# Copying remote files to local

We can use the same "**fetch**" Ansible module to copy remote files and directories to the local Ansible controller. The "**fetch**" Ansible module is part of the "**ansible.builtin**" Ansible collection. Refer to *Chapter 4, Ansible for Linux,* section *File System* for an extensive overview of the "**fetch**" Ansible module. The following "**win_copy_from.yml**" Ansible playbook retrieves a copy of the **example.txt**:

```
---
- name: Fetch module
  hosts: all
  vars:
    myfile: 'C:\Users\ansible\Desktop\example.txt'
    save_dir: "logs"
  tasks:
    - name: Fetch file
      ansible.builtin.fetch:
        src: "{{ myfile }}"
```

```
        dest: "{{ save_dir }}"
```

We can execute the "**win_copy_from.yml**" playbook using the following **ansible-playbook** command:

```
ansible-playbook win_copy_from.yml
```

At the end of the execution, the "**example.txt**" file from the Desktop of the "**ansible**" user is copied from the remote server to the local "**logs**" directory of the Ansible controller. Learn more about another usage of the Ansible "**win_copy**" module in the *Creating text file* section.

For retrieving multiple items, use the "**loop**" statement with a list of files or directories.

# Downloading a file

We can download a file from a remote server using the Ansible "**win_get_url**" module, which is part of the "**ansible.windows**" collection. It downloads files from HTTP, HTTPS, or FTP to the node. For Linux targets, use the "**ansible.builtin.get_url**" module. This module has the same parameters as the Ansible "**get_url**" module. Refer to *Chapter 4, Ansible for Linux,* section *File system* for more information. Please note that there are also additional parameters for the X509 authentication client certificate (.pfx). Enterprise users could also specify the "**proxy**" parameter to set a proxy server. The Ansible playbook "**win_get_url.yml**" retrieves a file, verifies the checksum, and saves it on the Desktop of the specified user:

```
---
- name: Downloading a file
  hosts: all
  vars:
    myurl: "https://releases.ansible.com/ansible/ansible-2.9.25.tar.gz"
    mycrc: "https://releases.ansible.com/ansible/ansible-2.9.25.tar.
gz.sha"
    mycrc_algorithm: "sha256"
    mydest: 'C:\Users\ansible\Desktop\ansible-2.9.25.tar.gz'
  tasks:
    - name: Download file
      ansible.windows.win_get_url:
        url: "{{ myurl }}"
        dest: "{{ mydest }}"
        checksum_algorithm: "{{ mycrc_algorithm }}"
        checksum_url: "{{ mycrc }}"
```

We can execute the "**win_get_url.yml**" using the following **ansible-playbook** command:

```
ansible-playbook win_get_url.yml
```

At the end of the execution, the expected file "**ansible-2.9.25.tar.gz**" is downloaded, verified the checksum using the "**sha256**" algorithm and saved in the Desktop of the "**ansible**" user, as shown in *Figure 5.8*:

***Figure** 5.8: The file downloaded and saved on the desktop*

# Backup with robocopy

To backup with robocopy usinsg the Ansible "**win_robocopy**" module, which is specifically designed for robocopy on Windows hosts. The module is part of the "**community.windows**" Ansible collection. We can follow these steps:

1. Define the source and destination directories in your playbook.
2. Use the "**win_robocopy**" module to copy the directories. You can set the "**recurse**" parameter to "**yes**" to include all subdirectories. We can also specify additional parameters to the robocopy command via the "**flags**" parameter.
3. Run the playbook to copy the directories.

Here is an example playbook that back up files from the *Desktop*folder or the current user of a remote Windows server to a local backup directory using "**win_robocopy**":

```
---
- name: Backup
  hosts: all
  become: false
  vars:
    source: "Desktop"
    destination: 'C:\Backups'
  tasks:
    - name: Backup files with robocopy
      community.windows.win_robocopy:
        src: '{{ source }}'
        dest: '{{ destination }}'
```

In this example, the "`win_robocopy`" module is used to copy the files from the source directory to the destination directory.

# Installing packages

Chocolatey[1] is a package manager for Windows. When we need to manage a large fleet of machines, it is not sustainable to maintain them manually. It has the largest online registry of Windows packages, and it is distributed under an open-source license. At the moment of writing this book, Chocolatey contains nearly 9600 Community maintained packages. Popular software packages include Adobe Acrobat, Google Chrome, Mozilla Firefox, and so on. The principal advantage is the full support of the software automation and the ability to keep a track of installed packages to simplify any upgrade processes. It also sells the **Chocolatey for Business** (**C4B**), offering advanced functionality for organizations. *Figure 5.9* shows the Chocolatey logo:

***Figure 5.9:*** *The Chocolatey logo*

1 https://chocolatey.org

**Tip: An alternative to Chocolatey is the Scoop package manager. We can automate using the "community.windows.win_scoop" Ansible module. At the moment of writing the book Ansible doesn't support the "Winget" Windows package manager[2]**

There are five Chocolatey modules included in the additional "**chocolatey.chocolatey**" Ansible collection. We can install the collection using the "**ansible-galaxy**" command line utility introduced in *Chapter 3, Ansible Language Extended,* section *Ansible Collection*. The "**chocolatey.chocolatey**" Ansible collection comprehends the following five modules:

- **win_chocolatey**: Manage packages using chocolatey.
- **win_chocolatey_config**: Manage Chocolatey config settings.
- **win_chocolatey_facts**: Gather facts from Chocolatey.
- **win_chocolatey_feature**: Manage Chocolatey features.
- **win_chocolatey_source**: Manage Chocolatey sources.

The Ansible "**win_chocolatey**" module automates the installation of the Chocolatey software and any software packages. It manages packages in Windows using Chocolatey. The following are the most useful parameters:

- **name**: string
- **state**: string (present, latest, absent, downgrade, reinstalled)
- **version**: string
- **pinned**: boolean
- **source**: string
- **proxy_url**: string, **proxy_username**: string, **proxy_password**: string

In the "**name**" parameter, you are going to specify the name of the package or a list of packages. If you would like to install a specific version, you could specify it in the "**version**" parameter. The state specifies the action that we would like to perform. To verify if a package is successfully installed, pick the "**present**" option. On the other hand, for verifying if that the package is up-to-date, use the "**latest**" value. It is worth mentioning some of the additional parameters that might be useful for you. The "**pinned**" parameter allows for pinning the Chocolatey package or not. Pin a package to suppress upgrades. During the next upgrade for all packages, Chocolatey will automatically skip the pinned packages. "**source**" allows specifying a local repository for packages if available. Enterprise users benefit from the proxy

---

2 **https://github.com/ansible-collections/community.windows/issues/89**

parameters and authentication mechanisms via the **proxy_url**, **proxy_username**, and **proxy_password** parameters.

The following "**win_chocolatey.yml**" Ansible playbook installs the "**git**" and "**notepadplusplus**" packages in a Windows target:

```
---
- name: Installing packages
  hosts: all
  vars:
    - packages:
      - git
      - notepadplusplus
  tasks:
    - name: Install packages
      chocolatey.chocolatey.win_chocolatey:
        name: "{{ packages }}"
        state: present
```

We can execute the "**win_chocolatey.yml**" using the following **ansible-playbook** command:

```
ansible-playbook win_chocolatey.yml
```

At the end of the execution, the software "Git" and "Notepad++" are successfully installed in the Windows target host, as shown in *Figure 5.10:*

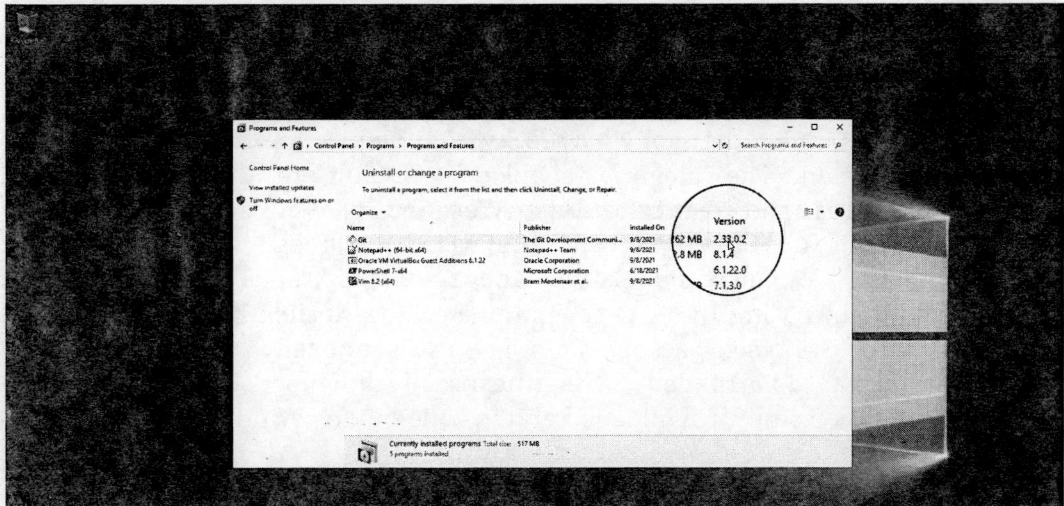


*Figure 5.10: The git and notepad++ software installed by Ansible*

# Rolling update

Rolling updates are an important step for fleet management. When the number of servers grows up, it is difficult to keep pace manually with the update process. Especially in the enterprise world, there are many alternatives. Ansible enables us a simple and efficient way to perform rolling updates and reports of our fleet.

We are going to use the Ansible "**win_updates**" module. It is included in the "**ansible.windows**" collection. The module works in Windows and Windows Server operating systems. This module is used to download and install Windows updates. To install packages in Linux targets, use the "**yum**" or "**dnf**" module for RedHat-like systems, "**apt**" for Debian-like, and "**zypper**" module for Suse-like, as described in *Chapter 4, Ansible for Linux*, section *Installing packages and rolling update*. To implement a full rolling update process, complement with the "**fork**" and "**serial**" statements in our playbook. Learn more about it in *Chapter 7, Ansible Advanced,* section *Ansible Orchestration*.

The seven parameters of the Ansible "**win_updates**" module are as follows:

- **category_names** string (**CriticalUpdates**, **DefinitionUpdates**, **DeveloperKits**, **FeaturePacks**, **SecurityUpdates**, **ServicePacks**, **UpdateRollups**)
- **state** string - (searched, downloaded, installed)
- **reboot** boolean
- **reboot_timeout** integer
- **log_path** path
- **accept_list** / **reject_list** list (titles or KB to whitelist or blacklist)
- **server_selection** string

The most important is "**category_names**," which defines the types of updates to install in the system. The categories enabled by default are "**CriticalUpdates**", "**SecurityUpdates**", and "**UpdateRollups**". We can add or remove different categories by the full list of "**CriticalUpdates**", "**DefinitionUpdates**", "**DeveloperKits**", "**FeaturePacks**", "**SecurityUpdates**", "**ServicePacks**", and "**UpdateRollups**". We can also define using the "**state**" parameter, the Ansible behavior about the update. It specifies if each package show is only "**searched,**" which means only listed in the log file, "**downloaded,**" which means only downloaded, or "**installed,**" which means successfully downloaded and installed in the Windows target system.

If you prefer only to download the code and perform the actual update a second time, you need to select the "**downloaded**" option. When the "**reboot**" parameter is enabled, Ansible can automatically reboot the remote host when it is required and continue to install updates after the reboot. There is a default timeout to wait for the host after a rebook of the **1200** seconds value. We can increase the value with the "**reboot_timeout**" option. We can save the status in the log file defined in the "**log_path**" option to save a log file on the disk. We could specify a list of update titles or KB numbers that specify which updates are to be searched or installed using the "**accept_list**" parameter as well as a list of exclusions in the "**reject_list**" parameter. We can also fetch content from the **Microsoft Windows Server Update Services (WSUS)** for the corporate environment. When dealing with WSUS, we should set the "**server_selection**" parameter to the "**managed_server**" value to use the WSUS catalog. On the other hand, we set it to the "**windows_update**" value to use the Microsoft Windows Update catalog. The following "**win_rolling.yml**" Ansible playbook update executes a rolling update on the Windows target for only the critical and security updates. It also reboots the machine when needed and saves the log in the "**C:\ansible.txt**" file. The full Ansible playbook looks like the following:

```
---
- name: Windows rolling update
  hosts: all
  tasks:
    - name: Install all critical and security updates
      ansible.windows.win_updates:
        category_names:
          - CriticalUpdates
          - SecurityUpdates
        state: installed
        reboot: true
        log_path: C:\ansible.txt
```

We can execute the "**win_rolling.yml**" using the following **ansible-playbook** command:

```
ansible-playbook win_rolling.yml
```

At the end of the execution, the Windows software updates are successfully installed in our system, and an "**ansible.txt**" log file is created, as shown in *Figure 5.12*. *Figure 5.11* shows the situation before Ansible triggers the Windows Update process.

Please refer to the following figure:

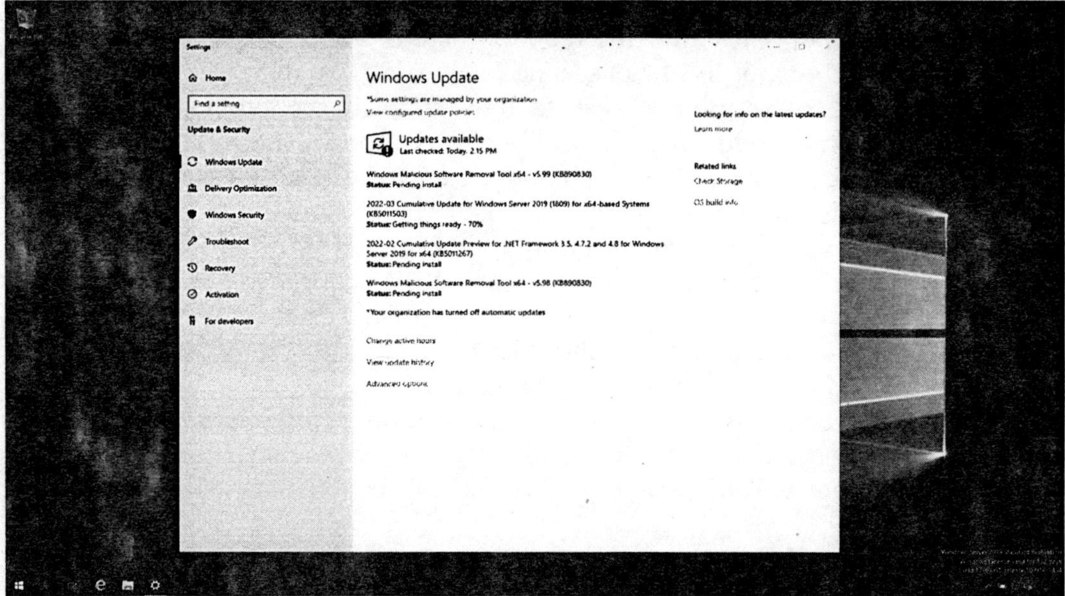


*Figure 5.11: The Windows target before the execution of the rolling update Playbook*

*Figure 5.12* shows the "**`ansible.txt`**" log file of the executed Windows updates on the target system:

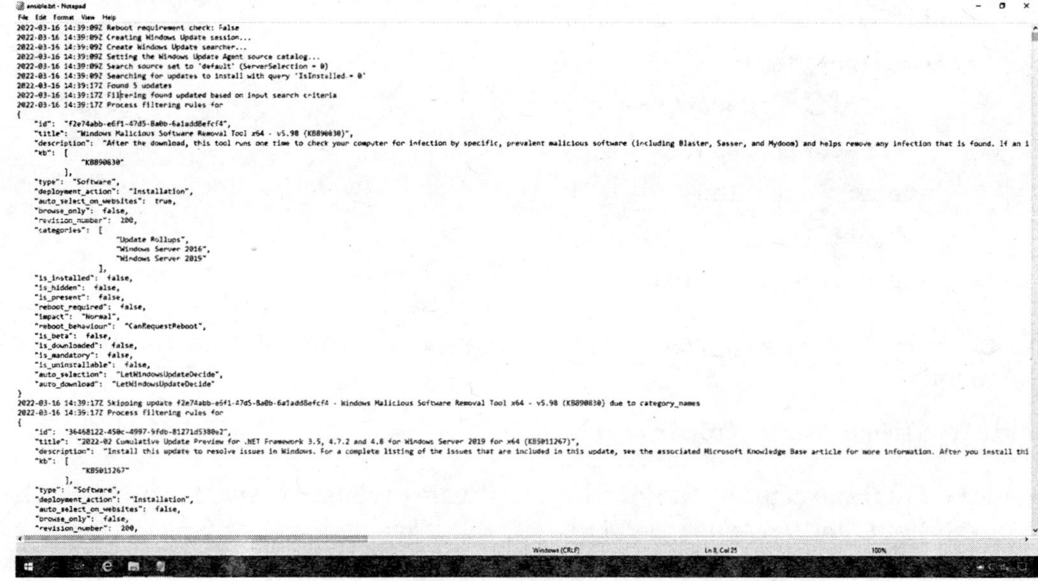


*Figure 5.12: Windows target after the execution of the rolling update Playbook*

# User management

We use the Ansible module "**win_user**" to manage local users and the "**win_group**" to create a local group. Both modules are part of the "**ansible.windows**" collection. The "**win_user**" module manages local Windows user accounts, whereas the "**win_group**" module adds and removes local groups. For Linux targets, use the "**user**" and "**group**" modules of the "**ansible.builtin**" collection instead. Refer to *Chapter 4, Ansible for Linux*, section *User management* for more information.

The "**ansible.windows.win_user**" module manages local Windows user accounts. Its parameters are:

- **name** string
- **state** string
- **password** string
- **description** string
- **groups** list
- **update_password** string (always or **on_create**)
- **password_never_expires** boolean
- **password_expired** string
- **account_locked** boolean
- **account_disabled** boolean

The only required parameter is "**name**", which is the user name of the account. The "**state**" parameter enables us to define the operation to verify if a user is present or not, in the target Windows system. In our use case, the default is already set to "**present**" to create a user. The "**password**" set the password in cleartext, and so we can easily specify what password assign to the user. No hash functions are needed. We can specify the password directly. The "**description**" parameter allows you to specify a description of the user. It is not mandatory, but sometimes it is useful. The "**groups**" parameter allows you to add or remove the user from this list of groups. The "**update_password**" parameter specifies when the module will update the user password. The "**always**" option updates passwords when they differ, and "**on_create**" sets the password only when a user is newly created. Let us also highlight some parameters about password expiration: "**password_never_expires**" sets the password never to expire, and "**password_expired**" forces the user to change the password at the next login. You could also lock or disable the account using the "**account_locked**" and "**account_disabled**" parameters.

The following "**win_user.yml**" Ansible playbook creates a user "**example**" in the Windows target system in the "**Users**" group with a password change on the first user access. The full "**win_user.yml**" Ansible playbook is like the following:

```
---
- name: Create a user account
  hosts: all
  vars:
    usr_name: 'example'
    usr_password: 'password'
    usr_groups: "Users"
  tasks:
    - name: User example exist
      ansible.windows.win_user:
        name: "{{ usr_name }}"
        password: "{{ usr_password }}"
        groups: "{{ usr_groups }}"
        update_password: on_create
        password_expired: true
```

We can execute the "**win_user.yml**" playbook using the following **ansible-playbook** command:

```
ansible-playbook win_user.yml
```

At the end of the execution, the local user "**example**" is created with the options specified in the Ansible playbook.

# Group management

The "**win_group**" module manages the local group(s) in the target Windows system. The main parameters of the Ansible "**win_group**" module are:

- **name** string: group name
- **state** string: present/absent
- **system** boolean: yes/no
- **gid** integer: GID to set for the group
- **local** string: "local" command alternatives

The required parameter is "**name**". This parameter specifies the group name. The "**state**" parameter enables us to verify if a group is present or absent in the Windows target system. In our use case, the default is already set to "**present**" to verify whether a group exists or not. The "**system**" parameter enables us to create a system group. By default, it is not. You could specify the "**GID**", the group identifier, by using the "**gid**" parameter. The "**local**" parameter enables us to use the "**local**" command alternatives on platforms that implement it. This is usually performed when a central authentication system is used. The following "**win_group.yml**" Ansible playbook creates a local group "**'accounting'**" in the Windows target system:

```
---
- name: Group add
  hosts: all
  vars:
    mygroup: 'accounting'
    mydescription: 'accounting group'
  tasks:
    - name: Create a new group
      ansible.windows.win_group:
        name: "{{ mygroup }}"
        description: "{{ mydescription }}"
        state: present
```

We can execute the "**win_group.yml**" playbook using the following **ansible-playbook** command:

```
ansible-playbook win_group.yml
```

At the end of the execution, the local group "**accounting**" is created in the target Windows system.

# Windows registry

Automating the Windows registry interaction with Ansible is very useful because we can obtain precise results and apply the playbook at a scale. We can use the "**win_reg_stat**" module to check the value of a specific key and add or remove keys using the "**win_regedit**" module.

# Checking registry

We can obtain information about the Windows registry using the Ansible "**win_reg_stat**" module. The module is included in the "**ansible.windows**" collection. The purpose is to retrieve information from Windows registry keys.

The main parameters of the module are:

- **path** string
- **name** string
- **type** string (string, none, binary, dword, expandstring, multistring, qword)
- **data** string
- **state** string (present, absent)

The only required parameter is "**path**". This parameter specifies the null registry key path including the hive to search for. The "**name**" specifies the name of the registry entry. The "**type**" parameter specifies the datatype: string, dword, qword, binary, multistring, and so on. Please note that some values are specified as a decimal number, a hex value or a multi-string specified as an Ansible list. We are able to specify the value of the registry entry by populating the "**data**" parameter. We can verify if a key exists using the "**state**" parameter with two options: "**present**" for existing or "**absent**" for not existing.

The following "**reg_check.yml**" Ansible playbook checks the .NET Framework version on Windows-like systems, by accessing the Windows Registry. More specifically, it checks the Windows Registry key "**Version**" located in "**HKEY_LOCAL_MACHINE\SOFTWARE\Microsoft\NET Framework Setup\NDP\v4\Full**".

The full "**reg_check.yml**" Ansible playbook looks like the following:

```
---
- name: Check .NET version
  hosts: all
  tasks:
    - name: Retrieve .NET version
      ansible.windows.win_reg_stat:
        path: 'HKLM:\SOFTWARE\Microsoft\NET Framework Setup\NDP\v4\Full'
        name: "Version"
      register: reg_val
    - name: Print .NET version
      ansible.builtin.debug:
        msg: "{{ reg_val }}"
```

We can execute the "**reg_check.yml**" playbook using the following **ansible-playbook** command:

```
ansible-playbook reg_check.yml
```

At the end of the execution, the current .NET 4.8 version of the target Windows system is printed on the screen. The output looks like this:

```
TASK [Print .NET version] *********************************************
*********************

ok: [WindowsServer] => {

    "msg": {

        "changed": false,

        "exists": true,

        "failed": false,

        "raw_value": "4.8.04161",

        "type": "REG_SZ",

        "value": "4.8.04161"

    }

}
```

# Adding Windows registry

As discussed previously, we can use the Ansible "**win_regedit**" module to verify if a key is already present and create it using Ansible "**win_regedit**" module if needed, by combining the parameters "**path**", "**name**", "**type**" and "**data**".

The following "**reg_create.yml**" Ansible playbook creates a "**Test**" hive entry under the "**HKEY_LOCAL_MACHINE**" under the "**Software**" folder. Under this entry, we create a key "**hello**" with the value "**world**" as a string. The full Ansible playbook looks like the following:

```
---

- name: Windows registry add

  hosts: all

  vars:

    mypath: 'HKLM:\Software\Test'

    mykey: 'hello'

    mytype: string

    myvalue: 'world'

  tasks:
```

```
  - name: Add key-value to registry
    ansible.windows.win_regedit:
      path: "{{ mypath }}"
      name: "{{ mykey }}"
      type: "{{ mytype }}"
      data: "{{ myvalue }}"
```

We can execute the "**reg_create.yml**" playbook using the following **ansible-playbook** command:

```
ansible-playbook reg_create.yml
```

At the end of the execution stage the key "**HKLM:\Software\Test**" is present on the target Windows system as shown in *Figure 5.13*:

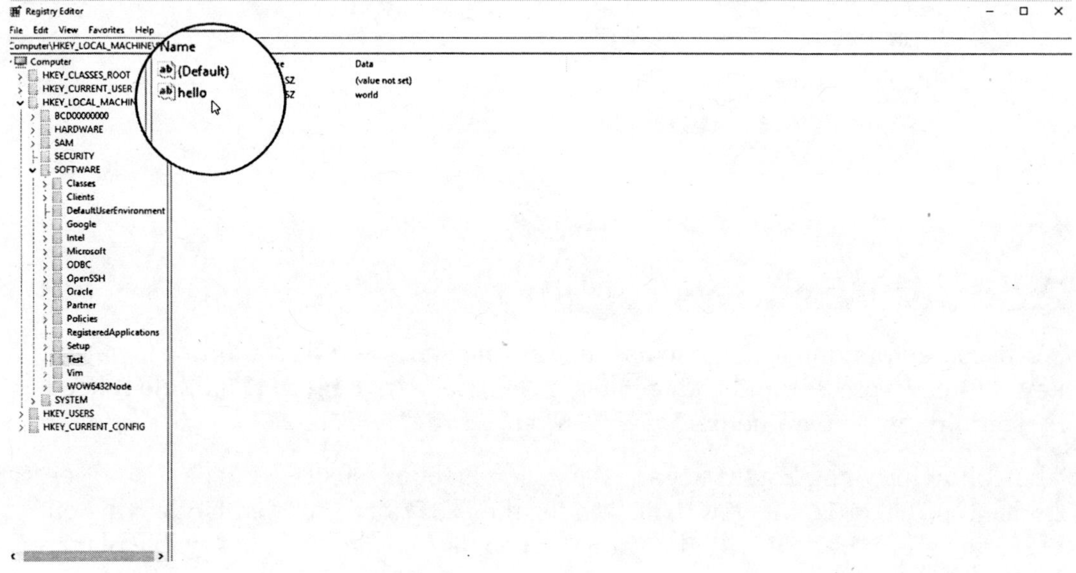


***Figure 5.13:*** *The Windows registry after the execution of the reg_create.yml Playbook*

## Removing Windows registry

Just as we added a Windows Registry key in the previous section, we can also remove a path or hive using the Ansible "**win_regedit**" module and setting the "**path**" parameter to "**absent**".

The following "**reg_remove.yml**" Ansible playbook creates a "**Test**" hive entry under the "**HKEY_LOCAL_MACHINE**" under the "**Software**" folder. Under this entry, we create a key "**hello**" with the value "**world**" as a string. The full Ansible playbook looks like the following:

```
---
- name: Windows registry remove
  hosts: all
  vars:
    mypath: 'HKLM:\Software\Test'
  tasks:
    - name: Registry remove path
      ansible.windows.win_regedit:
        path: "{{ mypath }}"
        state: absent
```

We can execute the "**reg_remove.yml**" playbook using the following **ansible-playbook** command:

```
ansible-playbook reg_remove.yml
```

At the end of the execution stage, the key "**`HKLM:\Software\Test`**" is removed on the target Windows system as shown in *Figure 5.14*. As we can see, the key "**`Test`**" is not present on the target system. Please refer to the following figure:

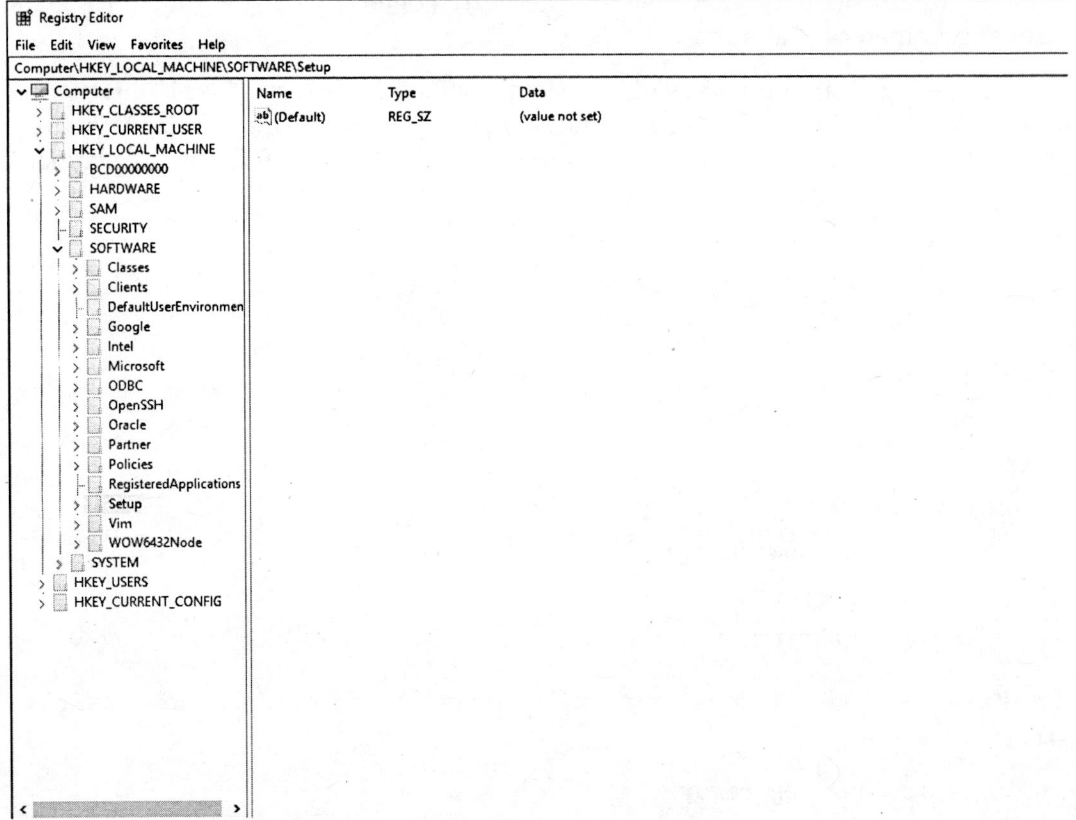


***Figure 5.14:*** *The Windows registry after the execution of the reg_create.yml Playbook*

# Executing commands

The "**`win_command`**" and "**`win_shell`**" are both Ansible modules for executing commands on Windows hosts, but they differ in their execution environment and syntax.

The Ansible "**`win_command`**" module runs commands in a Windows command shell, whereas the "**`win_shell`**" module runs commands in a PowerShell shell. The choice of module to use depends on the type of command you need to run.

If you need to run a simple command or batch file, you can use the **`win_command`** module. For example, to run a command to create a directory:

```
- name: Create directory
  win_command: mkdir C:\example
```

We can execute any PowerShell script using the "**win_shell**" Ansible module. The following script creates a new user:

```
- name: Create new user
  win_shell: New-LocalUser -Name "exampleuser" -Password (ConvertTo-SecureString "P@ssword1" -AsPlainText -Force)
```

The "**win_command**" Ansible module can be used for simple commands that do not need full shell capabilities. Either the "**win_shell**" Ansible module or "**win_command**" Ansible module executes commands on the Windows target host to execute a Windows PowerShell or cmd.exe but in a slightly different way. It is always the best idea to prefer a specific Ansible module when possible.

The "**win_shell**" Ansible module executes a PowerShell or cmd.exe interpreter with the full shell capabilities such as variables like "**$env:HOME**" and operations like "<", ">", "|", and ";". The "**win_command**" Ansible module executes the code without any shell capabilities; sometimes it is safer because it does not expose environment variables. The "**win_command**" Ansible module is intrinsically more secure than the "**win_shell**" Ansible module.

From the security point of view, the **win_command** module is more robust and has a more predictable outcome because it bypasses the shell. Both modules returned always changed status because Ansible is not able to predict if the execution has or has not altered the target system. For Linux targets, use the "**ansible.builtin.command**" and "**ansible.builtin.shell**" modules instead, as described in *Chapter 4, Ansible For Linux*, section *Executing commands*.

The Ansible "**win_command**" module executes a command on a remote Windows node. The "**win_command**" module will not be impacted by local "**win_shell**" variables because it bypasses the **win_shell**. At the same time, it may not be able to run **win_shell** built-in features and redirections.

The Ansible "**win_shell**" module executes shell commands on target hosts with the full shell context. The following examples demonstrate the capabilities of the "**win_command**" Ansible module and the "**win_shell**" Ansible module.

# Netstat playbook

This is an example of an Ansible playbook using the "**win_command**" module to run the "**netstat -e**" command on all hosts and register the output in the **command_output** variable. The "**ansible.builtin.debug**" module is then used to display the output of the "**command_output.stdout_lines**" variable.

In Windows, "**netstat**" is a command-line utility that displays the active TCP connections, ports on the listening connection host, Ethernet statistics, the IP routing table, and more. The "**-e**" option is used to display Ethernet statistics.

The "**win_command**" module is used to run commands on Windows hosts. It allows the execution of any command that can be run from a command prompt, including PowerShell commands.

The register keyword is used to capture the output of the "**netstat**" command in the **command_output** variable. This variable can be used later in the playbook for further processing or analysis.

The "**ansible.builtin.debug**" module is used to display the output of the "**command_output.stdout_lines**" variable, which contains the standard output of the "**netstat**" command as a list of strings. The output of this task will be printed to the console, providing information about the Ethernet statistics of each Windows host. The full Ansible "**netstat.yml**" playbook looks like the following:

```
---
- name: Netstat playbook
  hosts: all
  tasks:
    - name: Check netstat
      ansible.windows.win_command: "netstat -e"
      register: command_output
    - name: Command output
      ansible.builtin.debug:
        var: command_output.stdout_lines
```

We can execute the "**netstat.yml**" playbook using the following **ansible-playbook** command:

```
ansible-playbook netstat.yml
```

The output of the execution looks similar to the following:

```
TASK [Command output] **************************************************
*********************
ok: [WindowsServer] => {
    "command_output.stdout_lines": [
        "Interface Statistics",
        "                          Received            Sent",
        "Bytes                     13617365        10237530",
        "Unicast packets              53129           15035",
        "Non-unicast packets            293             274",
        "Discards                         0               0",
```

```
        "Errors                            0              0",
        "Unknown protocols               206"
    ]
}
```

# Get-Date playbook

This is an example of an Ansible playbook using the "**win_shell**" module to run multiple PowerShell commands on all hosts and register the output in the **command_output** variable. Like in the previous example, the "**ansible.builtin.debug**" module is then used to display the output of the "**command_output.stdout_lines**" variable.

In this example, two PowerShell commands are run on each Windows host. The first command is "**hostname**", which displays the hostname of the computer. The second command is "**Get-Date**", which displays the current date and time.

The Ansible "**win_shell**" module is used to run PowerShell commands on Windows hosts. It allows the execution of multiple PowerShell commands using a multiline string.

The register keyword is used to capture the output of the two PowerShell commands in the **command_output** variable. This variable can be used later in the playbook for further processing or analysis.

The "**ansible.builtin.debug**" module is used to display the output of the **command_output.stdout_lines** variable, which contains the standard output of the two PowerShell commands as a list of strings. The output of this task will be printed to the console, providing information about the hostname and current date and time of each Windows host. The full Ansible "**powershell.yml**" playbook looks like the following:

```
---
- name: Powershell playbook
  hosts: all
  tasks:
    - name: Check getdate
      ansible.windows.win_shell: |
        hostname
        Get-Date
      register: command_output
    - name: Command output
```

```
      ansible.builtin.debug:
        var: command_output.stdout_lines
```

We can execute the "**powershell.yml**" playbook using the following **ansible-playbook** command:

```
ansible-playbook powershell.yml
```

The output of the execution looks similar to the following:

```
TASK [Command output] **************************************************
*********************ok: [WindowsServer] => {
    "command_output.stdout_lines": [
        "demo",
        "",
        "Friday, April 8, 2022 18:19:36 AM",
        "",
        ""
    ]
}
```

# Wrong module

When we use the wrong module between the "**win_command**" and "**win_shell**" modules, we obtain a fatal error. Refer to *Chapter 6, Ansible Troubleshooting,* section *Ansible modules,* for further troubleshooting.

# Conclusion

Automating tasks on a Windows target system using Ansible enables us to be more productive and deliver more value to our fleet. Repetitive operations such as testing the availability, configuration management, file system, and user management, installation of packaging, rolling update, and Windows registry could be performed in a better way and obtain a more precise and accurate result.

In the next chapter, we are going to learn the Ansible best practices of how to troubleshoot, identify the root cause of the problem, and fix it.

# Points to remember

- We can execute automation scripts on most of the recent Windows and Windows Servers using Ansible. The connection is performed via WinRM, and the commands are executed using the PowerShell terminal.

- The simplest Ansible module is "**`win_ping`**" which tests the authentication and execution of a PowerShell code on a Windows target host
- Configuration management could be performed using the Ansible "**`win_lineinfile`**" module and Ansible "**`template`**" module.
- Many modules simplify file system management: check the existence of files and directories with the Ansible "**`win_stat`**" module, create files, and directories, with the Ansible "**`win_file`**" module, download contents with the Ansible "**`win_get_url`**" module, and checkout a Git repository using the Ansible "**`git`**" module.
- We can provision or install additional software using the Chocolatey package manager and maintain our fleet uniform.
- We maintain our fleet up to date using the Ansible "**`win_updates`**" module for rolling updates and also using the **Microsoft Windows Server Update Services** (**WSUS**) for the corporate environment.
- The Ansible "**`win_user`**" and "**`win_group`**" modules simplify the local user and group management.
- It is possible to check, create and remove keys, hives, and values from the Windows Registry using the Ansible "**`win_reg_stat`**" and Ansible "**`win_regedit`**" modules.

# Key terms

- **WinRM:** WinRM stands for Windows Remote Management, and it is a protocol that allows remote management of Windows machines. It enables communication between Windows machines over the network and provides a secure way to execute commands, access files, and perform other administrative tasks remotely.
- **PowerShell:** PowerShell is a command-line shell and scripting language designed for automating administrative tasks on Windows operating systems.
- **Chocolatey**: Chocolatey is a package manager for Windows that automates the installation and management of software packages. Read more about it at **https://chocolatey.org**.
- **WSUS**: **Windows Server Update Services** (**WSUS**) is a server role in Windows Server that allows the centralized management and distribution of Windows updates and patches within a network.

- **Windows Registry**: The Windows Registry is a hierarchical database that stores configuration settings and options for the Windows operating system and its installed applications.

# Multiple choice questions

1. **What are the requirements to configure a Windows target?**
    a. OpenSSH service running and Python interpreter
    b. WinRM service running and Python interpreter
    c. WinRM service running and PowerShell interpreter
    d. OpenSSH service running and PowerShell interpreter

2. **What is the best way to check if a file exists on a Windows target?**
    a. Ansible **`stat`** module
    b. Ansible **`win_stat`** module
    c. Ansible **`win_file`** module
    d. Ansible **`file`** module

3. **How can we install packages in an automated way on a Windows target?**
    a. Use the Chocolatey package manager.
    b. Manually install the package.
    c. Ansible **`package`** module
    d. It is not possible

4. **What are the two Ansible collections for Windows target?**
    a. They are the "**`aws..windows`**" and "**`ansible.windows`**" collections.
    b. They are the "**`aws.windows`**" and "**`community.windows`**" collections.
    c. They are the "**`ansible.builtin`**" and "**`community.windows`**" collections.
    d. They are the "**`ansible.windows`**" and "**`community.windows`**" collections.

# Answers

1. **c**
2. **b**
3. **a**
4. **d**

# Questions

1. What are authentication options for the Windows target?
2. What is the effect of the usage of the "**`ansible_winrm_transport`**" variable of the Ansible inventory?
3. What are the two different purposes of the Ansible "**`win_copy`**" module?
4. How can we check if a file or directory exists on the Windows target host?
5. What is the purpose of the Chocolatey open-source web archive?
6. When is it necessary to use the Ansible "**`command`**" and "**`shell`**" modules?

# CHAPTER 6
# Troubleshooting Ansible Deployments

## Introduction

This chapter outlines the most common Ansible issues. By the end of the chapter, we are going to learn the steps to troubleshoot, the root cause of the most common error, and some practical examples of the solution. We are going to become confident about checking the playbook syntax, using verbose and debug modes, checking for typos, verifying version compatibility, checking for dependencies, and using Ansible debug modules. By following these steps, we can solve common issues with Ansible and ensure efficient automation of IT infrastructure management tasks.

## Structure

In this chapter, we shall cover the following topics:

- Ansible troubleshooting
- Ansible debugging
- Ansible syntax
- Troubleshooting tools
- Ansible connection

- Ansible vault
- Ansible modules
- Ansible role
- Ansible collection
- Ansible for Linux
- Ansible for Windows

# Objectives

By the end of this chapter, the reader will be able to understand how to understand the most common Ansible error messages, troubleshoot the systems to find the root cause, and fix the problem for the future.

# Ansible troubleshooting

In Ansible, like any computer programming language and software tool, things can go wrong. In this chapter, we are going to learn the most common Ansible troubleshooting steps and techniques that we can use to solve any issues that may arise.

Let us now go over the 10 steps in Ansible troubleshooting:

1. **Check the Ansible documentation:** The Ansible documentation provides an extensive list of troubleshooting tips and tricks. It is always a good idea to start by reviewing the documentation to see if there are any known issues or limitations that may be causing our problem. If we are unable to find a solution in the documentation, proceed to the next step.

2. **Verify the inventory:** The inventory file is a critical part of Ansible's infrastructure. Ensure that the inventory file is correctly defined and that all hosts are reachable. If we are having trouble with a particular host, make sure that the host is up and running and that the SSH key authentication is correctly set up.

3. **Check the connectivity:** Verify that we can connect to the target hosts from the Ansible control node. Common connectivity issues can include firewall rules, network issues, or SSH key authentication problems. Use the **`ping`** command to verify connectivity to the host. If we are still having trouble, try using a different SSH port or setting up an SSH tunnel.

4. **Verify the playbook syntax:** Make sure that the playbook syntax is correct by running the playbook in check mode. This mode does not make any changes

to the system but only checks the syntax. Use the **`ansible-playbook`** command with the `--`check flag to run the playbook in check mode.

5. **Use verbose mode:** When executing an Ansible playbook, use the verbosity (**`-v`**) flag to get a more detailed output. This can help identify where the error is occurring. We can increase the verbosity by adding more **`-v`** parameters to the "**`ansible-playbook`**" command. For example, **`-vvv`** for three levels of verbosity for the "Debug". The full levels are summarized in the following *Table 6.1*. Refer to *Chapter 2, Ansible Language Core,* section *Ansible playbook,* for the complete Ansible verbosity levels.

| Levels | Description | ansible-playbook parameter |
|---|---|---|
| `0` | **`Normal`** | no parameter |
| `1` | **`Verbose`** | **`-v`** |
| `2` | **`More Verbose`** | **`-vv`** |
| `3` | **`Debug`** | **`-vvv`** |
| `4` | **`Connection Debug`** | **`-vvvv`** |

***Table 6.1:** Ansible verbosity levels*

6. **Debug mode:** Debug mode is the level three verbosity (**`-vvv`**) that provides even more detailed output. Use this mode to get more information about what is happening during the playbook execution. We can use the **`-vvv`** flag to turn on the debug verbosity mode.

7. **Check for typos:** Sometimes, errors can be caused by simple typos in the playbook, inventory file, or other configuration files. Review the files carefully for any typos or syntax errors. Use a text editor with syntax highlighting to make it easier to spot any errors.

8. **Check Ansible version compatibility:** Make sure that the Ansible version is compatible with the version of the operating system or software that we are managing. Some modules may not be supported on older versions of the software or operating system. Use the "**`ansible --version`**" command to check the version of Ansible we are running.

9. **Check for dependencies:** Ensure that any necessary dependencies or prerequisites are installed on the target host. Ansible will not be able to execute a task if the required packages or libraries are missing. Check the documentation for the specific module we are using, to see if any dependencies are required. See the *Ansible collection* section for more information about Python library dependencies.

10. **Use Ansible debug module:** The Ansible "**`debug`**" module can be used to output variables or other information during the playbook execution. Use this

module to troubleshoot issues with variables, templates, or other dynamic content. We can use the debug module by adding it to our playbook.

We explored some of the most common Ansible troubleshooting steps and techniques that we can use to solve any issues that may arise. Remember to always start by checking the documentation, verifying the inventory and connectivity, using verbose and debug modes, checking for typos, verifying version compatibility.

# Ansible debugging

Ansible has a 'check' mode, which allows users to run their playbooks without actually making any changes to the target system. Refer to *Chapter 2, Ansible Language Core*, sections *Check* and *Debugging*, to go over how to execute dry runs or increase the verbosity of using the debug messages.

When running in check mode, Ansible will go through the playbook and perform all the tasks as usual, but it will not execute any tasks that would modify the system in any way. Instead, Ansible will report back to the user what changes would have been made if the playbook were run normally. Using check mode can be helpful when users want to verify what changes would be made to the target system before running the playbook. This allows users to catch any potential issues or errors before making any changes to the system. Additionally, check mode can help users to avoid unintended changes to the target system by providing a dry run of the playbook before actually executing it. To run a playbook in check mode, users can add the `` `--check` `` parameter to their Ansible command:

```
ansible-playbook --check playbook.yml
```

This will run the playbook in check mode and report back any changes that would be made if the playbook were run normally. Users can then review the output to ensure that the changes are expected and desired before running the playbook normally.

It is important to note that check mode does not guarantee that the playbook will run successfully when run normally. There may be certain conditions or dependencies that only come up during actual execution, so users should still thoroughly test their playbooks before running them in a production environment.

The following "**`changeip.yml`**" Ansible playbook sets the IP address and netmask in a Linux target machine:

```
---
- name: Change IP Address of Remote Host
  hosts: all
  become: true
  vars:
```

```
    new_ip_address: 192.168.1.100
    netmask: 255.255.255.0
  tasks:
    - name: Update Network Configuration File
      ansible.builtin.lineinfile:
        path: /etc/network/interfaces
        regexp: '^address'
        line: 'address {{ new_ip_address }}'
      notify:
        - Restart Network Service
    - name: Update Netmask Configuration File
      ansible.builtin.lineinfile:
        path: /etc/network/interfaces
        regexp: '^netmask'
        line: 'netmask {{ netmask }}'
      notify:
        - Restart Network Service
  handlers:
    - name: Restart Network Service
      ansible.builtin.service:
        name: networking
        state: restarted
```

We use the check mode by adding the "**--check**" parameter to the "**ansible-playbook**" command. We can execute the "**changeip.yml**" Ansible playbook using the **ansible-playbook** command in the check mode, adding the "**--check**" parameter. The full command is the following:

```
ansible-playbook --check changeip.yml
```

The output of the execution of the Ansible playbook **shell.yml** is the following:

```
PLAY [Change IP Address of Remote Host] *********************************
***************************************


TASK [Gathering Facts] **************************************************
****************************ok: [demo.example.com]


TASK [Update Network Configuration File] ********************************
```

```
****************************************

changed: [demo.example.com]


TASK [Update Netmask Configuration File] *********************************
****************************************

changed: [demo.example.com]


RUNNING HANDLER [Restart Network Service] ******************************
*****************************************

changed: [demo.example.com]


PLAY RECAP *******************************************************
*********************demo.example.com           : ok=4    changed=3
unreachable=0    failed=0    skipped=0    rescued=0    ignored=0
```

As we can see, the output of the execution seems like a normal execution, but no changes are performed on the target host. Our Ansible Playbook can be parsed without any execution on the target node using the check mode.

# Ansible syntax

Ansible syntax is designed to be human-readable, simple, and easy to understand. The basic building block of Ansible syntax is a YAML file that contains a list of tasks to be executed on the target systems. Overall, Ansible syntax is designed to be easy to read, write, and understand, even for non-technical users. The use of YAML files, modules, variables, conditionals, loops, and roles provides a flexible and powerful framework for managing complex IT infrastructure and automating repetitive tasks.

Here are some common Ansible syntax errors that users may encounter and how to fix them:

- **YAML syntax errors:** Ansible uses YAML syntax to define playbooks and tasks. Users may encounter syntax errors such as missing or extra commas, incorrect indentation, or mismatched brackets. To fix these errors, users should review the YAML syntax carefully and ensure that all brackets, commas, and indentations are correct.
- **Undefined variables:** If a variable is not defined or misspelled, Ansible will not be able to find it and may throw an error. Users should ensure that all variables are defined correctly and that the variable names are spelled correctly.

- **Missing modules:** Ansible modules are pre-written scripts that perform various tasks on remote systems. If a module is not installed or misspelled, Ansible will not be able to find it and may throw an error. Users should ensure that all required modules are installed and that the module names are spelled correctly.
- **Incorrect indentation:** Ansible uses indentation to define the hierarchy of tasks and blocks. If the indentation is incorrect, Ansible will not be able to parse the playbook correctly and may throw an error. Users should ensure that all tasks and blocks are properly indented.
- **Missing quotes:** If a string is not enclosed in quotes, Ansible may interpret it as a variable or a command and throw an error. Users should ensure that all strings are properly enclosed in quotes.
- **Missing or extra brackets:** If a bracket is missing or extra, Ansible may not be able to parse the playbook correctly and may throw an error. Users should ensure that all brackets are correctly matched and balanced.
- **Invalid syntax in conditionals:** Ansible uses a simple **`if/then/else`** syntax to define conditionals. If the syntax is incorrect, Ansible may not be able to parse the conditional correctly and may throw an error. Users should ensure that the syntax of all conditionals is correct.

In general, to avoid syntax errors in Ansible, users should carefully review the syntax of their playbooks and ensure that all variables, modules, tasks, and blocks are properly defined and indented. Additionally, users should thoroughly test their playbooks before running them in a production environment.

# Troubleshooting tools

Ansible has many investigation tools that can help us speed up our workflow, by avoiding common pitfalls and following best practices.

The combination of Ansible syntax check, YAML linter, and Ansible linter create an exceptional army to troubleshoot Ansible Playbook.

# Errors playbook

We are going to explore all the troubleshooting processes and the information that we can obtain by the Ansible syntax check, YAML linter, and Ansible linter tools using some code.

The following Ansible "**`errors.yml`**" Ansible playbook contains some common errors that require further investigation:

```
---
```

```
- name: Troubleshooting example
  hosts: all
  become: true
  vars:
    servers:
      host01:
        ip: 192.168.1.11
        type: large
  tasks:
    - name: Print a fact
      ansible.builtin.debug:
        var: ansible_facts['architecture']

    - name: Latest apache2 package
      ansible.builtin.apt:
      name: apache2
        state: latest
        update_cache: true

    - name: Only large machines
      ansible.builtin.debug:
        msg: "{{ servers.values() | selectattr('type', 'eq', 'large') |
map(attribute='ip') | join(',') }}"
```

As we might already spot, the first task, "**`Print a fact`**" is not correctly aligned in the YAML document. The second task has two "**`name`**" statements at the same level, with two different meanings. The third task has text too long than the standard 80 characters.

We are going to use three command line tools to identify and correct each mistake.

## syntax check

Our investigation with automatic tools began with a simple syntax check. We can perform a syntax check on the playbook without executing it using the "**`--syntax-check`**" parameter of the **`ansible-playbook`** command:

```
ansible-playbook --syntax-check errors.yml
```

The execution returns the following error on the screen and a `4 (four)` return code:

```
ERROR! We were unable to read either as JSON or YAML, these are the errors we got from each:
JSON: Expecting value: line 1 column 1 (char 0)

Syntax Error while loading YAML.
  did not find expected key

The error appears to be in 'errors.yml': line 15, column 5, but may
be elsewhere in the file depending on the exact syntax problem.

The offending line appears to be:

    - name: Latest apache2 package
    ^ here
```

Refer to the following *Figure 6.1:*

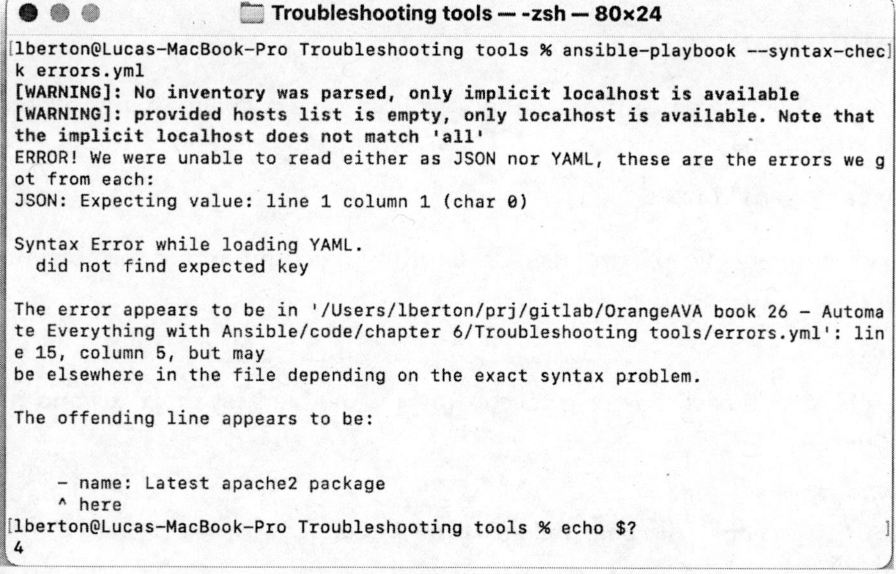


***Figure 6.1:*** *The syntax check output*

The colorful output of the "**`ansible-playbook`**" command is also shown in *Figure 6.1*. The error messages point in the right direction to troubleshoot and debug line 15 of the source code, but we need further investigation and corrections.

When we have a trained eye, it is easy to spot and correct some common errors on it. For a better experience, use some command line utilities to assist in our development journey.

The command line utilities "**yamllint**" and "**ansible-lint**" are useful to spot code errors and save time in our automation journey.

# YAML linter

The "**yamllint**" is a command line static code analyzer utility for all the YAML files. The purpose of the software is to be a "linter for YAML files" released under the MIT and open-source GPL-3.0 license. The latest version at the time of writing this book is the stable 1.30.0 release. The dependency requirements are a recent version of Python 3 and the "**pyyaml**" Python library. Refer to the official website for further information: "**https://github.com/adrienverge/yamllint**". The installation process is super easy because we only need to install the additional "**yamllint**" in the most recent operating system. When the utility is not installed in our system, we obtain the following error message:

```
command not found: yamllint
```

For example, we can install the "**yamllint**" package using the "**yum**" or "**DNF**" package manage in any "Red Hat"-like Linux distributions:

```
dnf install yamllint
```

On the other hand, we need to use the "**apt**" package manage in any "Debian"-like Linux distributions.

```
apt install yamllint
```

We can execute our "**yamllint**" using the following command in the current project directory:

```
yamllint .
```

The output shows each line error according to Ansible best practices and a 1 (**one**) return code:

```
./errors.yml
  11:3      error    wrong indentation: expected 4 but found 2
(indentation)
  15:5      error    syntax error: expected <block end>, but found '-'
(syntax)
  23:81     error    line too long (107 > 80 characters)  (line-length)
```

The colorful output of the "**yamllint**" command is also shown in *Figure 6.2*:

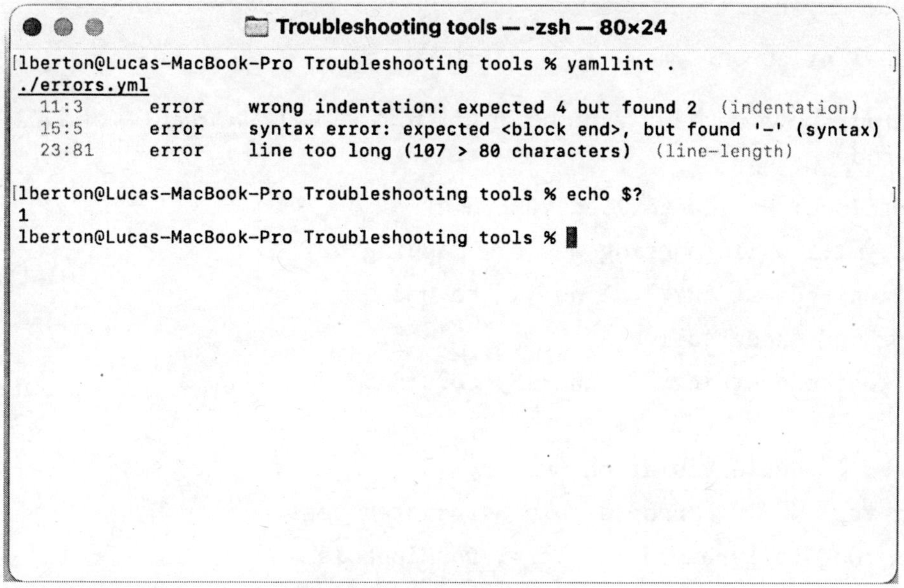

```
Troubleshooting tools — -zsh — 80×24
lberton@Lucas-MacBook-Pro Troubleshooting tools % yamllint .
./errors.yml
  11:3      error    wrong indentation: expected 4 but found 2  (indentation)
  15:5      error    syntax error: expected <block end>, but found '-' (syntax)
  23:81     error    line too long (107 > 80 characters)  (line-length)

lberton@Lucas-MacBook-Pro Troubleshooting tools % echo $?
1
lberton@Lucas-MacBook-Pro Troubleshooting tools %
```

*Figure 6.2: The yamlint output*

# Ansible linter

The "**ansible-lint**" is a command line static code analyzer utility specific for the Ansible language. The software aims to verify that the Ansible best practices and behavior are followed in our Ansible Playbook and spot potential problems. It is released under an open-source GPL-3.0 license. The latest version at the time of writing this book is the stable 6.14.3 release. The dependency requirements are a recent version of Python 3 and the Python libraries "**pyyaml**", "**pygments**" and the tools "**yamllint**" and "**ansible**". Refer to the official website for further information: "**https://ansible-lint.readthedocs.io/**". The installation process is super easy because we only need to install the additional "**ansible-lint**" in the most recent operating system. When the utility is not installed in our system, we obtain the following error message:

```
command not found: ansible-lint
```

For example, we can install the "**ansible-lint**" package using the "**yum**" or "**DNF**" package manage in any "Red Hat"-like Linux distributions, as shown:

```
dnf install ansible-lint
```

On the other hand, we need to use the "**apt**" package manage in any "Debian"-like Linux distributions, as follows:

```
apt install ansible-lint
```

We can execute the "**`ansible-lint`**" using the command in the current project directory:

```
ansible-lint errors.yml
```

The output shows each line error according to Ansible best practices and a `2 (two)` return code:

```
load-failure: Failed to load YAML file
errors.yml:1 while parsing a block mapping
  in "<unicode string>", line 11, column 5
did not find expected key
  in "<unicode string>", line 15, column 5

              Rule Violation Summary
 count tag          profile rule associated tags
     1 load-failure min     core, unskippable

Failed after : 1 failure(s), 0 warning(s) on 1 files.
```

The colorful output of the "**`ansible-lint`**" command is shown in *Figure 6.3*:

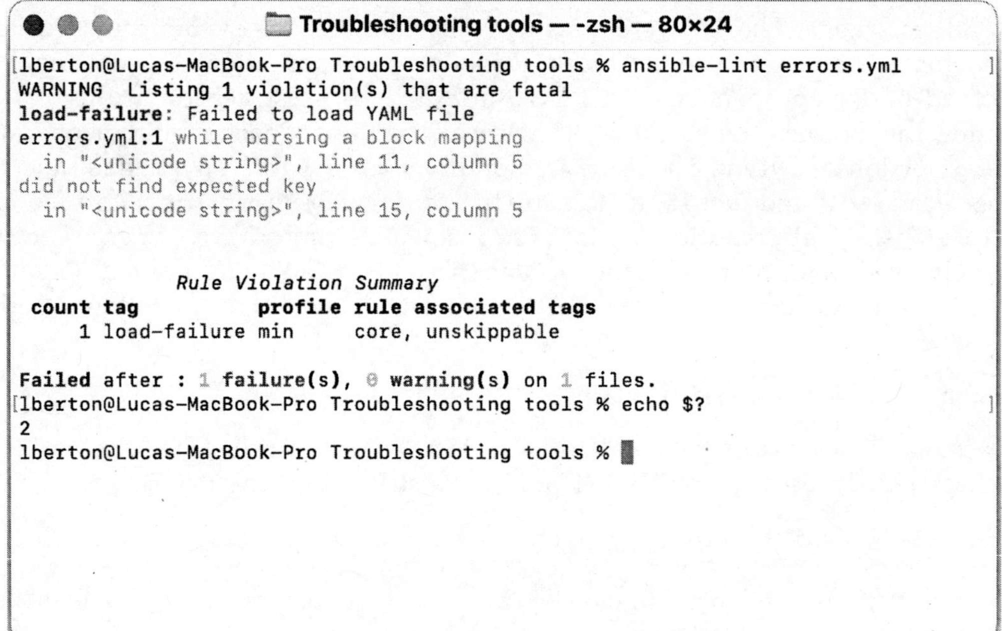


*Figure 6.3: The ansible-lint output*

After fixing the Playbook main errors, we produce the **fix.yml** playbook. We can execute again the "**ansible-lint**" in the current project directory:

```
ansible-lint fix.yml
```

The output shows two suggestions to improve our code according to the Ansible best practices:

```
WARNING  Listing 2 violation(s) that are fatal
name[casing]: All names should start with an uppercase letter.
fix.yml:10 Task/Handler: print a fact

package-latest: Package installs should not use latest.
fix.yml:14 Task/Handler: Latest apache2 package

Read documentation for instructions on how to ignore specific rule
violations.

               Rule Violation Summary
 count tag            profile  rule associated tags
     1 name[casing]   moderate idiom
     1 package-latest safety   idempotency

Failed after basic profile, 1/5 star rating: 2 failure(s), 0 warning(s)
on 1 files.
```

Refer to the following *Figure 6.4:*

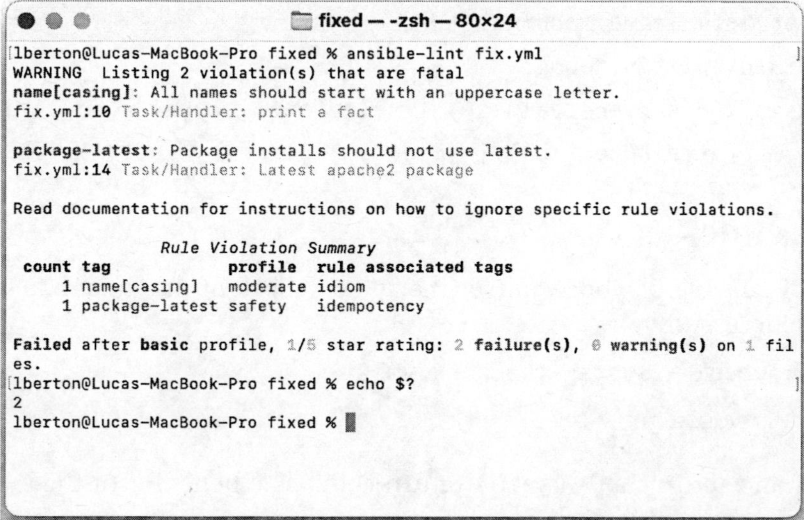


*Figure 6.4: The ansible-lint output*

## Fixed playbook

After correcting all the errors, we obtain the following "**fix.yml**" Ansible playbook:

```
---
- name: Troubleshooting example
  hosts: all
  vars:
    servers:
      host01:
        ip: 192.168.1.11
        type: large
  tasks:
    - name: Print a fact
      ansible.builtin.debug:
        var: ansible_facts['architecture']

    - name: Latest apache2 package
      ansible.builtin.apt:
        name: apache2
        state: present
        update_cache: true

    - name: Only large machines
      ansible.builtin.debug:
        msg: "{{ servers.values() | selectattr('type', 'eq', 'large') |
          map(attribute='ip') | join(',') }}"
```

## Syntax check

The **fix.yml** Ansible playbook passes the syntax check of the "**ansible-playbook**" command successfully:

```
ansible-playbook --syntax-check fix.yml
playbook: fix.yml
```

This command returns a 0 **(zero)** return code. The behavior of the syntax check command is shown in *Figure 6.5*:

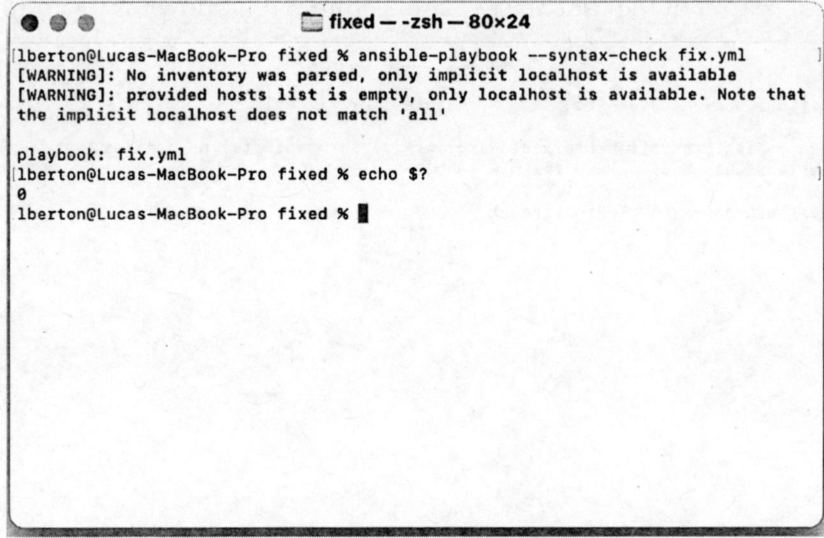


***Figure 6.5:** The syntax check output*

# YAML linter

The "**`yamllint`**" execute at the project level:

```
yamllint .
```

The behavior of the "**`yamllint`**" command is also shown in the previous *Figure 6.5*. When we execute the "**`yamllint`**" command line utility, we obtain successful empty output and a 0 (zero) return code.

# Ansible linter

We are going to analyze the playbook using the "**`ansible-lint`**" command line utility:

```
ansible-lintfix.yml
```

The output shows a successful execution according to Ansible best practices and a **`0 (zero)`** return code:

```
ansible-lintfix.yml


Passed with production profile: 0 failure(s), 0 warning(s) on 1 file.
```

The colorful output of the "**`ansible-lint`**" command is shown in *Figure 6.6*:

```
[lberton@Lucas-MacBook-Pro fixed % ansible-lint fix.yml

Passed with production profile: 0 failure(s), 0 warning(s) on 1 files.
[lberton@Lucas-MacBook-Pro fixed % echo $?
0
lberton@Lucas-MacBook-Pro fixed %
```

***Figure 6.6:*** *The ansible-lint output*

# Visual Studio code

**Visual Studio Code** (**VSCode**) is a free and open-source integrated development environment (IDE) developed by Microsoft. It supports a wide range of programming languages, and provides a rich set of features for code editing, debugging, and version control. We can download the editor from **https://code.visualstudio.com/** for the most common operating systems: MacOS in Universal binary, Windows x64, and Linux x64 as an RPM and DEP package format.

VSCode is the first-class citizen for Ansible code development because it drastically boosts the productivity of developers. However, it is possible to use any text editor.

Ansible integration with VSCode allows developers to leverage the powerful features of both tools. This integration enables developers to write, test, and deploy Ansible playbooks from within the VSCode environment. It provides an intuitive interface for creating and editing playbooks, as well as a range of debugging and testing features.

Some of the key benefits of Ansible VSCode integration include the following:

- **Code completion and syntax highlighting:** VSCode provides auto-completion for Ansible modules and syntax highlighting for Ansible YAML files, making it easier for developers to write and debug Ansible code.

- **IntelliSense and linting:** The VSCode Ansible extension provides IntelliSense and linting for Ansible modules and playbooks. This ensures that the code is error-free and adheres to best practices.
- **Debugging:** VSCode allows developers to debug Ansible code using breakpoints, variable inspection, and step-by-step execution. This makes it easier to identify and fix issues in complex playbooks.
- **Ansible Galaxy integration:** VSCode provides integration with Ansible Galaxy, a repository of Ansible roles and collections. This makes it easy for developers to discover, download, and use pre-built Ansible content.
- **Continuous Integration/Continuous Deployment (CI/CD) support:** The VSCode Ansible extension supports integration with popular CI/CD tools like Jenkins, Travis CI, and GitLab CI. This allows for automated testing and deployment of Ansible playbooks.

Ansible VSCode integration provides a powerful and intuitive interface for developing and deploying Ansible playbooks. It improves productivity, ensures code quality, and simplifies the management of complex systems. To get the best experience, ensure that the Ansible extension by Red Hat is installed, as shown in *Figure 6.7*:

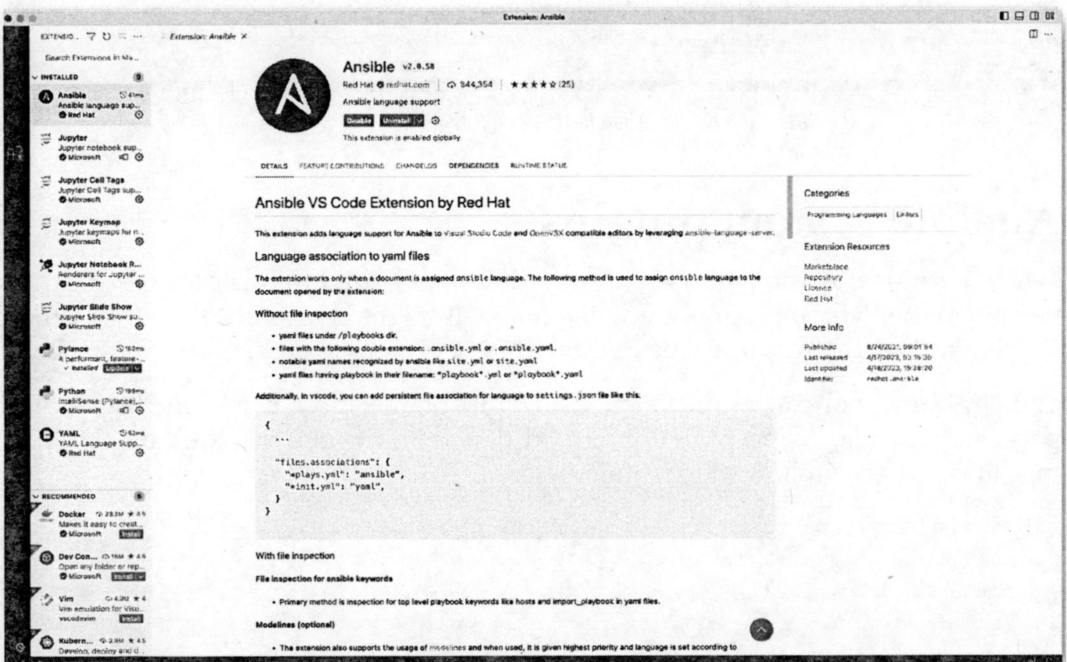


*Figure 6.7: The Ansible VSCode extension*

Under the hood, the Ansible extension uses the same "**ansible-lint**" rules to highlight best practices and assist during programming. Each line with a suggestion is underlined with a red mark, and when we move our mouse cursor over it, we receive the hint as shown in *Figure 6.8* for code line 7:

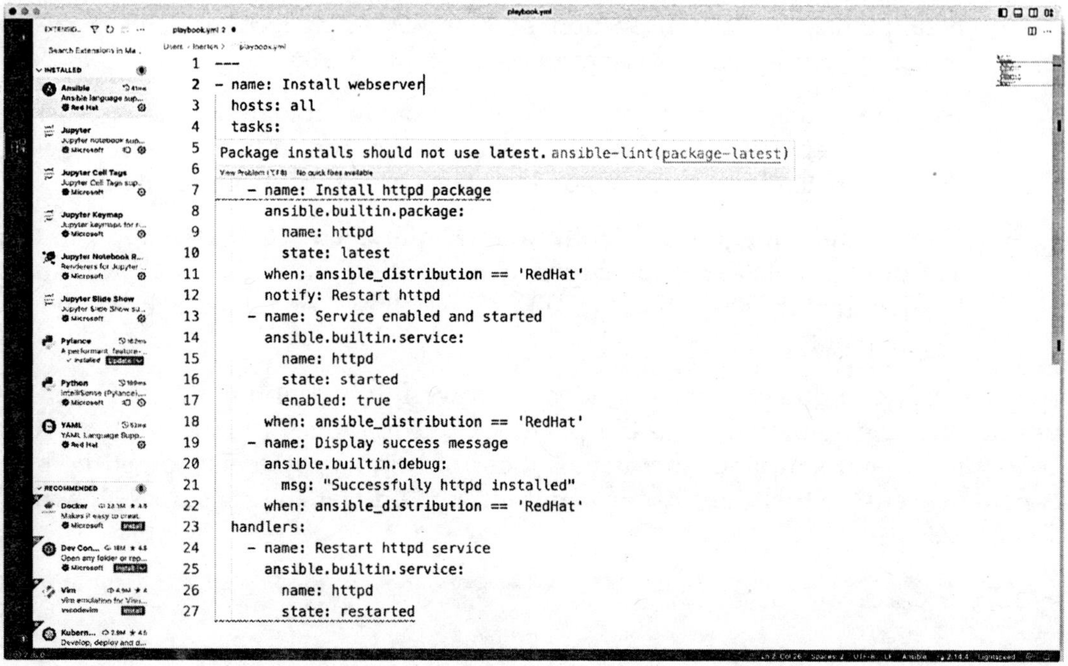

```
1  ---
2  - name: Install webserver
3    hosts: all
4    tasks:
5  Package installs should not use latest. ansible-lint(package-latest)
6  View Problem  No quick fixes available
7      - name: Install httpd package
8        ansible.builtin.package:
9          name: httpd
10         state: latest
11       when: ansible_distribution == 'RedHat'
12       notify: Restart httpd
13     - name: Service enabled and started
14       ansible.builtin.service:
15         name: httpd
16         state: started
17         enabled: true
18       when: ansible_distribution == 'RedHat'
19     - name: Display success message
20       ansible.builtin.debug:
21         msg: "Successfully httpd installed"
22       when: ansible_distribution == 'RedHat'
23   handlers:
24     - name: Restart httpd service
25       ansible.builtin.service:
26         name: httpd
27         state: restarted
```

*Figure 6.8: The Ansible VSCode integration suggestions*

# Ansible custom plugins

When additional Ansible plugins and modules are added to our projects, they are written in the Python programming language. It might be useful to use the Python Linter like "**pylint**" to verify the Python files.

The "**pylint**" tool can be installed using pip or the most common distribution package manager. Using pip, all required dependencies are installed on the local machine using the following command:

```
pip install pylint
```

The output of the execution is shown in the following *Figure 6.9*:

```
Troubleshooting tools — -zsh — 84×28
(venv) lberton@Lucas-MacBook-Pro Troubleshooting tools % pip install pylint
Collecting pylint
  Using cached pylint-2.17.3-py3-none-any.whl (536 kB)
Collecting platformdirs>=2.2.0 (from pylint)
  Using cached platformdirs-3.5.0-py3-none-any.whl (15 kB)
Collecting astroid<=2.17.0-dev0,>=2.15.4 (from pylint)
  Using cached astroid-2.15.4-py3-none-any.whl (278 kB)
Collecting isort<6,>=4.2.5 (from pylint)
  Using cached isort-5.12.0-py3-none-any.whl (91 kB)
Collecting mccabe<0.8,>=0.6 (from pylint)
  Using cached mccabe-0.7.0-py2.py3-none-any.whl (7.3 kB)
Collecting tomlkit>=0.10.1 (from pylint)
  Using cached tomlkit-0.11.8-py3-none-any.whl (35 kB)
Collecting dill>=0.3.6 (from pylint)
  Using cached dill-0.3.6-py3-none-any.whl (110 kB)
Collecting lazy-object-proxy>=1.4.0 (from astroid<=2.17.0-dev0,>=2.15.4->pylint)
  Using cached lazy_object_proxy-1.9.0-cp311-cp311-macosx_13_0_arm64.whl
Collecting wrapt<2,>=1.14 (from astroid<=2.17.0-dev0,>=2.15.4->pylint)
  Using cached wrapt-1.15.0-cp311-cp311-macosx_11_0_arm64.whl (36 kB)
Installing collected packages: wrapt, tomlkit, platformdirs, mccabe, lazy-object-pro
xy, isort, dill, astroid, pylint
Successfully installed astroid-2.15.4 dill-0.3.6 isort-5.12.0 lazy-object-proxy-1.9.
0 mccabe-0.7.0 platformdirs-3.5.0 pylint-2.17.3 tomlkit-0.11.8 wrapt-1.15.0
(venv) lberton@Lucas-MacBook-Pro Troubleshooting tools % pylint --version
pylint 2.17.3
astroid 2.15.4
Python 3.11.3 (main, Apr  7 2023, 20:13:31) [Clang 14.0.0 (clang-1400.0.29.202)]
(venv) lberton@Lucas-MacBook-Pro Troubleshooting tools %
```

***Figure 6.9:** The PyLint installation*

# CI/CD pipeline

We can combine all the tools for Ansible syntax check, YAML linter, Ansible linter, and Python linter in a CI pipeline, in order to spot the errors as soon as possible, for every commit in our repository or to ensure that every release does not contain any error that might generate any failure or unexpected behavior in a production environment. Integrating all the tools in a CI pipeline enables us to create a workflow to approve our changes before any execution. We can use several tools for the CI pipeline; the most popular are Jenkins, GitLab, GitHub Actions, and so on.

## Ansible connection

The most common Ansible connection error is related to SSH authentication. Here are some details on this error:

- **SSH authentication error:** This error occurs when Ansible is unable to authenticate to the remote server over SSH. This may be due to incorrect login credentials or missing SSH keys.

- **Host key verification error:** This error occurs when the remote server's host key is not recognized by Ansible. This may happen if the remote server is being accessed for the first time or if the host key has changed.
- **Network connectivity error:** This error occurs when Ansible is unable to connect to the remote server due to network connectivity issues such as firewall blocking or network congestion.
- **SSH timeout error:** This error occurs when the connection times out before authentication can be completed. This may happen due to slow network connectivity or other network issues.
- **Connection refused error:** This error occurs when the remote server is not accepting SSH connections. This may happen due to the SSH daemon not running or listening on a different port.

To resolve the most common Ansible connection error, users should first ensure that the login credentials are correct and that the SSH keys are present and valid. They should also verify the host key and add it to the "**`known_hosts`**" file if it is not already there. Users should also check the network connectivity between the Ansible control node and the remote server and ensure that the firewall is not blocking SSH connections. Additionally, they should check if the SSH daemon is running and listening on the correct port.

## The error

Connection failed errors are one of the most common Ansible problems and are very annoying. The root cause of these types of problems might be the networking connection, firewall, some SSH configuration parameter, or even a misspelled Ansible hostname in our Ansible inventory.

The outcome is a fatal connection failed error, and we often see an "**`operation timed out`**" message on our execution log.

When we are dealing with virtual machines, verify the connection of the virtual network card and that the SSH service is enabled in the firewall. A manual SSH connection to the target host test might be useful for the connection test.

## Example

Let us now simulate and solve the misspelled hostname as the target machine. The right hostname is "**`server01.example.com`**", but let us suppose we type an extra "**`e`**" and the final hostname becomes "**`serveer01.example.com`**". Please note the additional letter e in the hostname. This is a trivial and often occurred error.

The following "**inventory_error.ini**" Ansible inventory file has a misspelled target hostname error for the "**serveer01.example.com**" instead of "**server01.example.com**":

```
serveer01.example.com
```

We can verify the Ansible inventory **inventory_error** using the **ansible-inventory** command that is included in every Ansible installation. The full command for the list view is as follows:

```
ansible-inventory -i inventory_error.ini --list
```

The preceding command produces the following output:

```
{
    "all": {
        "children": [
            "ungrouped"
        ]
    },
    "ungrouped": {
        "hosts": [
            "serveer01.example.com"
        ]
    }
}
```

Once the right hostname is typed ("**server01.example.com**") we can see a successful command:

```
server01.example.com
```

We can verify the Ansible inventory file using the **ansible-inventory** command:

```
ansible-inventory -i inventory --list


{
    "all": {
        "children": [
            "ungrouped"
        ]
    },
```

```
    "ungrouped": {
        "hosts": [
            "server01.example.com"
        ]
    }
}
```

With the correct Ansible inventory file, we obtain the list of correct hosts.

## Password authentication

When trying to connect to the host using password authentication, we might encounter the following error message:

```
to use the 'ssh' connection type with passwords, you must install the sshpassprogram
```

We need to install the "**sshpass**" software on the Ansible controller. For "Red Hat"-like operation system:

```
dnf install sshpass
```

For the Debian-like distributions:

```
apt install sshpass
```

See the *Ansible for Linux* section for further information about the "**sshpass**" command line.

# Ansible Vault

Ansible Vault is a feature in Ansible that allows users to encrypt sensitive data such as passwords, API keys, and other secrets. Here are some common Ansible Vault errors that users may encounter and how to fix them:

- **Incorrect password:** If the user enters an incorrect password when decrypting an Ansible Vault file, Ansible will not be able to decrypt the file and may throw an error. Users should ensure that they enter the correct password when decrypting the Ansible Vault file.
- **Missing or misplaced Vault tags:** Ansible Vault uses special tags to indicate which variables or files should be encrypted. If these tags are missing or misplaced, Ansible will not be able to encrypt or decrypt the data correctly and may throw an error. Users should ensure that they use the correct syntax and placement of Vault tags.

- **Encryption errors:** If the encryption process encounters an error, Ansible may not be able to encrypt the data correctly and may throw an error. Users should ensure that they are using a supported encryption algorithm and that the data they are encrypting does not exceed the maximum length allowed.
- **File permission errors:** If the file permissions are incorrect, Ansible may not be able to read or write to the Ansible Vault file and may throw an error. Users should ensure that the file permissions are set correctly and that they have the necessary permissions to access the file.
- **Conflicting encryption methods:** If the user is using multiple encryption methods in their playbooks, they may encounter conflicts that prevent Ansible Vault from working correctly. Users should ensure that they use only one encryption method in their playbooks.
- **Encryption key rotation:** If the encryption key is changed or rotated, users may not be able to decrypt their Ansible Vault files and may encounter errors. Users should ensure that they have a secure process in place for rotating encryption keys and that they update their playbooks accordingly.

In general, to avoid Ansible Vault errors, users should ensure that they use strong and unique passwords, correctly place Vault tags, use supported encryption algorithms, set correct file permissions, and follow best practices for encryption key management. Additionally, users should thoroughly test their playbooks that use Ansible Vault before running them in a production environment.

## Create

The following two errors might occur when using the **`ansible-vault create`** command.

When the two passwords do not match, we obtain the following error on the screen by the **`ansible-vault`** command:

```
New Vault password:

Confirm New Vault password:

[WARNING]: Error in vault password prompt (default): Passwords do not
match

ERROR! Passwords do not match
```

We obtain the following error message if we specify an already existing filename by the **`ansible-vault`** command:

```
New Vault password:

Confirm New Vault password:

ERROR! secret.yml exists, please use 'edit' instead
```

# Encrypt

When the **vault-password.txt** file does not exist, we obtain the following "**password file not found**" error message:

```
[WARNING]: Error getting vault password file (default): The vault password file /vault-password.txt

was not found

ERROR! The vault password file /vault-password.txt was not found
```

As expected, the file **secret.yml** already exists. Hence, the **ansible-vault** execution is aborted, and the file is not altered.

The solution is verifying the presence of the "**vault-password.txt**" file and redoing the "**ansible-vault**" command with the "**encrypt**" parameter.

# View

When the password is incorrect, we obtain the following output:

```
Vault password:

ERROR! Decryption failed (no vault secrets were found that could decrypt) on secret.yml for secret.yml
```

The solution is to use the correct password of the password file for the "**ansible-vault**" command with the "**view**" parameter.

# Playbook

We had a fatal error when we forgot to specify the Ansible Vault password. We can simulate using the following command:

```
ansible-playbookplaybook.yml
```

Produce the output of the **ansible-playbook** command without specifying any password:

```
TASK [include_vars] *****************************************************************************
```

```
fatal: [server01.example.com]:
FAILED! => {
    "ansible_facts": {},
    "ansible_included_var_files": [],
    "changed": false,
    "message": "Attempting to decrypt but no vault secrets found"
}
```

This was the output of the **ansible-playbook** command.

# Inline vault

When we copy and paste the output of the **ansible-vaultencrypt_string** command, please be mindful to remove the trailing character from the output (displayed as "%" character in MacOS). When the end character is not removed, the execution might end in one of the two scenarios.

## Encrypted variable

The output of the execution of the **vault_inline.yml** playbook file is displayed encrypted, as shown:

```
ok: [server01.example.com] => {
    "password": "$ANSIBLE_VAULT;1.1;AES256 33323438663430343838353432366
53335643262323462646334346430613934396565373362623637643137643136353538
34633232626539626561376664320a35663834376337626665346531356331616265616
638363866623962316166623537356164363032323266623761643931663732353034 34
65393533343063360a636461396139646335326463343666393062666430386334383235
666662 6632%"
}
```

## Fatal error

The output of the execution of the **vault_inline.yml** playbook file displayed the "**Vault format unhexlify error**" message on the screen:

```
[WARNING]:
There was a vault format error: Vault format unhexlify error: Odd-length
string


The error appears to be in 'vault_inline.yml': line 5, column 15, but
may
```

```
be elsewhere in the file depending on the exact syntax problem.

The offending line appears to be:

  vars:
    password: !vault |
              ^ here
fatal: [localhost]: FAILED! => {"msg": "Vault format unhexlify error:
Odd-length string\n\nThe error appears to be in 'vault_inline.yml':
line 5, column 15, but may\nbe elsewhere in the file depending on the
exact syntax problem.\n\nThe offending line appears to be:\n\n  vars:\n
password: !vault |\n              ^ here\n"}
```

Once the offending line is corrected in the **vault_inline.yml** file, the execution continues, and we obtain the result shown in *Chapter 3 Ansible Language Extended,* section *Ansible Vault* output.

# Ansible modules

Ansible modules are pre-built tasks that perform a specific function. Here are some of the most common Ansible module errors and how to resolve them:

- **Module not found:** This error occurs when Ansible is unable to locate the module that is being called in the playbook. Users should ensure that the module is installed on the Ansible control node and that the correct path is specified in the playbook.
- **Invalid module parameter:** This error occurs when a module parameter is not recognized by Ansible. Users should ensure that they are using the correct syntax for the module and that all required parameters are specified.
- **Permissions error:** This error occurs when Ansible does not have permission to perform the task specified by the module. Users should ensure that they have the necessary permissions to perform the task and that they are running Ansible as a privileged user if required.
- **Incorrect data type:** This error occurs when Ansible is expecting data of a certain type but receives data of a different type. Users should ensure that they are passing data in the correct format and that they are using the correct data types.
- **Connection errors:** This error occurs when Ansible is unable to establish a connection to the remote server using a connection plugin. Users should ensure that they have the correct login credentials, that the remote server is reachable, and that SSH access is enabled.

- **Incorrect module version:** This error occurs when Ansible is using an outdated or incompatible version of the module. Users should ensure that they are using the correct version of the module that is compatible with their Ansible version.

To resolve these Ansible module errors, users should ensure that they have a clear understanding of the syntax and requirements of the module they are using. They should also ensure that the correct permissions are set, that the necessary modules are installed, and that they are using the correct data types. Additionally, users should test their playbooks thoroughly and verify that the tasks specified in the playbook are executing as expected.

# Missing module parameter

The Ansible "`Missing Module Parameter`" error occurs when a required parameter is missing from a module in an Ansible playbook. This error typically occurs when the module has specific required parameters that must be defined in order for the task to execute successfully.

For example, the "`copy`" module (part of the "`ansible.builtin`" collection) requires the "`src`" and "`dest`" parameters to be defined. If either of these parameters is missing, Ansible will report a "`Missing Module Parameter`" error.

To resolve this error, users should review the module's documentation to determine which parameters are required for the module to execute successfully. They should then add the missing parameters to the playbook or ensure that they are defined in the inventory file.

It is also important to ensure that the parameters are defined correctly, using the appropriate syntax and data types. Users can use the Ansible debug module to print out variable values and verify that they are set correctly.

Overall, the "`Missing Module Parameter`" error is a common error that can be easily resolved by reviewing the module's documentation and ensuring that the required parameters are defined correctly in the playbook or inventory file.

# Ansible service

The Ansible "`Service is in unknown state`" error occurs when Ansible is unable to determine the current state of service on the target host. This error can occur when using the Ansible "service" module to start, stop or restart a service.

For example, the following error messages show an "unknown state" for the nginx web service on the target machine:

```
TASK [reload nginx] **************************************************
************************

fatal: [server01.example.com]: FAILED! => {"changed": false, "msg":
"Service is in unknown state", "status": {}}
```

Here are the steps to troubleshoot and solve the "`Service is in unknown state`" error:

1. **Check the service name:** Verify that the service name in the playbook matches the name of the service on the target host. If the service name is misspelled or incorrect, Ansible will not be able to determine the state of the service.

2. **Verify service status:** Check the status of the service on the target host using the system's service management commands. This will help determine whether the service is running, stopped, or has failed to start.

3. **Check system logs:** Check the system logs on the target host for any errors related to the service. This can provide insight into why the service is in an unknown state.

4. **Verify privilege escalation:** Verify that Ansible is running with sufficient privileges to manage the service on the target host. This may require running the playbook with elevated privileges or configuring `sudo` permissions for the Ansible user.

5. **Ensure service module is installed:** Verify that the Ansible service module is installed on the control node. If the module is missing, Ansible will not be able to manage the service.

6. **Try a different module:** If the "`service`" module is not working, try using a different module to manage the service. For example, the "`command`" module can be used to execute service management commands directly on the target host.

Overall, the "`Service is in unknown state`" error can be resolved by verifying the service name, checking the service status, reviewing system logs, ensuring template privilege escalation, verifying the service module is installed, and trying a different module.

# Ansible template

The Ansible template might generate a fatal error at runtime when the following five conditions might arise on the Ansible controller or on the Ansible target nodes.

- When the destination path ("`/home/devops/`") does not exist, Ansible returns the following fatal error:

```
fatal: [server01.example.com]: FAILED! => {"changed": false, "checksum": "96d448ee43c8498088c12c8b1b44e9a022443257", "msg": "Destination directory /home/devops does not exist"}
```

For reference, see *Chapter 2, Ansible Language Core,* section *Ansible template,* playbook "**template_helloworld.yml**" code. The solution is to verify that the destination path ("**/home/devops/**") exists.

- When the Ansible template file is missed or misspelled in the controller, a failed execution returns a fatal error message similar to the following for the "**templates/helloworld.txt.j2**" file:

  We can reproduce renaming the **helloworld.txt.j2** file to **helloworld2.txt.j2**.

  The full fatal error message looks like the following:

  ```
  An exception occurred during task execution. To see the full traceback, use -vvv. The error was: If you are using a module and expect the file to exist on the remote, see the remote_srcoption

  fatal: [server01.example.com]: FAILED! => {"changed": false, "msg": "Could not find or access 'templates/helloworld.txt.j2'\nSearched in: REDACTED.\nIf you are using a module and expect the file to exist on the remote, see the remote_src option"}.
  ```

  For reference, see *Chapter 2, Ansible Language Core,* section *Ansible Template,* playbook "**template_helloworld.yml**" code. The solution is to verify that the template file ("**templates/helloworld.txt.j2**") exists before the execution of the Ansible playbook.

- When the Ansible template file uses an undefined or misspelled variable, a failed execution returns the "**AnsibleUndefinedVariable**" fatal error message similar to the following for the "**type**" variable:

  ```
  {% for server in servers.items() if type == 'large' %}
  ```

  The full fatal error message looks like the following:

  ```
  An exception occurred during task execution. To see the full traceback, use -vvv. The error was: ansible.errors.AnsibleUndefinedVariable: 'type' is undefined. 'type' is undefined

  fatal: [server01.example.com]: FAILED! => {"changed": false, "msg": "AnsibleUndefinedVariable: 'type' is undefined. 'type' is undefined"}
  ```

  For reference, see *Chapter 2, Ansible Language Core,* section *Ansible Template,* playbook "**template_type.yml**" code. The solution is to verify the spell of the "**type**" variable used in the template file before the execution of the Ansible playbook.

- When the Ansible template file uses an undefined or misspelled variable, a failed execution returns the "**AnsibleUndefinedVariable**" fatal error message similar to the following for the "**server.type**" variable:

  ```
  'tuple object' has no attribute 'type'
  {% for server in servers.items() if server.type == 'large' %}
  ```

  The full fatal error message looks like the following:

  ```
  An exception occurred during task execution. To see the full traceback, use -vvv. The error was: ansible.errors.AnsibleUndefinedVariable: 'tuple object' has no attribute 'type'. 'tuple object' has no attribute 'type'

  fatal: [server01.example.com]: FAILED! => {"changed": false, "msg": "AnsibleUndefinedVariable: 'tuple object' has no attribute 'type'. 'tuple object' has no attribute 'type'"}
  ```

  For reference, see *Chapter 2, Ansible Language Core,* section *Ansible template,* playbook "**template_type.yml**" code. The solution is to verify the spell of the "**server.type**" variable used in the template file before the execution of the Ansible playbook.

- When the Ansible template file performs a comparison between two different data types, a failed execution returns the "**AnsibleError: template error while templating string**" fatal error message. We can reproduce with the following line 1 in the **type.txt.j2** file:

  ```
  {% for key, value in servers.items() if value.type is 'large' %}
  ```

  The full fatal error message looks like the following:

  ```
  An exception occurred during task execution. To see the full traceback, use -vvv. The error was: . expected token 'name', got 'string'

  fatal: [server01.example.com]: FAILED! => {"changed": false, "msg": "AnsibleError: template error while templating string: expected token 'name', got 'string'. String: {% for key, value in servers.items() if value.type is 'large' %}\n{{ key }} is large\n{% else %}\n{{ key }} is {{ value.type }}.\n{% endfor %}\n. expected token 'name', got 'string'"}
  ```

For reference, see *Chapter 2, Ansible Language Core,* section *Ansible template,* playbook "**template_type.yml**" code. The solution is to verify the operation between the **toggle** variable before the execution of the Ansible playbook.

# Ansible command

When we use the wrong module between the "**command**" and "**shell**" modules, we obtain a fatal error. The Ansible novices found it difficult to troubleshoot.

If we try to access shell capabilities with the "**command**" module, we obtain a fatal error. Sometimes analyzing the error code might be challenging as there is no clear indication of the usage of the wrong Ansible module. The exact message is as follows:

```
"stderr": "ls: cannot access '*': No such file or directory", "stderr_
lines":
["ls: cannot access '*': No such file or directory"], "stdout": "",
"stdout_lines": []
```

We obtain the error when using the "**command**" module instead of the "**shell**" Ansible module. The fatal error code is produced by the following "**command_wrong.yml**" Ansible playbook. As we could notice, the code is similar to the "**shell.yml**" file with the command module instead. The entire "**command_wrong.yml**" file looks like the following:

```
---
- name: wrong module demo
  hosts: all
  tasks:
    - name: list file(s) and folder(s)
      ansible.builtin.command: 'ls -l *'
      register: command_output
    - name: command output
      ansible.builtin.debug:
        var: command_output.stdout_lines
```

We can execute our code using the **ansible-playbook** command line command:

```
ansible-playbook -i inventory command_wrong.yml
```

The "**commmand_wrong.yml**" playbook execution produces the following output:

```
TASK [List file(s) and folder(s)] ****************************************
*********************
fatal: [server01.example.com]: FAILED! => {"changed": true, "cmd":
```

```
["ls", "-l", "*"], "delta": "0:00:00.005169", "end": "2022-11-16
23:21:58.397262", "msg": "non-zero return code", "rc": 2, "start":
"2022-11-16 23:21:58.392093", "stderr": "ls: cannot access '*': No such
file or directory", "stderr_lines": ["ls: cannot access '*': No such file
or directory"], "stdout": "", "stdout_lines": []}
PLAY RECAP ************************************************************
****************
server01.example.com: ok=1    changed=0    unreachable=0    failed=1
skipped=0    rescued=0    ignored=0
```

The fatal error with the "**command**" module is standard because it has limited capabilities.

# Ansible role

The Ansible role error can occur when there is an issue with the role structure or execution. Here are the steps to troubleshoot and solve the Ansible role error:

1. **Check the role directory structure:** Verify that the directory structure of the role follows the recommended structure. A typical Ansible role has a **main.yml** file inside the tasks directory, a **meta/main.yml** file for dependencies, and other directories such as handlers, templates, and files.
2. **Verify the role syntax:** Check the syntax of the role's YAML files for syntax errors using the `ansible-playbook --syntax-check` command. If there are syntax errors, fix them before running the playbook.
3. **Verify the role execution:** Check that the role is being executed properly. Ensure that the role is included in the playbook and that the role name and path are correct.
4. **Check for missing dependencies:** If the role has dependencies, ensure that they are installed. Use the `ansible-galaxy install` command to install dependencies from the Ansible Galaxy.
5. **Check for missing variables:** Ensure that all required variables are defined and set correctly. Check the variable files and templates in the role's directory.
6. **Verify file permissions:** Verify that file permissions are set correctly on any files that the role is trying to access. Incorrect file permissions can prevent the role from executing properly.
7. **Debug the role execution:** Use the Ansible debug module to print out variable values and troubleshoot the role execution.

Overall, the Ansible role error can be resolved by checking the role directory structure, verifying the role syntax, ensuring proper role execution, checking for missing dependencies and variables, verifying file permissions, and using the debug module to troubleshoot.

When Ansible is not able to find "**role1**", we obtain the following **role not found** error:

```
ERROR! the role 'role1' was not found in /home/devops/roles/roles:/
root/.ansible/roles:/usr/share/ansible/roles:/etc/ansible/roles:/home/
devops/roles
```

The shown error is very common and it simply communicates to us that **role1** is not found in the directory listed after by Ansible. The solution is to verify to be in the correct directory for the execution or customize the role path in **ansible.cfg** file. Learn more about the usage of the **roles_path** parameter in the **ansible-galaxy** command or **ansible.cfg** file in *Chapter 8, Ansible Advance,* section *Ansible Configuration Settings*.

# Molecule

The molecule tools provide a simple and consistent way to test Ansible roles and collections, ensuring that they are working correctly before they are deployed to production. It is widely used in the Ansible community and is recommended for anyone developing and testing Ansible roles. Ansible Role Molecule is a tool used for testing Ansible roles. It provides a way to validate the functionality of Ansible roles by simulating different scenarios and testing the role in various environments. Molecule uses a combination of Docker or Vagrant to create virtual machines, Ansible to configure the virtual machines, and a testing framework such as Testinfra or Inspec to run tests against the virtual machines. Using Molecule, developers can test their roles in different environments and ensure that the roles work as expected in each environment. Molecule automates the entire testing process, from creating virtual machines to running tests and generating test reports.

The Molecule testing process is broken down into several stages, including:

1. **Create:** This stage creates the virtual machines, installs the necessary software, and configures them according to the role being tested.
2. **Converge:** This stage applies the Ansible role to the virtual machines and configures them.
3. **Verify:** This stage runs the tests against the virtual machines to ensure that the role is working as expected.
4. **Destroy:** This stage removes the virtual machines.

Molecule provides a simple and consistent way to test Ansible roles, ensuring that they are working correctly before they are deployed to production. It is widely used in the Ansible community and is recommended for anyone developing and testing Ansible roles.

# Ansible collection

Ansible collections are a way to package and distribute playbooks, roles, and modules, along with other related content, as a single unit. We can use the molecule tool to test Ansible collections. Here are some steps we can take to troubleshoot Ansible collection-related issues:

1. **Check the Ansible version:** Make sure we are using a version of Ansible that supports the collection we are using. Different collections require different minimum versions of Ansible.

2. **Check the collection path:** Verify that the collection is installed and located in the correct path. We can check the collection path by running the following command:

   ```
   ansible-config dump | grep COLLECTIONS_PATHS
   ```

3. **Check the collection name:** Verify that the collection name is specified correctly in the playbook or command that we are running. Collection names are case-sensitive and should be specified in the format "**namespace.collection_name**".

4. **Check the collection dependencies:** If the collection we are using has dependencies, make sure they are installed. We can use the "**ansible-galaxy collection install**" command to install dependencies.

5. **Check the module path:** If we are using a module from a collection, make sure that the module path is set correctly in the Ansible configuration file. We can set the module path by adding the following line to the **ansible.cfg** file:

   ```
   module_utils = /path/to/collection/plugins/modules
   ```

6. **Check the documentation:** Consult the documentation for the collection we are using to see if there are any known issues or troubleshooting steps specific to that collection.

7. **Debug the playbook:** Use the "**-vvv**" option to run the playbook or command in verbose mode, which can help us identify where the issue is occurring.

By following these steps, we can troubleshoot and resolve issues with Ansible collections.

## Missing collection

When our Ansible controller has not installed the Ansible collection, we end with the following error. Please note that the error reports the missing module **`'community.general.iso_create'.`** It simply indicates that Ansible does not know how to process our request. The collection is missing errors look like the following:

```
ERROR! couldn't resolve module/action 'community.general.iso_create'.
This often indicates a misspelling, missing collection, or incorrect
module path.
The error appears to be in '/home/devops/collections/collection.yml':
line 5, column 7 but may
be elsewhere in the file depending on the exact syntax problem.
The offending line appears to be:
  tasks:
    - name: Create an ISO file
      ^ here
```

The solution is to install the missing collection using the **`ansible-galaxy`** command:

```
ansible-galaxy install community.general
```

## Missing Python library

When running Ansible, we may encounter a "**`missing Python library`**" error if one of the required Python libraries is not installed. Ansible relies on a number of Python libraries to function properly, and if one of these libraries is missing or outdated, we may encounter errors. Here are some steps we can take to troubleshoot a "missing python library" error in Ansible:

1. **Identify the missing library:** The error message should indicate which library is missing. Look for the name of the library in the error message.

2. **Install the missing library:** Use our system's package manager or pip (Package Installer for Python) to install the missing library. The package name may vary depending on our operating system. For example, on Ubuntu, we can install Python packages using the apt package manager by running "**`apt install python3-<package_name>`**", while on CentOS or Red Hat Enterprise Linux, we can use "**`yum install python3-<package_name>`**". For PIP, we can use "**`pip install <package_name>`**" to install the missing library.

3. **Check the library version:** Ensure that the installed library version is compatible with the version of Ansible we are using. Different versions of

Ansible require different versions of Python libraries, and hence, make sure to check the Ansible documentation to see which versions are supported.

4. **Verify the library location:** Check that the library is installed in the correct location and that Ansible can find it. We can use the "**pip show <package_name>**" command to verify the location of the installed library.

5. **Check the library dependencies:** Make sure that the missing library does not have any dependencies that are also missing. If there are dependencies, we will need to install those as well.

By following these steps, we should be able to install the missing Python library and resolve the "**missing python library**" error in Ansible.

The following Ansible playbook uses the "**iso_create**" module that requires the "**pycdlib**" Python library:

```
TASK [Create an ISO file] **********************************************
***********************

An exception occurred during task execution. To see the full traceback,
use -vvv.
The error was: ModuleNotFoundError: No module named 'pycdlib'
fatal: [server01.example.com]: FAILED! => {"changed": false,
"msg": "Failed to import the required Python library (pycdlib) on Python
/usr/bin/python3. Please read the module documentation and install it in
the appropriate location.
If the required library is installed, but Ansible is using the wrong
Python interpreter, please consult the documentation on ansible_python_
interpreter"}
```

For example, the **iso_create** module requires the **pycdlib** Python library. This requirement is specified in the collection documentation on the Ansible Galaxy website. We can install it using the pip, the Python package manager in our system.

First of all, let us upgrade the pip utility to the latest version using the following command:

```
pip install --upgrade pip
```

After upgrading pip, we can install the **pycdlib** Python library using the following command:

```
pip install pycdlib
```

The PIP utility produces the following output:

```
Collecting pycdlib
```

```
  Using cached pycdlib-1.13.0-py2.py3-none-any.whl (211 kB)
Installing collected packages: pycdlib
Successfully installed pycdlib-1.13.0
```

When the Python library is already installed, we obtain the following message:

```
Requirement already satisfied:
pycdlib in /usr/local/lib/python3.8/dist-packages (1.13.0)
```

# Ansible for Linux

The `'sshpass'` is a utility tool that allows us to pass the password to the **`ssh`** command while executing it non-interactively. It is used to automate password authentication in SSH connections. `'sshpass'` can be used to pass the password to the **`ssh`** command via the standard input (stdin) stream.

When we use the SSH connection type with Ansible, we may need to provide the password for the SSH connection. Ansible provides several ways to pass the password, such as using SSH keys or specifying the password in the inventory file. However, if we want to pass the password directly to the **`ssh`** command, we need to use `'sshpass'`. Additionally, `'sshpass'` can be used to automate other authentication mechanisms that require a password, such as **`pkcs11_provider`**.

Refer to *Figure 6.10:*

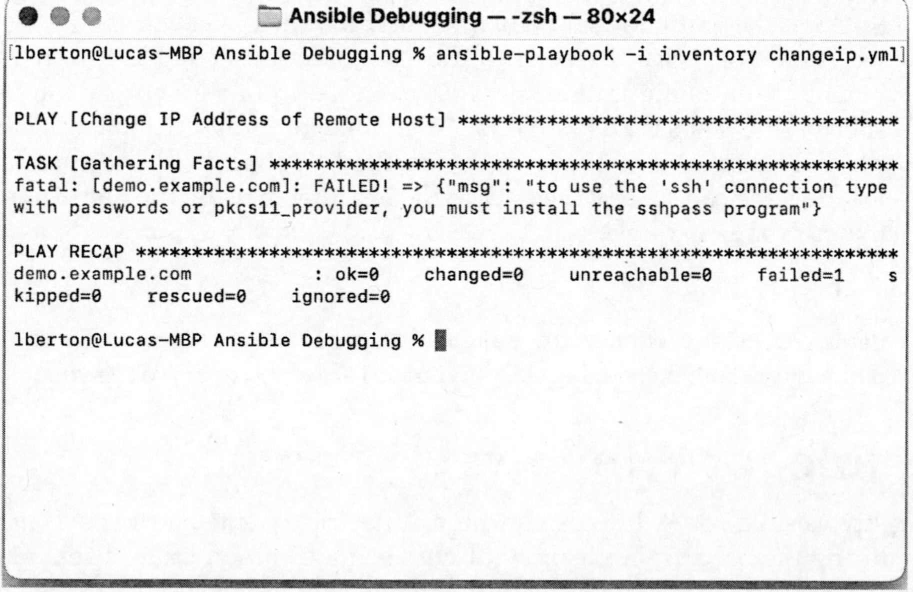


***Figure 6.10:*** *The SSH connection with password error*

We can troubleshoot the "**`to use the 'ssh' connection type with passwords or pkcs11_provider, you must install the sshpass program`**" error, as shown in *Figure 6.10* when executing an Ansible inventory with a Linux SSH password authentication.

If we encounter the "**`to use the 'ssh' connection type with passwords or pkcs11_provider, you must install the sshpass program`**" error while using Ansible, here are the steps we can follow to troubleshoot the issue:

1. **Check if 'sshpass' is installed on the remote system:** The first step is to check if **`'sshpass'`** is installed on the remote system. We can do this by logging into the remote host and running the following command:

   ```
   sshpass -V
   ```

   If the command is not found, it means that **`'sshpass'`** is not installed. In this case, we need to install it.

2. **Install `'sshpass'` on the remote system:** The next step is to install **`'sshpass'`** on the remote system. Depending on our operating system, we can use the appropriate package manager to install it. For example, if we are using Ubuntu or Debian, we can install it by running the following command:

   ```
   apt-get install sshpass
   ```

   If we are using a different Linux distribution, we can use the corresponding package manager to install **`'sshpass'`**.

3. **Specify the path to 'sshpass' in Ansible:** Once **`'sshpass'`** is installed, we need to specify the path to the **`'sshpass'`** executable in our Ansible inventory or configuration file. For example, in our inventory file, we can specify the **`'ansible_ssh_pass'`** variable to provide the password for the SSH connection. If we have installed **`'sshpass'`** in a non-standard location, we can specify the path to the executable using the **`'ansible_ssh_executable'`** variable.

   ```
   [servers]

   demo.example.com ansible_ssh_user=myuseransible_ssh_
   pass=mypasswordansible_ssh_executable=/usr/local/bin/sshpass
   ```

# Ansible for Windows

Setting up Ansible for Windows can be a little tricky, and users may encounter errors during the process. Let us now discuss some common issues users may face when troubleshooting Ansible for Windows and provide some tips on how to resolve them.

**Issue: Unable to install Ansible on Windows**

One of the most common issues users encounter when installing Ansible on Windows is an installation error. The error message may state that a package or module is missing.

**Solution: Install the required modules**

To resolve this issue, users should check the requirements for Ansible on Windows. Ansible requires Python, Git, and PowerShell to be installed on the Windows host. Users should ensure that these packages and modules are installed on their system before attempting to install Ansible.

**Issue: Unable to connect to Windows Host**

Another issue that users may encounter when using Ansible on Windows is the inability to connect to the Windows host. This error may be caused by several factors, including network connectivity, configuration issues, and authentication problems.

**Solution: Check configuration and authentication settings**

To resolve this issue, users should check their Ansible configuration settings and ensure that the Windows host is configured to accept incoming connections. Users should also check their authentication settings and ensure that the correct username and password are being used to authenticate with the Windows host.

**Issue: PowerShell execution policy blocks execution**

Another issue that users may encounter when running Ansible on Windows is the PowerShell execution policy blocking the execution of Ansible scripts.

**Solution: Change the execution policy**

To resolve this issue, users should change the PowerShell execution policy to allow the execution of Ansible scripts. Users can change the execution policy by running the following command in PowerShell:

```
Set-ExecutionPolicy Unrestricted
```

**Issue: SSH not enabled on Windows Host**

If users are trying to use the SSH connection type in Ansible, they may encounter an error indicating that SSH is not enabled on the Windows host.

**Solution: Enable SSH on Windows Host**

To resolve this issue, users should enable SSH on the Windows host. This can be done by installing the OpenSSH Server feature on the Windows host. Users can install the OpenSSH Server feature by running the following command in PowerShell:

```
Add-WindowsCapability -Online -Name OpenSSH.Server~~~~0.0.1.0
```

Setting up Ansible for Windows can be a little tricky, but with a little troubleshooting, users can resolve most issues. The key to resolving issues is to check configuration and authentication settings, ensure that required packages and modules are installed, and change PowerShell execution policies if necessary. With these tips, users should be able to use Ansible on Windows successfully.

# Ansible facts

When working with Ansible on Windows, we may encounter issues with gathering facts about Windows hosts. Here are some steps we can take to troubleshoot Ansible facts in Windows:

1. **Check the Ansible version:** Make sure we are using a version of Ansible that supports fact-gathering for Windows hosts. Fact gathering for Windows hosts is supported in Ansible 2.8 or later.
2. **Check the WinRM configuration:** Ensure that the **Windows Remote Management (WinRM)** service is running on the target Windows host and that it is configured to allow connections from the Ansible control node. We may need to add a firewall exception or configure WinRM to use HTTPS instead of HTTP.
3. **Check the Ansible configuration:** Verify that the `ansible_user` and `ansible_password` variables are correctly set in the Ansible configuration file for the target Windows host. These variables should specify the credentials that Ansible will use to authenticate with the Windows host.
4. **Check the Python version:** Verify that Python is installed on the target Windows host and that it is a supported version. Ansible requires Python 2.7 or later to be installed on the target Windows host for fact-gathering to work.
5. **Check the fact caching:** If we are using fact caching in Ansible, make sure that the cache is not stale or corrupt. Try disabling fact caching to see if that resolves the issue. More details are in *Chapter 8, Ansible Advanced*, section *Ansible configuration settings*.
6. **Check the fact-gathering modules:** Ansible uses modules to gather facts about Windows hosts. Verify that the `setup` module is installed on the target Windows host and that it is not disabled by any group or host variables.
7. **Verify the fact-gathering process:** Run the `ansible -m setup <hostname>` command to manually run the fact-gathering process for a specific Windows host. This command should output a JSON document containing all the facts that Ansible has gathered about the target Windows host.

By following these steps, we can troubleshoot and resolve issues by gathering facts about Windows hosts in Ansible. Sometimes we might still have problems retrieving

Ansible Facts when the execution on a Windows target host terminates on the "`gather_facts`" task. We might need to disable the facts gathering because they are not supported in the Windows target ("`gather_facts: false`").

# Module failure

When we encounter a Module Failure error in Ansible for Windows, it can be frustrating. Here are some steps to help us troubleshoot and resolve the issue:

1. **Verify the module:** Ensure that the module we are trying to use is supported on Windows. Some modules that work on Linux may not work on Windows or may require additional configuration.
2. **Check the module version:** Verify that we are using the correct version of the module. Ansible modules are updated frequently, and using an outdated module version can cause errors.
3. **Check the module path:** Ensure that the module path is set correctly. The module path can be set in the Ansible configuration file, and if it is not set correctly, Ansible may not be able to find the module.
4. **Check the remote machine configuration:** Verify that the remote machine is configured correctly. Windows requires additional configuration to enable remote management via Ansible, such as enabling PowerShell remoting and configuring WinRM.
5. **Check the module arguments:** Verify that the module arguments are set correctly. Incorrect or missing arguments can cause the module to fail.
6. **Check for dependencies:** Some modules require additional software or dependencies to be installed on the remote machine. Ensure that all required dependencies are installed.
7. **Check the error message:** The error message may provide useful information about the cause of the failure. Read the error message carefully and try to understand what caused the failure.
8. **Debug the module:** Use the Ansible debug module to troubleshoot the module failure. Add the debug module to the playbook and use it to print out variable values and debug information.

Overall, troubleshooting module failures in Ansible for Windows requires a careful review of the module, its dependencies, and the remote machine configuration. By following the preceding steps and debugging the module using the debug module, we should be able to identify and resolve the issue.

# Windows subsystem for Linux

When running Ansible on Windows with the **Windows Subsystem for Linux** (**WSL**), we may encounter the error **0x80370102**. This error occurs when the Windows Subsystem for Linux is not installed, is not enabled or the target machine does not support nested virtualization. Virtualization technologies enable to consistently speed up the virtualization of Linux operating systems, especially when version 2 of the Windows Subsystem for Linux is used.

To troubleshoot this error, follow these steps:

1. **Ensure WSL is installed:** Verify that WSL is installed on our Windows machine. If it is not installed, we can install it from the Windows Features control panel.

2. **Enable WSL:** Verify that WSL is enabled on our Windows machine. To enable WSL, open a PowerShell prompt as an administrator and run the following command:

   ```
   dism.exe /online /enable-feature /featurename:Microsoft-Windows-Subsystem-Linux /all /norestart
   ```

   By the end of the execution, the following features are installed in our Windows target machine: Windows Subsystem for Linux, Hyper-V Platform and Hyper-V Hypervisor. If the latest version of the Windows Subsystem for Linux is not working, we can always downgrade to version 1 using the following command:

   ```
   wsl --set-default-version 1
   ```

   Windows Subsystem for Linux is a bit slower because it does not use the nested virtualization feature. However, it is able to execute in most environments.

3. **Install a Linux distribution:** Once WSL is enabled, we need to install a Linux distribution. We can install a Linux distribution from the Microsoft Store or by downloading a distribution package and running it on our machine.

4. **Set the default WSL distribution:** If we have multiple Linux distributions installed, we need to set the default distribution. The default is the Ubuntu Linux distribution. To do this, open a PowerShell prompt and run the following command:

   ```
   wslconfig /setdefault<distribution name>
   ```

5. **Verify the Ansible configuration:** Ensure that our Ansible configuration is set up to use WSL. Check the `ansible.cfg` file and ensure that the `ansible_connection` variable is set to `wsl`. Learn more about the usage of the **ansible_connection** parameter in *Chapter 8, Ansible Advanced,* section *Ansible Configuration Settings.*

6. **Test the Ansible configuration:** Test our Ansible configuration by running a simple playbook against a target Windows host. If the playbook runs successfully, we have resolved the WSL error.

By following these steps, we can troubleshoot and resolve the WSL error when running Ansible on Windows.

# Ansible Windows command

It could happen that we are using the "**win_command**" Ansible module instead of the "**win_shell**" Ansible module. The two modules enable us to execute commands on the Ansible target but they are not as similar as learnt in Chapter 5, *Ansible For Windows,* section *Executing commands*.

The "**win_command**" Ansible module does not execute multiple PowerShell lines. The following example uses the "hostname" and "**Get-Date**" PowerShell commands to print on the screen the hostname and the current date. Here is the "**win_date_command.yml**" playbook:

```
---
- name: Execute command
  hosts: all
  tasks:
    - name: Check getdate
      ansible.windows.win_command: |
        hostname
        Get-Date
      register: command_output
    - name: Command output
      ansible.builtin.debug:
        var: command_output.stdout_lines
```

We can execute the "**win_date_command.yml**" using the following **ansible-playbook** command:

```
ansible-playbookwin_date_command.yml
```

The execution does not return an error but only a part of the command is actually executed:

```
PLAY [win_command module demo] ******************************************
***************************

TASK [Gathering Facts] **************************************************
```

```
**********************ok: [WindowsServer]

TASK [check getdate] ***************************************************
********************

changed: [WindowsServer]

TASK [command output] **************************************************
*********************ok: [WindowsServer] => {

    "command_output.stdout_lines": [

        "demo"

    ]

}

PLAY RECAP *************************************************************
***********

WindowsServer   : ok=3    changed=1    unreachable=0    failed=0
skipped=0    rescued=0    ignored=0
```

To execute all the commands on a multiline, we need to switch from the "`win_command`" to the "`win_shell`" Ansible module instead.

# Conclusion

As we learned in this chapter, we could avoid most of the errors by being more careful while writing code and using some programs to simplify the syntax check and testing. Using an accurate testing strategy, we can avoid problems in production and implement our **Infrastructure as a Service** (**IaaS**).

In the next chapter, we are going to learn about the Ansible Automation Platform, Morpheus, usage of Configuration Management, Graphical User Interface and **Role-Based Access Control** (**RBAC**).

# Points to remember

- We can execute syntax check, yamlint and ansible-lint to statically verify the code correctness in our project.
- We can use the check and verbosity options of the "`ansible-playbook`" command to execute a dry run or increase the amount of information on the screen during the execution.
- We can use the molecule tool to test the execution of our Ansible role before sharing the code inside and outside the organization.
- Having a robust test environment and strategy, saves time troubleshooting corner cases and unexpected scenarios in a production environment.

# Key terms

- **"syntax-check":** "`ansible-playbook --syntax-check`" is a command used to check the syntax of Ansible playbooks without running them.
- **Yamlint:** "`Yamlint`" is a command-line tool that analyzes YAML files and checks for syntax errors, style consistency, and other issues.
- **ansible-lint:** Ansible linter is a tool that analyzes Ansible code to detect and report potential issues and errors.
- **molecule:** Molecule is a tool that helps with the development and testing of Ansible roles and collections in multiple environments.
- **Visual Studio Code** (**VSCode**) is a free source-code editor made by Microsoft that is highly customizable and supports various programming languages and frameworks.

# Multiple choice questions

1. **What is the maximum for the Verbose mode?**
    a. "`-v`"
    b. "`-vv`"
    c. "`-vvv`"
    d. "`-vvvv`"
2. **How can we execute a dry run execution?**
    a. Using the "`-v`" parameter
    b. Using the "`--dry-run`" parameter
    c. Using the "`--check`" parameter
    d. It is not possible
3. **What tools can we use to verify our Ansible playbooks?**
    a. `ansible playbook --syntax-check`, `yamlint` and `ansible-lint`
    b. `molecule`
    c. `yamlint` and `ansible-lint`
    d. CI/CD pipeline

4. **What are the key components of the molecule test?**
    a. The "create" stage creates the virtual machines, installs the necessary software, and configures them according to the role being tested.
    b. The "converge" playbook applies to the role, while the "verify" playbook checks for correct behavior.
    c. The "destroy" stage destroys the virtual machines being used during the tests.
    d. None of the previous answers.

## Answers

1. **d**
2. **c**
3. **a**
4. **b**

# Questions

1. What is the best strategy to test our Ansible Playbook?
2. How can we test the idempotency property of our Ansible Playbook?
3. How can we properly test and troubleshoot an Ansible Role?
4. What software can assist us in our Ansible code creation?

## Join our book's Discord space

Join the book's Discord Workspace for Latest updates, Offers, Tech happenings around the world, New Release and Sessions with the Authors:

**https://discord.bpbonline.com**

# CHAPTER 7
# Scaling Up with Ansible Enterprise

## Introduction

In this chapter, we will learn more about enterprise-grade and graphical user interfaces for Ansible. This includes learning how to use Ansible within our organization, integrating it with other tools, using authentication services **Lightweight Directory Access Protocol** (**LDAP**) and Active Directory, and implementing security best practices. Ansible for Enterprise is designed to work with more complex architectures and environments, such as distributed systems and microservices.

## Structure

In this chapter, we shall cover the following topics:

- Ansible use cases
- GitOps
- Ansible Automation Platform
- Morpheus
- Configuration management (CM)
- Graphical user interface

# Objectives

By the end of this chapter, the reader will be able to understand the Ansible enterprise users' use cases and how to interact with Ansible using graphical user interfaces and the Ansible Automation Platform.

# Ansible use cases

Advanced and enterprise users need to take care of maintaining mission-critical systems for the organization. In IT, the terms Day 0, Day 1, and Day 2 refer to different phases of the software life cycle that apply to the phases of the software lifecycle, as shown in the following *Figure 7.1*. We use this model for the lifecycle of any software application. Ansible is beneficial for Day 1 and Day 2 operations. Please refer to the following figure:

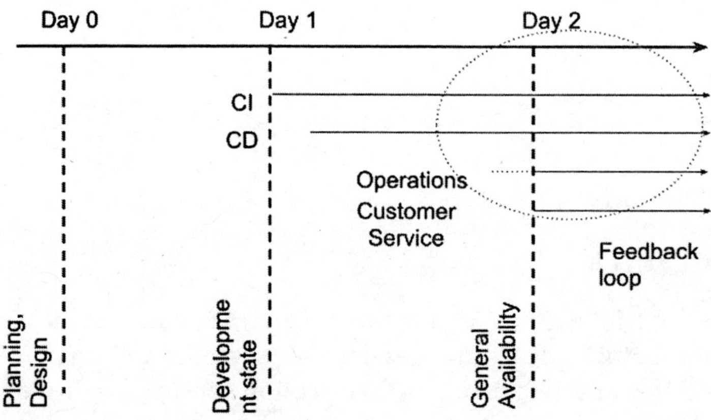


*Figure 7.1: The Day 0, Day 1, Day 2 model*

In today's rapidly evolving software landscape, the terms Day 0, Day 1, and Day 2 have gained prominence as stages of the software development lifecycle. These phases hold immense significance in the context of effective software development and maintenance. Let us deep dive into the following phases to understand each day and explore how cloud computing has transformed traditional software development and maintenance processes.

# Day 0 - Design phase

Day 0 represents the design phase of the software development lifecycle. It is akin to the initial day of training, where recruits enter their formative stage in the military. In software development, Day 0 encompasses the planning and design process, where project requirements are specified, and the architecture of the solution is determined. This phase involves careful planning of the system's infrastructure, resource allocation, and milestone setting. Testing and quality assurance are also integral components of Day 0, ensuring a solid foundation for the subsequent stages.

## Day 1 - Development and deployment

Day 1 signifies the development and deployment phase of the software lifecycle. It brings the initial design to life and involves creating the application itself, along with the necessary infrastructure, networks, and external services. In the cloud era, Day 1 is characterized by an agile approach to software development, where design and development stages seamlessly integrate. **Continuous Integration/Continuous Delivery** (**CI/CD**) practices play a vital role in ensuring a smooth and efficient Day 1. The focus is on adopting best practices, such as the Twelve-Factor Apps methodology, and utilizing cloud-native tools and container orchestration systems like Kubernetes. Ansible can simplify the deployment process and be integrated with the deployment pipelines.

## Day 2 - Maintenance and optimization

Day 2 marks the maintenance and optimization phase, which begins once the software is live and customers start using it. This stage involves monitoring the system, gathering feedback, and implementing necessary improvements based on customer requirements. The goal is to establish a feedback loop that continually analyzes the system's behavior, identifies areas of improvement, and implements changes to enhance performance and user experience. Automation and monitoring tools are essential during Day 2 to ensure efficient maintenance and timely issue resolution. **Application Performance Monitoring** (**APM**) solutions, ticketing systems for customer support, and automation tools like Ansible or Kubernetes aid in managing and optimizing the software throughout its lifecycle. Ansible can even process real-time events using Event-Driven Architecture (see *Event-driven Ansible* section).

# The cloud computing influence on the software lifecycle

The advent of cloud computing has revolutionized the software development lifecycle. The traditional separation between the phases of Day 0, Day 1, and Day 2 has given way to a more integrated and agile approach. Cloud-based development and deployment have become a top priority for organizations, enabling them to leverage the benefits of scalability, flexibility, and cost-effectiveness. Cloud computing allows for dynamic response to changing requirements, continuous improvement through CI/CD practices, and the elimination of handovers between development and operations teams. The shift-left approach in DevOps, where tasks traditionally left until the end are performed earlier, has reshaped the boundaries of Day 1 and Day 2, leading to overlapping phases and continuous optimization.

The concepts of Day 0, Day 1, and Day 2 provide a framework for understanding the various stages of the software development lifecycle. These phases, when effectively managed, contribute to the success of software projects. Cloud computing has played a pivotal role in transforming traditional software development and maintenance processes, enabling seamless integration, continuous improvement, and efficient automation. Embracing the principles of Day 0, Day 1, and Day 2, along with cloud-native practices, empowers organizations to deliver high-quality software products and services, while remaining responsive to customer needs in an ever-evolving digital landscape. Ansible is even more important in each of these phases because it simplifies and creates a standard in the automation journey.

# GitOps

It is very convenient to organize our source code in a repository, usually based on the Git popular version control system. The repository becomes the only source of truth for all the team operations. GitOps descends from **Site Reliability Engineering** (**SRE**), DevOps culture, **Infrastructure as Code** (**IaC**), and **Configuration as Code** (**CaC**) patterns that enable us to store the configuration of our infrastructure under a repository, usually managed by the Git technology. The following *Table 7.1* illustrates the recommended directory layout based on Ansible's best practices:

| File | Description |
|---|---|
| **`site.yml`** | master playbook |
| **`webservers.yml`** | playbook for the **`webservers`** inventory group |
| **`production`** | inventory file for the production environment |
| **`staging`** | inventory file for the staging environment |
| **`group_vars/`** | group variables (see *Chapter 2, Ansible Language Core,* section *Ansible Inventory*) |
| **`host_vars/`** | host variables (see *Chapter 2, Ansible Language Core,* section *Ansible Inventory*) |
| **`library/`** | (optional) custom libraries and modules |
| **`module_utils/`** | (optional) custom **`module_utils`** to support modules |
| **`filter_plugins/`** | (optional) custom filters |
| **`roles/`** | (optional) custom roles |

***Table 7.1:*** *The GitOps directory layout*

When organizing our source code and infrastructure configurations in a Git repository, following best practices is crucial. Ansible provides guidelines for structuring our directory layout. While the specific layout may vary depending on our project's requirements, the following directory structure is commonly recommended by Ansible best practices:

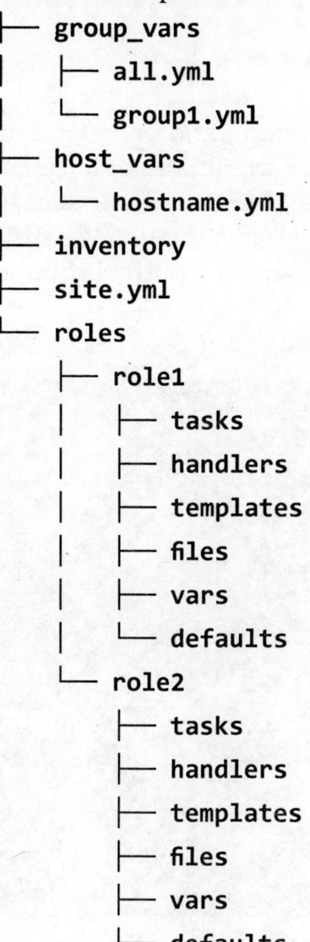

```
├── group_vars
│   ├── all.yml
│   └── group1.yml
├── host_vars
│   └── hostname.yml
├── inventory
├── site.yml
└── roles
    ├── role1
    │   ├── tasks
    │   ├── handlers
    │   ├── templates
    │   ├── files
    │   ├── vars
    │   └── defaults
    └── role2
        ├── tasks
        ├── handlers
        ├── templates
        ├── files
        ├── vars
        └── defaults
```

In this directory layout, the "**group_vars**" directory contains variables specific to different groups, while the "**host_vars**" directory stores variables specific to individual hosts. The "**inventory**" file represents the inventory of hosts or groups. The "**site.yml**" file serves as the entry point for executing Ansible tasks. It is the first Ansible playbook to be executed.

The roles directory contains reusable Ansible roles with encapsulated tasks, handlers, templates, files, variables, and defaults. Each role is organized into subdirectories corresponding to these different components. Following this directory structure helps maintain a clean and organized codebase, making it easier to understand and manage our Ansible playbooks and roles. Leveraging Git for managing source code and infrastructure configurations is highly beneficial. GitOps extends this practice further by treating the Git repository as the single source of truth for infrastructure configurations. When using Ansible, adhering to best practices for directory layout ensures consistency and maintainability in our automation workflows.

# Ansible Automation Platform

Enterprises need more than automation; they need coordination and orchestration at scale. If we are working in an enterprise, we need those different lines of business to work together with different skill sets and to have a straightforward interface in order to coordinate the available resources. Red Hat created the collaborative **Ansible Automation Platform** (**AAP**) as a solution with a focus on security, portability, and reliability. Refer to the following *Figure 7.2:*

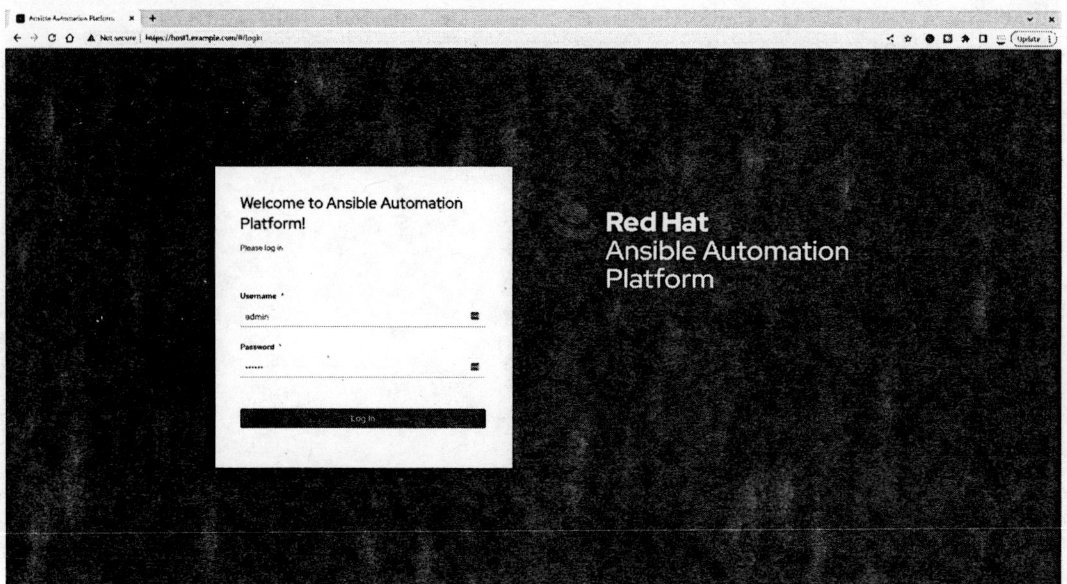


***Figure 7.2:*** *The login screen of the Ansible Automation Controller*

It combines the best value of the Ansible open source: simplicity, powerful, and agentless, unique certified technology with a nice web user interface and a powerful RESTful API interface. It also reduces time to deliver solutions based on automation. Ansible is the leader in infrastructure automation, according to international IT analysts. It is able to solve problems of day 1 (provision and deploying software) and day 2 automation (configuration, rolling updates, maintaining, monitoring, and optimizing the system).

The Ansible Automation Platform is the premium product of Red Hat (part of IBM) targeted at Enterprise users of Ansible.

The following are the significant benefits of adopting the Ansible Automation Platform in our organization:

- **Simplify complex tasks:** One of the main benefits of using the Ansible Automation Platform is the ability to simplify complex tasks. With this platform, we can automate tasks across multiple systems with a single interface. This means that we can automate complex tasks, such as configuring network devices or deploying applications, with ease. This reduces the time and effort required to perform these tasks manually, freeing up our team's time to focus on more strategic initiatives.
- **Scalability:** Another significant benefit of using the Ansible Automation Platform is its scalability. The platform can manage and automate tasks across thousands of machines, making it ideal for large-scale IT infrastructures. As our infrastructure grows, the Ansible Automation Platform can grow with us, ensuring that our automation workflows remain efficient and effective.
- **Efficiency:** Automation is all about improving efficiency, and Ansible Automation Platform is designed to do just that. By streamlining workflows and reducing manual effort, the platform can help us achieve greater efficiency in our IT operations. We can automate routine tasks, such as software updates or system configurations, freeing up our team's time to work on more valuable tasks.
- **Security:** Ansible Automation Platform is built with security in mind. It provides a secure way to automate tasks across different systems and environments, ensuring compliance with security policies and best practices. With the Ansible Automation Platform, we can automate tasks while maintaining the integrity and confidentiality of our IT systems.
- **Integration:** The platform integrates with a wide range of tools and technologies, making it easy to automate tasks across our entire infrastructure. This means that we can use the Ansible Automation Platform to manage and automate tasks across our entire IT ecosystem, including cloud platforms, virtualization platforms, and container platforms.
- **Customization:** One of the great things about the Ansible Automation Platform is its flexibility. The platform is highly customizable, allowing us to create customized workflows, modules, and playbooks to suit our specific needs. We can tailor the platform to meet the unique requirements of our IT infrastructure, ensuring that we get the most out of our automation workflows.
- **Collaboration:** Ansible Automation Platform supports collaboration among teams, enabling multiple users to work on the same tasks and workflows simultaneously. This means that we can share knowledge and expertise

across our team, improving the quality and efficiency of our automation workflows.

- **Visibility:** Ansible Automation Platform provides visibility into automation tasks, enabling us to track progress, monitor performance, and troubleshoot issues in real-time. This visibility gives us a complete picture of our automation workflows, allowing us to make informed decisions about how to improve our IT operations.

Refer to *Figure 7.3:*

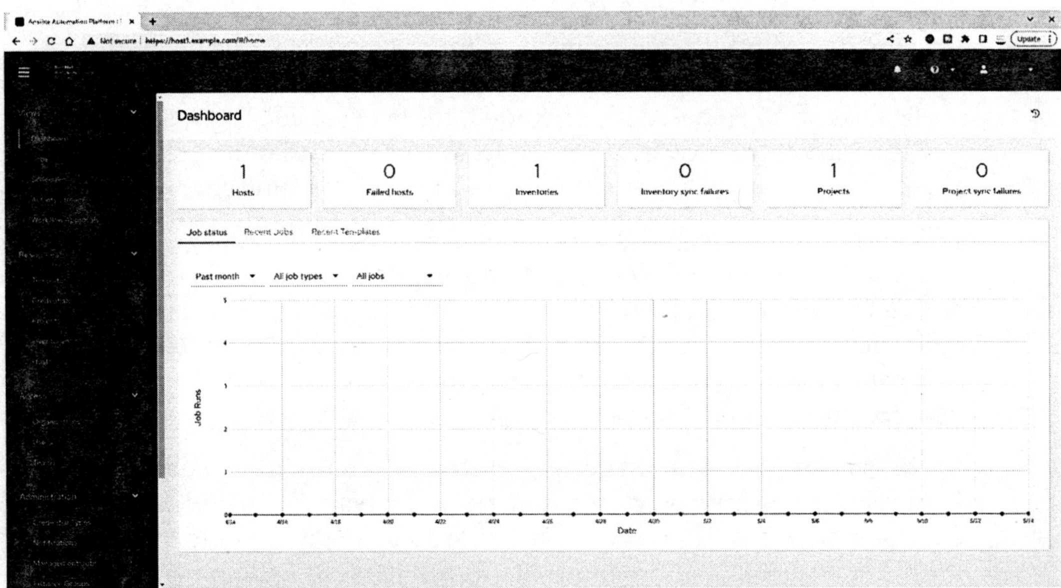


***Figure 7.3:*** *The dashboard of the Ansible Automation Controller*

Ansible Automation Platform is a powerful tool that can transform our IT infrastructure. The platform can help us achieve greater agility and responsiveness in our IT operations by simplifying complex tasks, improving scalability, and increasing efficiency. With its security features, integration capabilities, customization options, collaboration support, and visibility, the Ansible Automation Platform is the perfect tool for any organization looking to streamline and automate its IT workflows. The Ansible Automation Platform requires a subscription from Red Hat. The Ansible Automation Platform takes advantage of the GitOps project organization to fulfill the automation need of our team.

The typical use cases of the Ansible Automation Platform are hybrid cloud automation, edge automation, network automation, security automation, infrastructure automation, provisioning, configuration management, application deployment, continuous delivery, and orchestration.

The latest release of the Red Hat Ansible Automation Platform includes the project signing feature that allows users to sign and verify the security of project-based content, ensuring the integrity and authenticity of automation workflows, playbooks, and inventories relying on the "`ansible-sign`" command line tool and GnuPG asymmetric keys (private and public keys).

The Ansible Automation Platform is composed of multiple software. The latest release of the Ansible Automation Platform includes the following products:

- Automation controller (formerly Ansible Tower)
- Automation hub private and hosted service
- Automation services catalog
- Insights for Ansible Automation Platform as a hosted service

# Node requirements

The system requirements for any Ansible Automation Platform nodes (controller, database, execution, and hop nodes) are as follows:

- 16 GB+ of RAM
- 4+ CPUs
- 150 GB+ disk space for database nodes or 40 GB+ disk space for non-database nodes
- DHCP reservations use infinite leases to deploy the cluster with static IP addresses
- DNS records for all nodes
- Operating system Red Hat Enterprise Linux 8 or later 64-bit (x86) with Python 3.8+
- NTP service Chrony configured for all nodes

# Ansible automation hub

Ansible automation hub is a platform provided by Red Hat that offers a curated and trusted repository for Ansible Content Collections. It simplifies the process of discovering and downloading Ansible content by providing pre-built and certified collections of modules, plug-ins, roles, and documentation from Red Hat and certified Red Hat partners. It is the most powerful version of the Ansible Galaxy. We can choose to acquire content from the Automation Hub or mix it with Ansible Galaxy. The following are the benefits of using Ansible Automation Hub:

- **Red Hat-certified content:** Ansible automation huboffers direct access to trusted Content collections from Red Hat and certified Red Hat partners. These collections cover a wide range of topics and partners, ensuring that the content has been vetted and certified by Red Hat.
- **Reuse code and get started faster:** Ansible collections in the automation hub provide bundled modules and roles for specific domains and IT platforms. This allows us to get up and run with pre-built content quickly.
- **Ansible private automation hub:** If we create our own Ansible content, it enables us to publish and collaborate on it within our organization, either behind our firewall or on disconnected systems. This provides a centralized source of truth and allows for easy management and control of the lifecycle of our Ansible content.
- **Premium support:** Ansible automation hub is created and managed by Red Hat, and it offers standard and premium support options. If we encounter any issues with official Red Hat Ansible collections or certified partner collections, Red Hat's support team will assist us directly. For other items in Ansible Automation Hub, Red Hat will guide us to get the support we need.
- **Included with a Red Hat subscription:** Ansible automation hub is included as part of our Red Hat subscription. If we are Red Hat subscribers, we have free and unlimited access to any content available in the Automation Hub.

By leveraging Ansible Automation Hub, users can benefit from certified content, faster development through code reuse, private hub capabilities, premium support options, and the inclusion of Automation Hub with their Red Hat subscription. Since 2022, Ansible automation hub has supported digitally signed collections for an entire chain of trust from the creator to the execution node from Red Hat Ansible and Certified Partners.

# Ansible execution environment

Ansible **Execution Environments** (EE) are containerized environments designed to provide a consistent and portable runtime for executing Ansible automation jobs. They encapsulate all the necessary components, dependencies, and configurations required to run Ansible playbooks.

An execution environment typically consists of the following components:

- **Base container image:** The base container image forms the foundation of the execution environment. It includes the operating system and other essential components required for running Ansible.

- **Ansible Core:** Ansible Core is the central component of the execution environment. It provides the Ansible engine, which interprets and executes Ansible playbooks.
- **Ansible Runner:** Ansible Runner is a tool used by Ansible to execute playbooks in a more controlled and structured manner. It helps with features like job control, parallel execution, and result tracking.
- **Python:** Ansible is written in Python, so the execution environment includes the necessary Python runtime environment. It ensures that Ansible can leverage Python modules and libraries.
- **Ansible Collections:** Ansible Collections are pre-packaged units of Ansible content that provide additional modules, plugins, and roles. The execution environment may include specific collections required for the automation tasks.
- **Required Python libraries:** The execution environment may include specific Python libraries that are needed by the Ansible playbooks or modules being executed. These libraries can be installed as part of the execution environment to ensure their availability during playbook execution.

The purpose of Ansible execution environments is to provide a consistent and isolated runtime environment for Ansible automation. By packaging all the necessary components into a container image, execution environments ensure that automation jobs can be executed reliably across different systems and environments. They help in maintaining consistent behavior and eliminating potential compatibility issues.

Execution environments also enable portability, as the containerized format allows the execution environment to be easily shared, replicated, and deployed across different systems and infrastructures. This is particularly useful in scenarios where automation needs to be executed in disconnected or air-gapped environments, where internet access or external dependencies may be limited. Overall, Ansible execution environments simplify the deployment and execution of Ansible automation by providing a defined and consistent runtime environment, ensuring that automation jobs can be executed reliably and consistently across different systems and environments.

Using the "**`ansible-builder`**" command line utility creates a customized execution environment in our system. We can also create execution environment images for unconnected or air-gapped environments using the optional step 5. We can create a customized Ansible execution environment with these steps:

1. **Install ansible-builder utility:** First, we can install the **`ansible-builder`** tool from the Red Hat RPM repository:

```
dnf install ansible-builder
```

As an alternative, install the **ansible-builder** tool from the upstream Python repository:

```
pip install ansible-builder
```

2. **Create an execution-environment.yml file:** Create a YAML definition file called **execution-environment.yml** that specifies the base container image, the Ansible configuration, dependencies, and additional build steps. Here is an example:

```
---
version: 1
build_arg_defaults:
        EE_BASE_IMAGE:     'automationhub.example.com/ee-minimal-
rhel8:latest'
ansible_config: 'ansible.cfg'
dependencies:
  galaxy: requirements.yml
  python: requirements.txt
  system: bindep.txt
additional_build_steps:
  prepend: |
    RUN pip3 install --upgrade pip setuptools
  append:
    - RUN ls -al /
```

Make sure to customize the **EE_BASE_IMAGE** with the appropriate container registry source. The "**requirements.yml**" file specifies the Ansible collection dependencies in the format learned in *Chapter 3, Ansible Language Extended,* section *Ansible collection.* The "**requirements.txt**" file specifies the Python dependencies as learned in *Chapter 6, Ansible Troubleshooting,* section *Ansible Collection.* The "**bindep.txt**" file specifies the operating system packages to install for the RPM and DEB format using the RPM and DPKG command line tool. For the installation of the "**git**" tool, we are going to use the following " **bindep.txt**" file:

```
git [platform:rpm]
git [platform:dpkg]
```

3. **Build the container image:** Use the **`ansible-builder build`** command to build the container image based on the **`execution-environment.yml`** file. Specify a tag for the image. For example:

   ```
   ansible-builder build --tag my_custom_ee
   ```

   This will create a build context and generate a **`Containerfile`**.

4. **Create the container image:** Use the container engine (for example, Podman or Docker) to create the container image from the build context. For example:

   ```
   podman build -f context/Containerfile -t my_custom_ee context
   ```

5. **Transfer the container image (optional):** If we are in an unconnected environment, we need to transfer the container image to the target system. We can either create an archive of the container image and transfer it using a secure method or build the image directly on the target system using the transferred dependencies.

6. **Load and use the container image:** Once the container image is available on the unconnected system, load it using the container engine. For example:

   ```
   podman load -i my_custom_ee-1.0.tar
   ```

   We can then use the custom execution environment image for executing Ansible playbooks and automation jobs in the unconnected environment.

Remember to follow the appropriate tagging and pushing process if we want to store the container image in a private automation hub or another supported container registry.

Please note that the example commands provided here may vary based on our specific environment and configuration. Refer to the official documentation for the Ansible Automation Platform and **`ansible-builder`** for more detailed instructions and options.

## Ansible automation mesh

Automation mesh is a new feature introduced in the Ansible Automation Platform 2.1 release. It aims to simplify and improve the scalability of automation across different platforms and locations, including on-premises environments, hybrid clouds, and edge devices. Automation mesh provides a flexible design that can be deployed in single-site installations or across multiple global locations, catering to various automation requirements. The challenges of scaling automation across different environments, managing platforms centrally, and automating remote areas with limited connectivity are addressed by automation mesh. By delivering and running automation closer to the devices that require it, interruptions and inconsistencies in execution can be minimized, leading to improved reliability and reduced downtime for IT services.

In the past, scaling automation across multiple regions and complex networks was challenging with Ansible Tower and isolated node architectures. Ansible Tower's tightly coupled execution and control capacity made scalability difficult, and the monolithic design limited execution capacity to a single cluster, sensitive to network latency and disruptions. Isolated nodes provided localized execution but had limitations in communication and required additional tools like SSH proxies and jump hosts.

Automation mesh, in conjunction with the automation controller, overcomes these limitations. It simplifies the distribution of automation across multiple sites and reduces operational overhead. Automation mesh removes the dependency on ancillary tools like jump hosts and SSH proxies by localizing automation. It offers design flexibility, allowing deployments from a single site to global installations. Automation mesh utilizes a multi-directional, multi-hopped overlay network to deliver automation across constrained networks and remote endpoints. It enables scaling control and execution capacity independently, providing fault tolerance, redundancy, and improved resilience to network disruptions and latency.

Security is a crucial aspect of automation mesh, and it incorporates features like **Access Control Lists** (**ACL**), **Transport Layer Security** (**TLS**) authentication, and encryption. The centralized management via automation controller allows leveraging features such as **Role-Based Access Control** (**RBAC**) and authentication to secure the automation mesh.

The key benefits of automation mesh include simplifying operations, design flexibility, scalability, reliability, and enhanced security. By leveraging automation mesh, organizations can scale automation globally, improve reliability, and securely manage their entire enterprise IT estate. The default firewall port used for the Ansible mesh networks on all nodes is TCP 27199.

# Role-based access control

**Role-based access control** (**RBAC**) is a security model that provides access control based on the roles assigned to users or groups. The Ansible Automation Platform supports RBAC to provide a secure and granular access control mechanism to manage automation workflows and resources.

Refer to *Figure 7.4:*

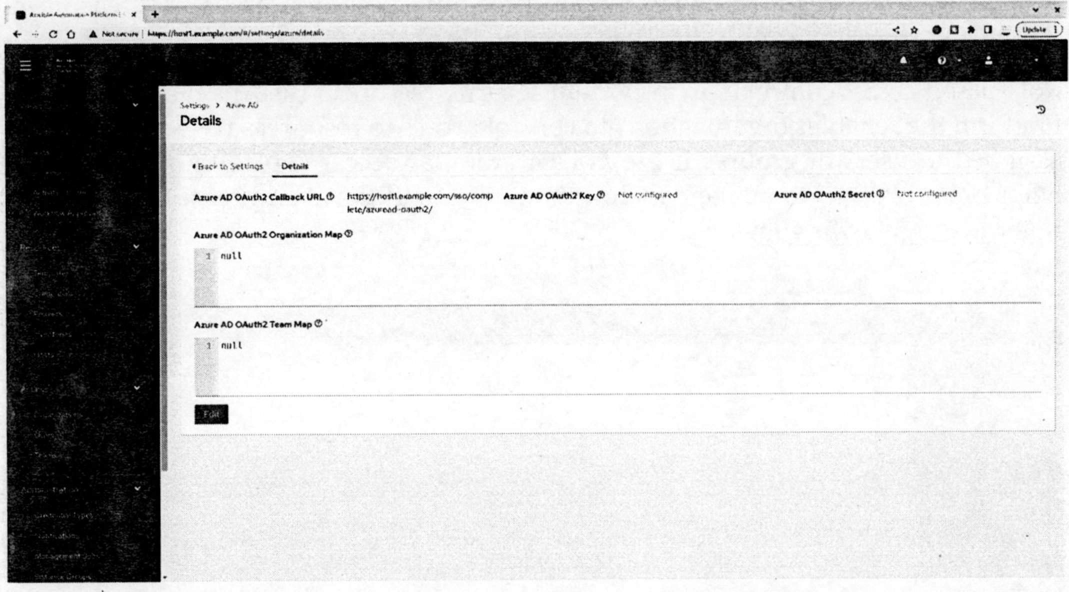


***Figure 7.4:*** *The Azure AD integration of the Ansible Automation Controller*

RBAC is an essential component of the Ansible Automation Platform that enables organizations to restrict users' access to specific features, resources, or actions based on their roles. The platform provides predefined roles, such as Administrator, Operator, and Viewer, which can be assigned to users or groups:

- The Administrator role has full access to all the features and resources of the Ansible Automation Platform, including the ability to create, modify, and delete users, groups, and roles.
- The Operator role has limited access and can only perform specific actions, such as running jobs or managing inventories.
- The Viewer role has read-only access to the Ansible Automation Platform, which allows users to view the status of resources, but they cannot modify them.

RBAC also allows organizations to create custom roles and assign them to users or groups.

Custom roles can be defined based on the specific requirements of the organization. For example, an organization may create a custom role for developers that allows them to run playbooks but restricts them from managing inventories or creating new users. Ansible Automation Platform RBAC also provides permission levels that control the level of access for specific resources. For example, users with the permission level "**read**" can view the resource but cannot modify it, whereas users with the permission level "**write**" can modify the resource.

Role-based access control is an important security feature of the Ansible Automation Platform that enables organizations to control access to resources based on the roles assigned to users or groups. It provides a granular access control mechanism that helps organizations to manage their automation workflows and resources securely. Refer to the following *Figure 7.5:*

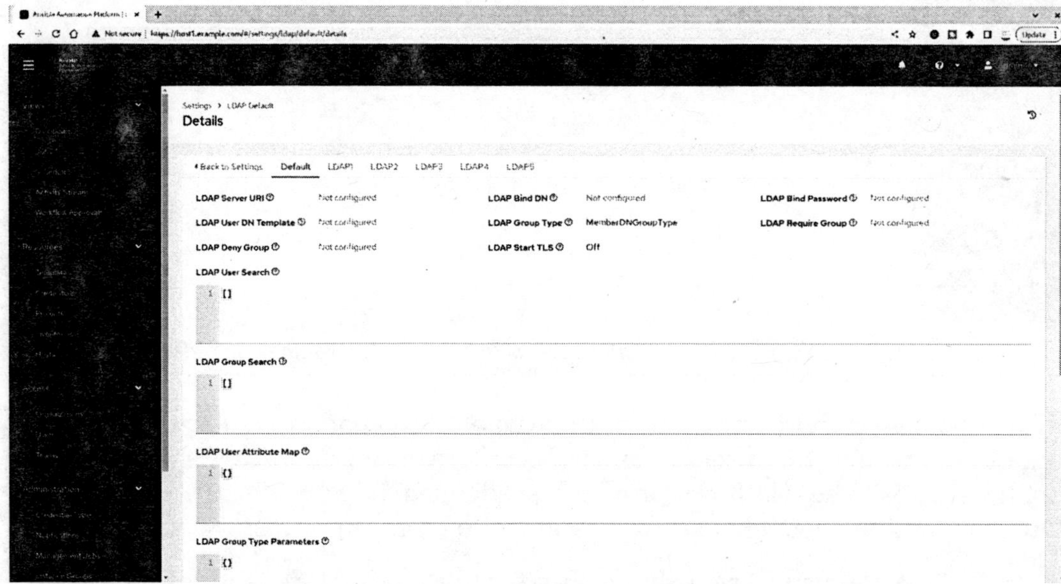


***Figure 7.5:*** *The LDAP integration of the Ansible Automation Controller*

In the context of the Ansible Automation Platform, RBAC allows us to control access to Ansible resources such as inventories, playbooks, and jobs based on the roles assigned to users or groups. To implement RBAC in the Ansible Automation Platform, we can integrate it with our enterprise directory systems, such as Microsoft Active Directory (as shown in *Figure 7.4*) or LDAP (refer to *Figure 7.5*). This integration enables us to manage access to Ansible resources based on the roles assigned to users or groups in our enterprise directory system.

The integration process involves the following steps:

1. **Set up our enterprise directory system:** To integrate the Ansible Automation Platform with our enterprise directory system, we first need to set up our directory system and ensure that it is configured correctly.

2. **Configure Ansible Automation Platform:** We then need to configure Ansible Automation Platform to use our enterprise directory system for

authentication and authorization. This involves configuring the platform to communicate with our directory system using LDAP or Active Directory protocols. See the Azure AD integration in *Figure 7.4* and LDAP in *Figure 7.5*.

3. **Define roles and permissions:** Once the integration is set up, we can define roles and permissions in the Ansible Automation Platform based on the roles assigned to users or groups in our enterprise directory system. We can create roles such as "**Admin**", "**Developer**", or "**Operator**" and assign permissions to each role based on the tasks and workflows they are responsible for.

4. **Assign roles to users or groups:** Finally, we can assign roles to users or groups in our enterprise directory system, which will automatically grant them the appropriate permissions in the Ansible Automation Platform. With RBAC integration, we can ensure that only authorized users have access to Ansible resources and that they can only perform tasks that are within their scope of responsibility. RBAC also helps us to manage and maintain a clear audit trail of who has accessed which resources and when, improving security and compliance. Integrating the Ansible Automation Platform with our enterprise directory system for RBAC allows us to manage access to resources based on roles and permissions, ensuring that only authorized users have access to the resources they need to perform their tasks.

# Morpheus

Ansible Morpheus is an integration between Ansible and the Morpheus cloud management platform. Morpheus is a cloud application management platform that helps IT teams to manage and automate infrastructure across multiple clouds, data centers, and DevOps tools.

With the Ansible integration, Morpheus allows users to leverage Ansible's powerful automation capabilities to manage and provision infrastructure resources across a wide range of platforms. The integration allows for the creation of dynamic infrastructure, with automated provisioning, scaling, and management, through the use of Ansible playbooks.

Morpheus provides a unified platform to manage IT resources, with support for cloud-native and traditional workloads, and the integration with Ansible adds even more flexibility and power to the platform. The integration allows IT teams to automate their infrastructure and cloud management tasks, enabling faster and more reliable deployment of applications and services.

The integration between Morpheus and Ansible offers a number of benefits for IT teams, including:

- **Increased efficiency:** The integration enables IT teams to automate infrastructure management tasks, reducing the amount of manual work required and increasing efficiency.
- **Simplified management:** The integration provides a unified platform for managing IT resources, with support for cloud-native and traditional workloads.
- **Enhanced flexibility:** The integration with Ansible adds even more flexibility and power to the Morpheus platform, enabling IT teams to automate their infrastructure and cloud management tasks more efficiently.
- **Improved scalability:** Ansible is known for its scalability, and the integration enables IT teams to scale their infrastructure management tasks as needed quickly.
- **Better reliability:** The automation capabilities provided by Ansible help to ensure that infrastructure management tasks are performed consistently and reliably, reducing the risk of errors and downtime.

# Using the Morpheus and Ansible Integration

To use the latest Morpheus and Ansible integration, users must first configure the Ansible endpoint in Morpheus. This involves providing the necessary credentials and configuring the endpoint settings.

Once the endpoint is configured, users can create Ansible playbooks and use them to automate infrastructure management tasks within Morpheus. For example, users can create a playbook to provision and configure virtual machines or to deploy and manage applications on cloud platforms.

Users can also leverage the Morpheus automation features, such as workflows and integrations with other DevOps tools, to further enhance the capabilities of the platform.

# Configuration management

Ansible is a powerful **Configuration Management** (**CM**) tool that allows us to automate the management of our IT infrastructure. It allows us to define and enforce the desired state of our systems and applications by writing Ansible playbooks, which are essentially scripts that automate the configuration of our systems.

Configuration management with Ansible involves the following steps:

1. **Define the desired state:** The first step in using Ansible for configuration management is to define the desired state of our IT infrastructure. This

involves defining the configuration settings that we want our systems and applications to adhere to. This could include things like package versions, network configurations, user accounts, and firewall rules.

2. **Write Ansible playbooks:** Once we have defined the desired state, we can write Ansible playbooks to automate the configuration of our systems and applications. Playbooks are written in YAML format and contain a set of tasks that describe how to configure our systems. Playbooks can be run against individual systems or groups of systems, making it easy to manage large-scale IT infrastructures.

3. **Run Ansible playbooks:** After writing the playbooks, we can run them using the Ansible command-line tool. Ansible will connect to our systems and execute the tasks defined in the playbook, ensuring that our systems are configured to adhere to the desired state.

4. **Verify and monitor configuration:** Once the playbooks have been executed, we can verify that our systems are configured correctly. Ansible provides tools for verifying the configuration of our systems and monitoring their state to ensure that they remain in compliance with the desired state.

Ansible also provides features that make configuration management more accessible and more efficient. For example, Ansible allows us to create reusable roles and templates, which can be used across multiple playbooks and systems. This makes it easy to maintain consistency and avoid duplication of effort.

Ansible configuration management allows us to automate the management of our IT infrastructure, ensuring that our systems are configured to adhere to the desired state. By defining the desired state, writing Ansible playbooks, and running them against our systems, we can streamline our IT operations and improve efficiency.

# Graphical user interface

When the amount of servers grows up, it is beneficial having a visual breakdown of each step of the execution process and a complete analysis of the workflow process. Ansible does not have a built-in **Graphical User Interface** (**GUI**), as its primary interface is command-line-based. However, there are some third-party tools and platforms that provide a GUI on top of Ansible to enhance the user experience and simplify the management of Ansible automation. These GUI tools typically offer visual representations of Ansible playbooks, inventories, and job execution, making it easier to interact with Ansible for users who prefer a graphical interface. Here are a few examples of Ansible GUI tools:

- **Ansible automation controller:** is part of the Ansible Automation Platform subscription, a comprehensive solution for IT automation that includes a web-based GUI. It provides a centralized interface for managing Ansible playbooks, inventories, credentials, and job scheduling. The GUI allows users to create and manage automation workflows, monitor job status, and view detailed logs and reports.

- **AWX:** AWX is the open-source version of Ansible Tower, which offers a similar GUI experience. It provides a web-based interface for managing Ansible automation, including the ability to define inventories, create job templates, and schedule jobs. AWX is a community-driven project and can be deployed on-premises or in the cloud.
- **Semaphore** is an open-source project that provides a web-based GUI for managing Ansible playbooks and automation tasks. It supports various databases such as MySQL, PostgreSQL, and BoltDB. With Semaphore, we can build, deploy, and roll back applications or configurations using Ansible. It allows us to group playbooks into projects and manage environments, inventories, repositories, and access keys. The responsive UI enables playbook execution from the browser, even on mobile devices. Semaphore offers features such as scheduled playbook runs, detailed logs, notifications, and user delegation. It is written in Go and is available for Windows, MacOS, and Linux platforms.
- **Rundeck:** Rundeck is an open-source automation platform that can integrate with Ansible and provide a GUI for managing and executing Ansible playbooks. It offers a web-based interface where users can define job workflows, execute playbooks, and monitor job execution.
- **Foreman:** Foreman is a lifecycle management tool for physical and virtual servers. It has integration with Ansible and provides a GUI for managing and orchestrating Ansible playbooks. The Foreman GUI allows users to define hosts, assign Ansible roles, and execute playbooks against targeted hosts.

These GUI tools aim to simplify the management and execution of Ansible automation by providing a visual interface for interacting with Ansible components. They offer features such as inventory management, job scheduling, logging, and reporting, making it easier to track and manage automation tasks. However, it is important to note that while these GUI tools enhance the user experience, the underlying functionality and capabilities are still based on Ansible's command-line interface.

# Ansible Semaphore

Ansible Semaphore is the modern UI for Ansible. It is a web-based tool designed explicitly for Ansible projects. It provides a graphical interface that enables users to define and manage their playbook execution. Semaphore integrates with version control systems like Git and provides execution automation of the Ansible playbooks. It enables an easy-to-use interface for projects, task templates, tasks, key stores, inventory, environment, and repositories. We can use Semaphore in our CI/CD processes because it supports the build and deploys tasks. It allows users to define and manage CI/CD pipelines for their Ansible playbooks and infrastructure code.

Semaphore supports MySQL, PostgreSQL, and BoltDB (embedded key/value) databases. We can install Semaphore in four different ways: snap, distribution package manager, Docker, and binary file.

The fastest way is to use the snap package that setup everything needed in our system:

```
snap install semaphore
```

After a successful installation of the program, we can configure the database and other parameters using the command:

```
semaphore setup
```

After a successful installation, the Semaphore Dashboard looks like *Figure 7.6*:

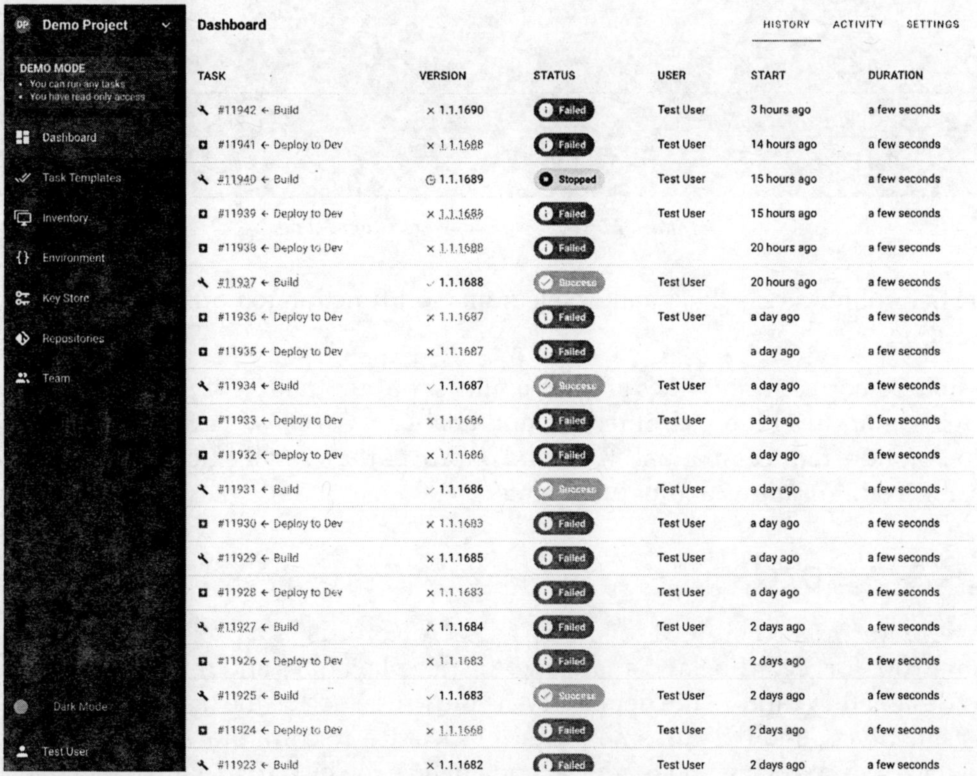

**Figure 7.6:** *The Semaphore dashboard*

We can investigate the status of each execution, as shown in *Figure 7.7*:

***Figure 7.7:** The Semaphore execution details*

One helpful feature is the email or telegram alert function to notify the status of the execution.

Ansible Semaphore simplifies and streamlines the automation of Ansible projects by providing an intuitive web interface and enabling CI/CD workflows. It enhances collaboration, reduces manual effort, and improves the overall efficiency of managing Ansible configurations and deployments.

# ARA records

**Ansible Records Ansible**, also known as **ARA Records**, is a project that provides a framework for recording and analyzing Ansible playbooks and their execution data. It is designed to capture the details of Ansible runs, such as the tasks performed, the hosts involved, and the outcomes of each task. ARA Records stores this information in a database, allowing you to review and analyze the historical data of your Ansible runs. This can be useful for troubleshooting, auditing, performance analysis, and understanding the impact of changes made through Ansible.

## Installation

ARA records require any modern Linux distribution or MacOS with Python installed. By default, it uses a local SQLite server to store the performance data. However, when more than one Ansible controller is running, we can use an API server to store the execution data. The architecture requires an API server running as a service and configuring the ARA Ansible callback plugin to use the HTTP API client with the API server endpoint. Learn more about the Ansible callback plugin in *Chapter 8, Ansible Advanced*, section *Callback plugin*. This is a simple installation of ARA Records without an API server:

1. Install the ARA server via PIP:

   ```
   python3 -m pip install "ara[server]"
   ```

2. **Configure the ARA callback plugin:** Set the Ansible callback plugin to use ARA. The easiest way to is to perform this is via the "**ANSIBLE_CALLBACK_PLUGINS**" environment variable:

   ```
   export ANSIBLE_CALLBACK_PLUGINS="$(python3 -m ara.setup.callback_plugins)"
   ```

3. **Run an Ansible playbook:** Every execution of the "**ansible-playbook**" command is going to send data to the ARA service:

   ```
   ansible-playbook playbook.yml
   ```

4. **Interact with the ARA tool:** We can use the "**ara**" command to list and analyze the result of the execution using ARA:

   ```
   ara playbook list
   ```

5. **Start the built-in development server:** ARA provides a built-in development server to browse the recorded results and analyze the executions:

   ```
   ara-manage runserver
   ```

The result of the execution is displayed in a dashboard of a Web user interface, like the following *Figure 7.8*:

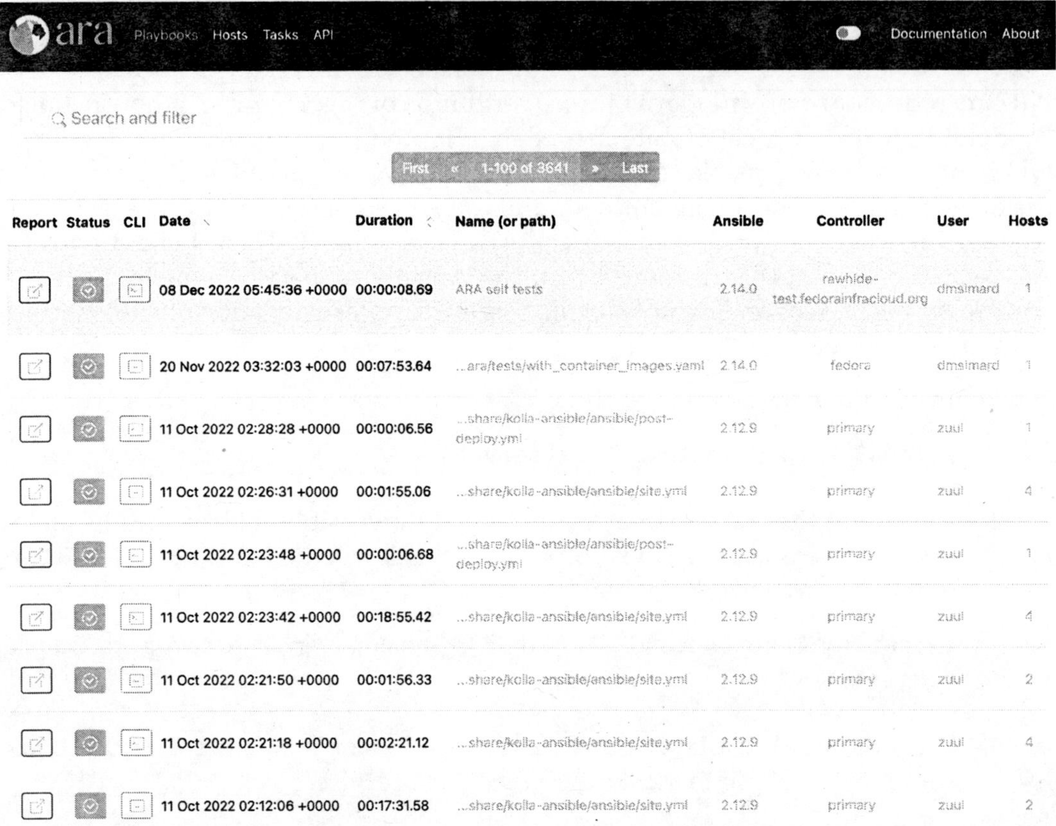


| Report | Status | CLI | Date | Duration | Name (or path) | Ansible | Controller | User | Hosts |
|---|---|---|---|---|---|---|---|---|---|
| | | | 08 Dec 2022 05:45:36 +0000 | 00:00:08.69 | ARA self tests | 2.14.0 | rawhide-test.fedorainfracloud.org | dmsimard | 1 |
| | | | 20 Nov 2022 03:32:03 +0000 | 00:07:53.64 | ...ara/tests/with_container_images.yaml | 2.14.0 | fedora | dmsimard | 1 |
| | | | 11 Oct 2022 02:28:28 +0000 | 00:00:06.56 | ...share/kolla-ansible/ansible/post-deploy.yml | 2.12.9 | primary | zuul | 1 |
| | | | 11 Oct 2022 02:26:31 +0000 | 00:01:55.06 | ...share/kolla-ansible/ansible/site.yml | 2.12.9 | primary | zuul | 4 |
| | | | 11 Oct 2022 02:23:48 +0000 | 00:00:06.68 | ...share/kolla-ansible/ansible/post-deploy.yml | 2.12.9 | primary | zuul | 1 |
| | | | 11 Oct 2022 02:23:42 +0000 | 00:18:55.42 | ...share/kolla-ansible/ansible/site.yml | 2.12.9 | primary | zuul | 4 |
| | | | 11 Oct 2022 02:21:50 +0000 | 00:01:56.33 | ...share/kolla-ansible/ansible/site.yml | 2.12.9 | primary | zuul | 2 |
| | | | 11 Oct 2022 02:21:18 +0000 | 00:02:21.12 | ...share/kolla-ansible/ansible/site.yml | 2.12.9 | primary | zuul | 4 |
| | | | 11 Oct 2022 02:12:06 +0000 | 00:17:31.58 | ...share/kolla-ansible/ansible/site.yml | 2.12.9 | primary | zuul | 2 |

***Figure 7.8:** The ARA records dashboard*

For each job, we can analyze step by step the execution of the playbook, as shown in the example in *Figure 7.9*:

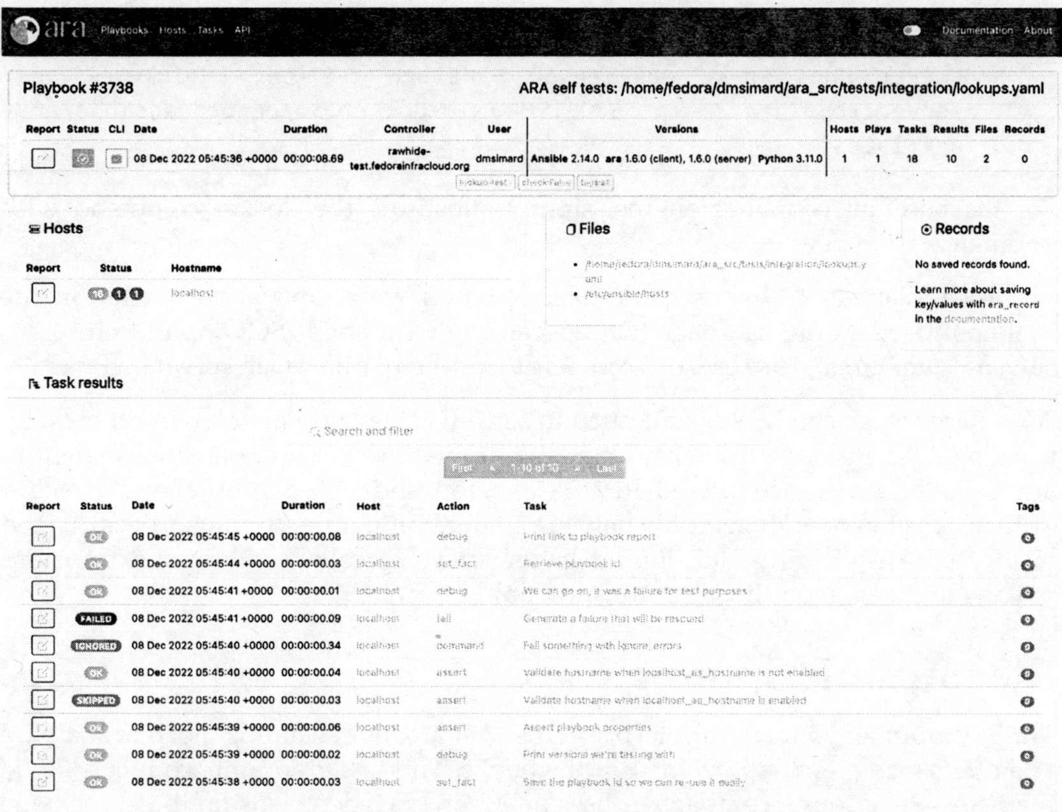


***Figure 7.9:*** *The ARA Records detail of execution*

# Customization

We can customize the behavior of the ARA utility setting environment variables or use the "**[ara]**" section of the "**ansible.cfg**" configuration file.

For example, the following two environment variables send data to the ARA HTTP API server named "**ara.example.com**" which receives data from multiple nodes.

```
export ARA_API_CLIENT="http"

export ARA_API_SERVER="http://ara.example.com:8000"
```

We can run the ARA server using the image published in DockerHub using the podman or Docker command:

1. Create a local directory to store settings and the SQLite database:

   ```
   mkdir -p ~/.ara/server
   ```

2. Start the API server with docker using the local directory:

```
docker run --name api-server --detach --tty  --volume ~/.ara/
server:/opt/ara:z  -p  8000:8000    docker.io/recordsansible/ara-
api:latest
```

For the podman container engine, simply substitute the docker command with podman.

The ARA Records API server is a Django-based web application written in the Python programming language that we can run with any WSGI application server such as "**gunicorn**", "**uwsgi**", or "**mod_wsgi**" for the popular web server software.

ARA Records is beneficial for production as well as development environments. By utilizing ARA Records, users can track the progress of Ansible playbooks, identify any issues or errors encountered during execution, and have a comprehensive record of their Ansible operations. This helps in maintaining an accurate and centralized history of Ansible runs, facilitating better analysis, collaboration, and decision-making in managing infrastructure and deployments.

# Steampunk Spotter

The Steampunk Spotter is an enterprise Ansible Playbook scanning tool that analyzes and offers recommendations for our playbooks. This is a premium product sold via the XLAB Steampunk company. It uses a CLI or VSCode extension to get the code and present the information directly on the terminal or in a nice web user interface.

Steampunk Spotter and Ansible Lint (refer to *Chapter 6, Ansible Troubleshooting,* section *Troubleshooting tools*) are complementary tools that work together to improve the quality and reliability of Ansible Playbooks. While Ansible Lint focuses on catching programming errors, bugs and stylistic errors, and enforcing best practices, Steampunk Spotter goes beyond syntax checking. Spotter analyzes the Ansible content itself, including modules, roles, and collections, to identify hard-to-catch issues, provide module-specific suggestions, and automatically fix some problems.

The following benefits of using the Steampunk Spotter alongside Ansible Lint:

- **Spotting elusive errors:** Steampunk Spotter can identify hidden obstacles and time-consuming errors that Ansible Lint may not catch. It helps you catch issues that go beyond basic syntax and style checks.
- **Module-specific suggestions:** Spotter provides suggestions that are specific to particular modules, user environment setups, and other factors. This allows for more tailored recommendations and improvements.
- **Convenient features:** Steampunk Spotter offers convenience features like generating a **requirements.yml** file and pointing you to the documentation

of specific module versions. These features can save you time and make your automation process more efficient.

- **Collaboration and repository scanning:** Spotter comes with an app that allows you to scan public Git repositories, collaborate with your team, and keep track of your scan history, playbook execution frequency, common mistakes, and progress over time, additionally Spotter provides reports, so they get more insight in the used collections and modules.
- **Simplifying Ansible upgrades:** Spotter can help streamline the process of upgrading Ansible. It checks if your existing playbooks are compatible with a specific Ansible version, identifies issues that need to be resolved during the upgrade, and allows you to determine the target and source versions of Ansible. This makes the upgrade process faster and more efficient.

In summary, while Ansible Lint is a powerful tool for catching errors and enforcing best practices, Steampunk Spotter extends its capabilities by providing module-specific suggestions, identifying hard-to-catch errors, and offering convenient features for playbook improvement and automation enhancement. Using both tools together can help ensure reliable automation and improve the overall quality of your Ansible Playbooks.

Refer to the following *Figure 7.10:*

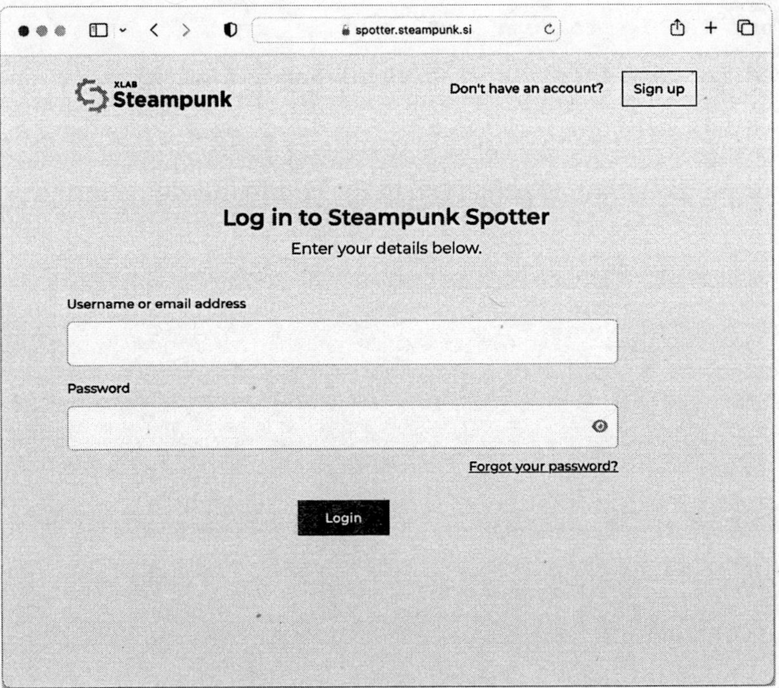


***Figure 7.10:*** *The login screen to Steampunk Spotter*

We can use the command line tool installed via the PIP package manager:

```
pip install steampunk-spotter
```

After installation, we can start using the command line interface performing login, and obtaining an API token:

```
spotter login
Username: AnsiblePilot
Password:
Login successful!
```

From now onward, we can proceed with any further scanning of our playbook. For example, the following command scans the "**fix.yml**" Ansible playbook:

```
spotter scan fix.yml
```

It produces the following output:

```
fix.yml:10:7: HINT: [H500] Use of module debug is discouraged in production.
fix.yml:20:7: HINT: [H500] Use of module debug is discouraged in production.
--------------------------------------------------------------------------
Spotter took 0.430 s to scan your input.
It resulted in 0 error(s), 0 warning(s) and 2 hint(s).
Overall status: HINT
```

The result of the execution is presented in the command line interface, as shown in *Figure 7.11*:

```
Graphical user interface — -zsh — 80×24
(spotter) lberton@Lucas-MacBook-Pro Graphical user interface % spotter login
Username: AnsiblePilot
Password:
Login successful!
(spotter) lberton@Lucas-MacBook-Pro Graphical user interface % spotter scan erro
rs.yml
while parsing a block mapping
  in "/Users/lberton/prj/gitlab/OrangeAVA book 26 - Automate Everything with Ans
ible/code/chapter 7/Graphical user interface/errors.yml", line 11, column 5
expected <block end>, but found '-'
  in "/Users/lberton/prj/gitlab/OrangeAVA book 26 - Automate Everything with Ans
ible/code/chapter 7/Graphical user interface/errors.yml", line 15, column 5
Spotter took 1.298 s to scan your input.
It resulted in 0 error(s), 0 warning(s) and 0 hint(s).
Overall status: SUCCESS
(spotter) lberton@Lucas-MacBook-Pro Graphical user interface % spotter scan fix.
yml
fix.yml:10:7: HINT: [H500] Use of module debug is discouraged in production.
fix.yml:20:7: HINT: [H500] Use of module debug is discouraged in production.
------------------------------------------------------------------------
Spotter took 0.430 s to scan your input.
It resulted in 0 error(s), 0 warning(s) and 2 hint(s).
Overall status: HINT
(spotter) lberton@Lucas-MacBook-Pro Graphical user interface %
```

*Figure 7.11: The Steampunk Spotter CLI*

The result of the execution in the graphical user interface is shown in the following *Figure 7.12*:

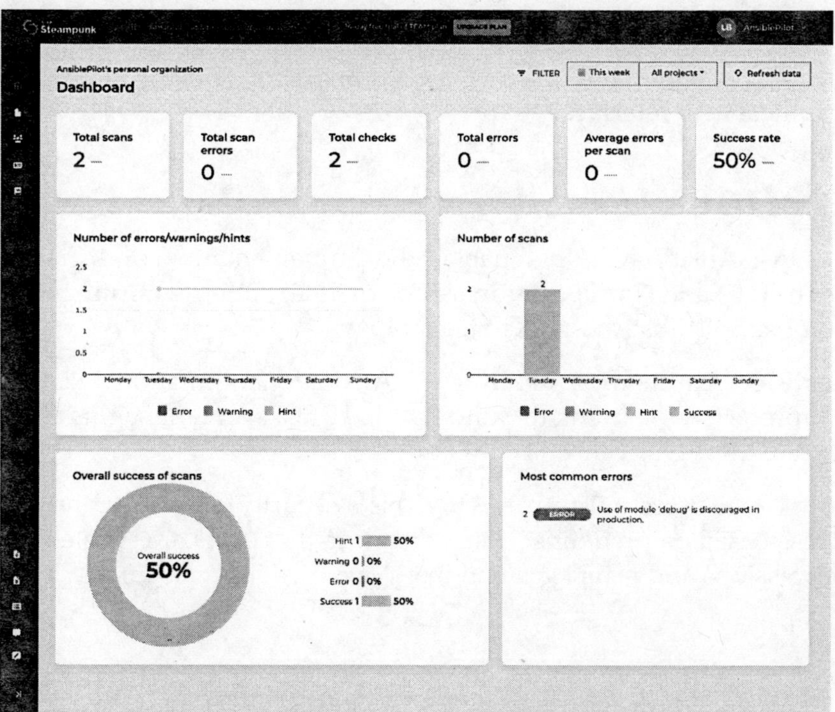


*Figure 7.12: The Steampunk Spotter dashboard*

# Conclusion

Ansible is an enterprise-grade automation platform that simplifies and accelerates IT operations by automating tasks, configurations, and application deployments. It enables consistent infrastructure management, reduces manual effort, promotes collaboration, and increases efficiency and scalability within enterprise environments. Many open-source projects and companies create products that integrate and simplify the management of a modern hybrid infrastructure using Ansible as a foundation. In this chapter, we learned how to take advantage of the Ansible Automation Platform and its alternatives that interact with centralized authentication systems implementing role-based access control.

In the next chapter, we are going to explore how to integrate with cloud computing providers, specifically Amazon Web Services and use Kubernetes technology to boost our cloud-native application deployment.

# Points to remember

- GitOps project design enables **Infrastructure as Code** (**IaC**) and **Configuration as Code** (**CasC**) by standardizing the file and directory structure of projects.
- Enterprise users should consider adopting the Ansible Automation Platform to centralize and optimize the execution of Ansible code.
- Ansible is a command line tool. However, there are many alternatives for the graphical user interface.

# Key terms

- **GitOps:** Ansible GitOps enables the implementation of **Infrastructure as Code** (**IaC**) and **Configuration as Code** (**CaC**) patterns storing information in a repository, mostly using Git technology.
- **Ansible Automation Platform**: Ansible Automation Platform is a comprehensive solution for automating IT tasks and managing infrastructure at scale through a centralized platform.
- **Role-based Access Control** (**RBAC**) is a security model that restricts system access based on predefined roles, ensuring that users are granted appropriate permissions and privileges within an organization's resources.

# Multiple choice questions

1. **What is not a component of the Ansible Automation Platform?**
   a. Automation controller
   b. Automation hub
   c. Ansible automation mesh
   d. Automation core

2. **What <u>is not</u> an Ansible graphical user interface?**
   a. Automation controller
   b. Semaphore
   c. ARA Records
   d. Foreman

3. **What <u>is not</u> a feature of the foundation of the GitOps?**
   a. It implements Infrastructure as Code (IaC)
   b. It is based on the Git popular version control system
   c. It has a fixed directory structure
   d. None of the above

4. **Is Ansible Automation Mesh part of the Ansible Automation Platform?**
   a. True
   b. False

# Answers

1. d
2. c
3. d
4. a

# Questions

1. What is the impact of enabling Ansible Pipelining in our system?
2. What is the GitOps directory layout?
3. What are the main components of the Ansible Automation Platform?
4. What are the Graphical User Interfaces for Ansible?

# CHAPTER 8
# Advanced Ansible Techniques

## Introduction

In this chapter, we are going to learn about more advanced features and techniques used in Ansible, such as custom modules, dynamic inventory scripts, complex playbooks, and advanced configuration management practices. This includes more in-depth topics such as scaling and performance tuning, using Ansible with cloud platforms, integrating with other tools, and implementing security best practices. Advanced Ansible users may also work with more complex architectures and environments, such as distributed systems and microservices.

## Structure

In this chapter, we shall cover the following topics:

- Third-party integrations, fragility, and agility
- Ansible orchestration
- Ansible configuration settings
- Latest trends

# Objectives

By the end of this chapter, the reader will be able to understand the possible Ansible integration, how to take advantage for the cloud computing & Kubernetes domain and the latest trends for developing our projects.

# Third-party integrations, fragility, and agility

In today's rapidly evolving technological landscape, organizations are constantly striving to optimize their IT infrastructure to achieve efficiency, reliability, and agility. Ansible, a powerful open-source automation platform, has emerged as a leading solution to address these needs. While Ansible offers a robust set of built-in features, its ability to seamlessly integrate with third-party tools and platforms takes its capabilities to new heights. Let us explore the significance of Ansible's third-party integrations in enhancing infrastructure fragility and agility, enabling organizations to embrace automation at scale:

- **The power of third-party integrations:** Ansible's third-party integrations empower organizations to extend their automation capabilities beyond their core functionalities. With a vast ecosystem of supported integrations, Ansible enables seamless interaction with a multitude of systems, applications, and services. This integration-centric approach ensures that organizations can automate complex workflows and harness the full potential of their existing infrastructure investments.

- **Fragility - Simplifying complex environments:** Complex IT environments can be inherently fragile, prone to manual errors and inconsistent configurations. Ansible's third-party integrations help alleviate these challenges by providing a standardized automation framework. By integrating with tools like monitoring systems, **Configuration Management Databases** (**CMDBs**), and incident management platforms, Ansible enables proactive monitoring, efficient change management, and automated incident response. This reduces the fragility of the infrastructure, minimizes downtime, and ensures consistent performance across the entire ecosystem.

- **Agility - Enabling rapid adaptation:** In today's fast-paced business landscape, agility is paramount. Ansible's third-party integrations play a pivotal role in fostering agility by enabling organizations to respond swiftly to evolving requirements. Integrations with cloud platforms such as **Amazon Web Services** (**AWS**), Microsoft Azure, or **Google Cloud Platform** (**GCP**) allow for dynamic provisioning of resources, auto-scaling, and seamless application deployments. Ansible also integrates with source control systems like Git, facilitating version control and enabling teams to roll out updates rapidly. By automating these processes, Ansible accelerates development cycles, enhances collaboration, and drives **Continuous Integration and Deployment** (CI/CD) practices.

- **A diverse integration ecosystem:** Ansible's integration ecosystem encompasses a wide range of technologies and tools. It seamlessly connects with configuration management systems such as Puppet and Chef, enabling organizations to leverage existing investments while benefiting from Ansible's orchestration capabilities. It integrates with networking devices, allowing the automation of network configurations and the provisioning of network services. Additionally, Ansible integrates with virtualization platforms, containerization technologies, databases, messaging systems, and many other components critical to modern infrastructure.
- **Extensibility and community contributions:** One of the key strengths of Ansible lies in its active community, which continuously contributes to the development and expansion of its integration ecosystem. The Ansible Galaxy community repository provides a vast collection of pre-built roles and playbooks, empowering users to accelerate automation by leveraging existing community-driven content. This extensibility ensures that Ansible can adapt and integrate with emerging technologies and tools, further enhancing its value proposition.

Ansible's third-party integrations are a game-changer when it comes to infrastructure automation. By seamlessly connecting with a diverse array of tools, platforms, and services, Ansible empowers organizations to enhance fragility, reduce errors, and embrace agility at scale. With an ever-growing ecosystem and a vibrant community, Ansible continues to evolve, making it a trusted choice for IT professionals looking to unlock the full potential of automation in their organizations. Embracing Ansible's third-party integrations is a strategic decision that can propel organizations toward a more efficient, reliable, and agile future.

# Callback plugin

In Ansible, callback plugins are a mechanism that allows us to extend the behavior and functionality of Ansible when responding to events during playbook execution. These plugins enable us to customize and control the output we see when running Ansible command line programs.

By default, callback plugins are responsible for managing the majority of the output displayed during the execution of Ansible commands. They control the formatting and presentation of information on the command line. However, callback plugins can also be utilized to add extra output, integrate Ansible with other tools or systems, and store or process events in a backend storage system.

Callback plugins are helpful for various purposes, such as:

- **Customizing output:** We can use callback plugins to modify or enhance the default output of Ansible, tailoring it to our specific requirements. This allows us to present information in a format that suits our needs.
- **Integration with external tools:** Callback plugins provide a way to integrate Ansible with other external tools, such as monitoring systems or logging frameworks. This enables us to incorporate Ansible events and information into our existing tooling ecosystem.
- **Event storage:** Callback plugins can be used to capture and store Ansible events in a storage backend. This allows us to maintain a historical record of playbook executions, analyze the data, and gain insights into the operations performed by Ansible.

If the existing callback plugins do not meet our needs, we have the flexibility to create custom callback plugins. This allows us to implement specific behaviors and responses tailored to our use case. By leveraging custom callback plugins, we can extend the Ansible capabilities and integrate them more effectively into our infrastructure and workflows.

# Dynamic inventories

Ansible dynamic inventories provide a powerful capability for managing infrastructure in a flexible and dynamic manner. Unlike static inventories that require manual updates, dynamic inventories automatically gather information about hosts and their attributes from external sources such as cloud providers, virtualization platforms, or custom scripts. With Ansible Dynamic Inventories, we can effortlessly adapt to changes in our infrastructure, including scaling up or down, provisioning new resources, or decommissioning existing ones. This flexibility enables us to efficiently automate tasks and configurations across our dynamic environment without the need for constant manual intervention.

Dynamic inventories allow us to define host groups and assign variables based on specific criteria such as tags, metadata, or network attributes. This dynamic grouping simplifies the organization and management of our infrastructure, making it easier to target specific hosts or groups for configuration management, deployment, or orchestration tasks. By leveraging Ansible Dynamic Inventories, we gain the ability to automate complex operations across diverse and evolving environments. It enables us to achieve consistency, scalability, and agility in our infrastructure management, ultimately saving time and effort while ensuring the accurate provisioning and configuration of resources. We can use or write custom dynamic inventory plugins using the Python, Java, Perl, Bash, Ruby, and Go programming languages and return a JSON object to Ansible. This feature enables us to list resources in fast pace environments such as virtual machines, cloud providers, or container orchestration platforms.

# VMware

To configure Ansible dynamic inventory for VMware and list all virtual machines within our VMware infrastructure, follow these steps:

1. **Install required dependencies:** Make sure we have the necessary dependencies installed, including the Python pyVmomi library, Python requests library, and vSphere Automation SDK (for tag feature).

   ```
   pip install PyVmomi
   ansible-galaxy install community.vmware
   ```

2. **Install the VMware dynamic inventory plugin:** Use the "`community.vmware.vmware_vm_inventory`" plugin, which interacts with VMware APIs to fetch information about virtual machines as inventory hosts.

3. **Create the inventory configuration file:** Create an inventory YAML configuration file with a name ending in `vmware.yml`, `vmware.yaml`, `vmware_vm_inventory.yml`, or `vmware_vm_inventory.yaml`.

4. **Configure the inventory file:** Specify the plugin as "`vmware_vm_inventory`" and provide the necessary parameters, such as the hostname of our VMware environment, username, password, and optional settings like certificate validation and tag support.

5. **Test the inventory:** Run the command "`ansible-inventory -i inventory.vmware.yml --list`" to list all the virtual machines as inventory hosts, along with their associated metadata.

6. **Visualize the inventory:** Optionally, we can use the command "`ansible-inventory -i inventory.vmware.yml --graph`" to generate a graphical representation of the inventory structure.

   The expected output looks like the following:

   ```
   @all:
     |--@VMs:
     |  |--example_92274719-810c-03ac-105b-14c372b4a210
     |--@centos64Guest:
     |  |--example_92274719-810c-03ac-105b-14c372b4a210
   ```

```
|--@poweredOff:
|  |--example_92274719-810c-03ac-105b-14c372b4a210
```

7. **Use the dynamic inventory in the playbook:**

```
ansible-playbook -i inventory.vmware.yml playbook.yml
```

By following these steps, we can successfully configure Ansible dynamic inventory for VMware, allowing us to leverage the power of Ansible automation across our VMware infrastructure.

# Citrix

Ansible interacts with Citrix **Application Delivery Controller** (**ADC**) and Citrix **Application Delivery Management** (**ADM**) using Ansible modules delivered by the Citrix collection.

Citrix ADC is a networking product that provides load balancing, application acceleration, security, and other functionalities for applications deployed in data centers or cloud environments. Ansible, on the other hand, is an open-source automation platform that enables you to automate IT tasks, including network configuration and management. The integration of Ansible with Citrix ADC allows users to automate the provisioning, configuration, and management of Citrix ADC instances using Ansible playbooks. Ansible provides a collection of modules specifically designed to interact with Citrix ADC, enabling users to automate various tasks such as creating virtual servers, configuring load-balancing policies, managing SSL certificates, and more.

By leveraging Ansible's declarative language and automation capabilities, users can define the desired state of their Citrix ADC infrastructure in Ansible playbooks and execute them to ensure consistent and repeatable configurations across multiple Citrix ADC instances. This integration simplifies the management of Citrix ADC deployments, reduces manual effort, and enhances operational efficiency. Additionally, Ansible's integration with Citrix ADC allows for seamless integration with other infrastructure components, such as network switches, routers, and virtualization platforms, enabling comprehensive automation and orchestration of the entire network infrastructure.

Citrix **Application Delivery Management** (**ADM**) is a centralized management and analytics platform provided by Citrix. It is designed to simplify the management, monitoring, and troubleshooting of application delivery infrastructure, including Citrix ADC instances. ADM offers a comprehensive set of features and functionalities that help administrators gain visibility into their application delivery infrastructure, optimize performance, ensure security, and streamline operations. It provides real-time monitoring and analytics capabilities, allowing administrators to monitor application traffic, identify performance bottlenecks, and troubleshoot issues proactively. Now, concerning the integration of Citrix ADM with Ansible, it enables administrators to automate the configuration and management of Citrix ADC instances using Ansible playbooks and modules. This integration allows for seamless orchestration and automation of Citrix ADC deployments within the broader IT infrastructure.

Overall, the integration of Ansible with Citrix ADC and ADM empowers network administrators and DevOps teams to automate the configuration and management of their Citrix ADC deployments, streamlining operations and enabling efficient management of application delivery services.

# Amazon Web Services

**Amazon Web Services (AWS)** is a comprehensive cloud computing platform offering a wide range of scalable and flexible services to help businesses build and deploy applications, store and analyze data, and manage their IT infrastructure.

The benefit of using Ansible with AWS is that it provides a powerful automation toolset to streamline and simplify the management and deployment of AWS resources, enabling infrastructure-as-code practices, improving operational efficiency, and promoting consistent and reproducible configurations.

## Dynamic inventory

Generating a dynamic inventory of a cloud provider, such as AWS resources, using Ansible offers several benefits. Firstly, it enables automation by eliminating manual updates to the inventory file and allowing for automated management and provisioning of AWS resources. The dynamic inventory adapts to changes in resource scale, ensuring seamless management at any level. It provides flexibility through grouping and tagging resources based on various criteria, enabling targeted control over resource management tasks. Real-time updates from AWS APIs ensure accurate and up-to-date information for Ansible tasks. By simplifying inventory management, dynamic inventory reduces administrative overhead, especially in dynamic AWS environments. It seamlessly integrates with other Ansible workflows, enhancing automation capabilities across AWS resources. Overall, using dynamic inventory with Ansible enhances agility, scalability, and efficiency in managing and automating tasks within AWS environments. *Figure 8.1* features the AWS logo:

***Figure 8.1:*** *The Amazon Web Services (AWS) logo*

To generate a dynamic inventory of resources in our AWS infrastructure using Ansible, follow these steps:

1. **Install the required dependencies:** Ensure that we have the necessary dependencies installed. The "**botocore**", and "**boto3**" Python libraries can be installed using the command:

   ```
   pip install botocore boto3
   ```

2. **Install the "amazon.aws" collection:** Use the command "**ansible-galaxy**" to install the "**amazon.aws**" collection. Verify the successful installation with the following command:

   ```
   ansible-galaxy collection list amazon.aws
   ```

3. **Create the AWS EC2 inventory configuration file:** Create an inventory configuration file named "**inventory.aws_ec2.yml**" with the necessary plugin configuration. Set the regions to query, define filters based on tags, and specify the keyed groups to create dynamic groups based on host variables.

4. **Enable the aws_ec2 inventory plugin:** Add the following configuration lines in our "**ansible.cfg**" file under the **"[inventory]"** section to enable the dynamic inventory plugin:

   "**enable_plugins = amazon.aws.aws_ec2**".

5. **Set AWS environment variables:** Make sure the **AWS_ACCESS_KEY_ID** and **AWS_SECRET_ACCESS_KEY** environment variables are defined with our AWS credentials.

6. **Interact with the dynamic inventory:** Use the "**ansible-inventory**" or "**ansible-playbook**" command with the **"-i inventory.aws_ec2.yml**" option to interact with the dynamic inventory. The "**ansible-inventory**" command generates a graph-style output, whereas "**ansible-playbook**" allows us to execute playbooks using the dynamic inventory.

By following these steps, we can generate an Ansible dynamic inventory of our Amazon Web Services infrastructure, allowing us to manage and automate tasks across our AWS resources using Ansible.

## Idempotence

When it comes to cloud deployment and managing infrastructure, idempotence is a critical concept. Idempotence means that running a task or playbook multiple times will not have any additional effects beyond the initial execution. In the context of cloud deployment using Ansible, idempotence ensures that the automation process does not disrupt existing infrastructure or create duplicate resources.

Each Ansible module, including those used for cloud deployment, has its own method of identifying and managing existing resources. It is essential to configure the module correctly so that it can identify and track the resources it creates. This ensures that subsequent runs of the automation process will recognize the existing resources and not recreate them.

Thinking in terms of groups of related resources can greatly simplify the management of entire environments. By organizing resources into logical groups, such as by application or environment type, it becomes easier to manage and coordinate their deployment, configuration, and scaling.

It is important to note that Ansible modules designed for specific cloud platforms, such as AWS, may have unique installation and configuration requirements. These modules are specifically tailored to interact with the APIs and services provided by the cloud provider.

It is crucial to follow the documentation and guidelines provided by the module to ensure proper installation and configuration for cloud-specific functionality. When using cloud deployment modules, the approach and usage may differ slightly from other modules due to the nature of working with cloud resources.

Cloud modules often involve interacting with infrastructure as code, managing virtual machines, networking, storage, and other cloud-specific resources. It is important to familiarize yourself with the specific documentation and best practices for working with cloud deployment modules to ensure effective and efficient management of your cloud infrastructure.

In summary, idempotence is crucial in cloud deployment to prevent disruptions and duplication of resources. Configuring modules correctly and organizing resources into logical groups can simplify management. Cloud deployment modules, such as those for AWS, may have unique requirements and are used differently compared to other modules. Understanding these concepts and practices is essential for successful cloud deployment automation with Ansible.

In AWS environments, Ansible provides several modules specifically designed to interact with AWS services. Many of these AWS modules have an additional "**`_info`**" module variant, which is used for collecting data without performing any actions or making changes to resources. Here are some key points about these AWS info modules:

- **Collecting data:** Info modules are used to gather information about specific AWS resources. They retrieve data without making any modifications or taking any actions on those resources. This allows you to inspect the current state of AWS resources before making any decisions or modifications.
- **Search functionality:** Info modules typically support search terms or filters, enabling you to retrieve information about a specific resource or a list of

resources that match certain criteria. This search functionality helps you narrow down the scope and collect the exact information you need.

- **AWS networks:** As an example, let us consider the AWS **Virtual Private Cloud** (**VPC**) related modules. The "`ec2_vpc_net`" module can be used to create or update a VPC. On the other hand, the "`ec2_vpc_net_info`" module is specifically used to collect information about existing VPCs. Both modules return similar data about VPCs, but the choice between them depends on whether you want your automation to create a new VPC or work with an existing VPC.
- **Key info modules:** The following *Table 8.1* summarizes the most important Ansible modules for information gathering for AWS.

| Module | AWS resources |
|---|---|
| `amazon.aws.ec2_ami_info` | Machine images (AMIs) |
| `amazon.aws.ec2_group_info` | Security groups |
| `amazon.aws.ec2_instance_info` | Instances (virtual machines) |
| `amazon.aws.ec2_vpc_net_info` | Networks and subnets within a VPC |
| `community.aws.ec2_asg_info` | Auto Scaling Groups |
| `community.aws.iam_user_info` | Identities and roles<br>AWS **Identity and Access Management** (**IAM**) |

***Table 8.1:*** *The AWS information-gathering modules*

By utilizing these "info" modules, you can gather comprehensive information about various AWS resources in your environment. This data can be used for decision-making, auditing, or to feed into subsequent automation tasks.

## Amazon EC2

We can easily automate the deployment of instances on the **Amazon Elastic Compute Cloud** (**Amazon EC2**). The following "`aws_ec2.yml`" Ansible playbook deploys an **Amazon Machine Image** (**AMI**) in our cloud computing environment:

```
---
- name: Deploy an EC2 instance
  hosts: all
  vars:
    ec2_name: "server-ec2"
    ec2_ssh: "my-ssh-key"
    ec2_vpc: "subnet-pub1234"
```

```
    ec2_type: "c5.large"
    ec2_sg: "default"
    ec2_ami: "ami-123456"
    ec2_tag: "Development"
    ec2_ip_public: true
  tasks:
    - name: Create an EC2 instance
      amazon.aws.ec2_instance:
        name: "{{ ec2_name }}"
        key_name: "{{ ec2_ssh }}"
        vpc_subnet_id: "{{ ec2_vpc }}"
        instance_type: "{{ ec2_type }}"
        security_group: "{{ ec2_sg }}"
        network:
          assign_public_ip: "{{ ec2_ip_public }}"
        image_id: "{{ ec2_ami }}"
        tags:
          Environment: "{{ ec2_tag }}"
```

The playbook defines a set of tasks to deploy an EC2 instance on AWS. Let us break down the playbook:

The first line, "`---`", is a YAML document separator used to separate multiple YAML documents within a single file. It is not necessary for this context.

The playbook starts with a play named "**`Deploy an EC2 instance`**," which will be executed on all hosts specified in the inventory. The play includes variables (under the **`vars`** keyword) that define various properties for the EC2 instance to be created.

Here are the variables defined in the playbook:

- **`ec2_name`**: Specifies the name for the EC2 instance, set to "**`server-ec2`**".
- **`ec2_ssh`**: Specifies the SSH key pair to use for accessing the instance, set to "**`my-ssh-key`**".
- **`ec2_vpc`**: Specifies the VPC subnet ID where the EC2 instance will be launched, set to "**`subnet-pub1234`**".
- **`ec2_type`**: Specifies the instance type, set to "**`c5.large`**".
- **`ec2_sg`**: Specifies the security group for the EC2 instance, set to "**`default`**".

- `ec2_ami`: Specifies the AMI ID to use for the instance, set to "`ami-123456`". We can get this value by searching on the Ubuntu Amazon EC2 AMI Locator (**https://cloud-images.ubuntu.com/locator/ec2**)
- `ec2_tag`: Specifies a tag for the EC2 instance, set to "`Development`".
- `ec2_ip_public`: Specifies whether to assign a public IP to the instance set to "`true`".

Following the variables, there is a task defined under the `tasks` keyword. The task is named "`Create an EC2 instance`" and uses the Ansible AWS EC2 module ("`amazon.aws.ec2_instance`") to launch the EC2 instance on AWS. The module takes several parameters to configure the instance based on the provided variables.

The parameters used in the task:

- `name`: Specifies the name of the EC2 instance using the value of the `ec2_name` variable.
- `key_name`: Specifies the SSH key pair name to use for accessing the instance, using the value of the `ec2_ssh` variable.
- `vpc_subnet_id`: Specifies the VPC subnet ID using the value of the `ec2_vpc` variable.
- `instance_type`: Specifies the instance type using the value of the `ec2_type` variable.
- `security_group`: Specifies the security group using the value of the `ec2_sg` variable.
- `network`: Specifies network-related configurations, including whether to assign a public IP to the instance, using the value of the `ec2_ip_public` variable.
- `image_id`: Specifies the AMI ID to use for the instance, using the value of the `ec2_ami` variable.
- `tags`: Specifies tags to be assigned to the EC2 instance, with the "`Environment`" tag set to the value of the `ec2_tag` variable.

Overall, this playbook aims to launch an EC2 instance on AWS with the specified configuration and tags using Ansible's AWS EC2 module.

# Google Cloud Platform and Azure

**Google Cloud Platform** (GCP) and Microsoft Azure are two popular cloud computing platforms that offer a wide range of services and resources for building, deploying, and managing applications and infrastructure in the cloud. Ansible, as a universal automation tool, can be integrated with both GCP and Azure to automate various tasks and configurations within these cloud environments.

With the Ansible integration with GCP, users can leverage Ansible's modules specifically designed for GCP to automate the provisioning and management of GCP resources. Ansible provides modules for GCP services such as computing instances, networks, storage, load balancers, and more. This integration allows users to define the desired state of their GCP infrastructure in Ansible playbooks and execute them to create, modify, or delete resources in GCP. They can automate tasks such as spinning up virtual machines, configuring network settings, managing storage, setting up load balancers, and even managing GCP projects and permissions.

Similarly, Ansible can be integrated with Azure to automate the configuration and management of Azure resources. Ansible provides modules for Azure services such as virtual machines, storage accounts, virtual networks, security groups, and more. Users can define Azure resource configurations in Ansible playbooks and execute them to automate the provisioning and management of Azure infrastructure. This integration allows tasks such as creating VMs, configuring networking, managing storage, and implementing security policies to be automated using Ansible.

In both cases, Ansible's declarative language and automation capabilities enable users to define the desired state of their infrastructure and ensure consistent configurations across multiple cloud resources. It helps to streamline operations, reduce manual effort, and improve efficiency. Furthermore, Ansible's integration with GCP and Azure can be combined with other Ansible modules and functionalities to enable comprehensive automation and orchestration across the entire IT infrastructure, including on-premises systems, other cloud platforms, and networking components.

Overall, the integration of Ansible with Google Cloud Platform and Azure provides users with powerful automation capabilities to manage and provision cloud resources, allowing for efficient and consistent infrastructure management within these cloud environments.

# API integration

Integrating Ansible in our organization workflow often requires interacting with some RESTful API services and using the data from that call to decide what to do next. We already know how to create custom temporary facts in our playbook using registered variables (refer to *Chapter 2, Ansible Language Core*, section *Registered Variables*) or "**`set_fact`**" (refer to *Chapter 2: Ansible Language Core*, section *Temporary Facts*) and how to process data using Ansible filters (refer to *Chapter 3, Ansible Language Extended*, section *Ansible filter*). We can interact with any API service using the Ansible "**`uri`**" module. It is part of the "**`ansible.builtin`**" collection. Using this module, we can perform HTTP requests and validations.

The "**uri**" Ansible module supports all the HTTP methods **GET**, **POST**, **PUT**, **DELETE**, and **HEAD** to interact with HTTP and HTTPS endpoints. The typical use cases include a wide range of tasks, including sending data to a web server, authenticating with a web service, and retrieving data from a web service.

These are the most important parameters of the module:

- **url**: Specifies the URL to be accessed. This parameter is mandatory and must be provided to the module.
- **method**: Specifies the HTTP method to be used. This parameter is optional and defaults to **GET**.
- **body**: Specifies the body of the HTTP request. This parameter is optional and can be used to send data to a web server.
- **headers**: Specifies any additional headers that should be included in the HTTP request. This parameter is optional and can be used for authentication or to pass custom headers.
- **timeout**: Specifies the amount of time to wait for a response before timing out. This parameter is optional and defaults to 30 seconds.
- **status_code**: Specifies the expected HTTP status code. This parameter is optional and can be used to verify that the response from the web server is as expected.

The "**uri**" module is very powerful and flexible, and it can be used in a wide range of scenarios. It can be used to check the health of a web server, retrieve data from an API, or upload a file to a cloud storage service. By using this module, Ansible automation experts can automate tasks that involve interacting with web services and APIs.

**Tip: We can use the Reqres API ("https://reqres.in") to test our Ansible code against a real API.**

## GET method

Ansible interacting with an API endpoint to retrieve data means often uses the **GET HTTP** method. Our web browser also uses the **GET HTTP** method to retrieve the HTML pages from a website. The following "**api_get.yml**" Ansible task retrieves data from an API endpoint using the GET method:

```
- name: Get data from API
  ansible.builtin.uri:
    url: https://api.example.com/data
    method: GET
  register: api_response
```

The **`url`** parameter specifies the API endpoint URL ("**https://api.example.com/data**"), and the **`method`** parameter specifies the HTTP method to be used, which is **`GET`** in this case. Finally, the register parameter allows us to store the API response in the "**`api_response`**" variable for later use or process with a filter. Interacting with API interfaces also means often dealing with JSON or YAML files.

The full "**`reqres_get.yml`**" Ansible code to retrieve the users of the second page of the Reqres API is as follows:

```
---
- name: API GET method
  hosts: all
  vars:
    server: "https://reqres.in"
    endpoint: "/api/users?page=2"
  tasks:
    - name: Reqres list users
      ansible.builtin.uri:
        url: "{{ server }}{{ endpoint }}"
        method: GET
        status_code: 200
        timeout: 30
      register: result

    - name: Reqres print
      ansible.builtin.debug:
        var: result.json.data
```

We can execute our code using the "**`ansible-playbook`**" command:

```
ansible-playbook reqres_get.yml
```

The code produces the following output:

```
TASK [Reqres print] *****************************************************
*************************ok: [server01.example.com] => {
    "result.json.data": [
        {
            "avatar": "https://reqres.in/img/faces/7-image.jpg",
            "email": "michael.lawson@reqres.in",
```

```
            "first_name": "Michael",
            "id": 7,
            "last_name": "Lawson"
        },
        {
            "avatar": "https://reqres.in/img/faces/8-image.jpg",
            "email": "lindsay.ferguson@reqres.in",
            "first_name": "Lindsay",
            "id": 8,
            "last_name": "Ferguson"
        },
        {
            "avatar": "https://reqres.in/img/faces/9-image.jpg",
            "email": "tobias.funke@reqres.in",
            "first_name": "Tobias",
            "id": 9,
            "last_name": "Funke"
        },
        {
            "avatar": "https://reqres.in/img/faces/10-image.jpg",
            "email": "byron.fields@reqres.in",
            "first_name": "Byron",
            "id": 10,
            "last_name": "Fields"
        },
        {
            "avatar": "https://reqres.in/img/faces/11-image.jpg",
            "email": "george.edwards@reqres.in",
            "first_name": "George",
            "id": 11,
            "last_name": "Edwards"
        },
        {
            "avatar": "https://reqres.in/img/faces/12-image.jpg",
```

```
            "email": "rachel.howell@reqres.in",
            "first_name": "Rachel",
            "id": 12,
            "last_name": "Howell"
        }
    ]
}
```

## JSON and YAML

Ansible integrates the Ansible filters to handle these file formats based on the PyYAML framework for the Python programming language. While using the standard Ansible string parsing "**`starts_with`**" and "**`contains`**" Ansible filters, it is more beneficial to use specific Ansible filters for the correct parsing of data structure. The most common are summarized in the following *Table 8.2*:

| Ansible filter | Behavior |
|---|---|
| **`to_json`** | Convert the input to a JSON document<br>• "**`indent=3`**" specifies space indentation<br>• "**`width=120`**" support longer lines<br>• "**`ensure_ascii=False`**" keep the Unicode format |
| **`to_yaml`** | Convert the input to the YAML document<br>• "**`indent=3`**" specifies space indentation<br>• "**`width=120`**" support longer lines |
| **`from_json`** | Interpret the input to the JSON document |
| **`from_yaml`** | Interpret the input to the YAML document |
| **`to_nice_json`** | Format the input to JSON document to be more human-readable |
| **`to_nice_yaml`** | Format the input to the YAML document to be more human-readable |
| **`from_yaml_all`** | Read the input and parse as multi-document YAML strings |
| **`json_query`** | Select a single element or a data subset from a complex data structure. It is part of the "**`community.general`**" collection. |

***Table 8.2:*** *The JSON or YAML Ansible filters*

## Bearer token

Sometimes we need an authentication token to access some web services. Let us suppose we already have a valid Bearer token saved in the "**`access_token`**" variable, and we would like to interact with an API. The OAuth 2.0 specification uses the bearer token as an authentication mechanism. The following "**api_get_bearer.yml**" Ansible task retrieves data from an API endpoint using the **GET** method using the bearer token authentication:

```
- name: Get data from API using Bearer Token
  ansible.builtin.uri:
    url: https://api.example.com/data
    method: GET
    headers:
      Authorization: "Bearer {{ access_token }}"
  register: api_response
```

The code looks similar to the "**api_get.yml**" Ansible task but with an additional "**headers**" parameter that specifies any additional headers needed in our HTTP request. In this case, we used the authentication token.

## POST and PUT methods

When we need to send data to an API service, we use the **POST** or **PUT** methods. Usually, we use these methods to enter data in an API. The difference between **POST** and **PUT** is that **PUT** requests are idempotent. In a well-designed API, calling the same **PUT** request multiple times produces the same result. However, calling a **POST** request repeatedly has the side effect of creating the same resource multiple times. Usually, the **POST** and **PUT** requested are protected by the Bearer Token.

The following Ansible task creates a new resource in an API using the "**resource_data**" as input and POST method:

```
- name: Create new resource in API
  ansible.builtin.uri:
    url: https://api.example.com/resource
    method: POST
    headers:
      Authorization: "Bearer {{ access_token }}"
    body: "{{ resource_data }}"
  register: api_response
```

Please note that we must specify the "**method: POST**" parameter to set the correct method to interact with the API. We specify in the **body** parameter, the data (the value of the **resource_data** variable) to be sent via the HTTP request.

The following "**reqres_token.yml**" interacts with the Reqres API to send the credential and retrieve an authentication token.

```
---
- name: API Bearer Token
  hosts: all
  vars:
    server: "https://reqres.in"
    endpoint: "/api/login"
  tasks:
    - name: Reqres login
      ansible.builtin.uri:
        url: "{{ server }}{{ endpoint }}"
        method: POST
        body_format: json
        body: '{
          "email": "eve.holt@reqres.in",
          "password": "cityslicka"
        }'
        status_code: 200
        timeout: 30
      register: result
    - name: Reqres token
      ansible.builtin.debug:
        var: result.json.token
```

We can execute our code using the "**ansible-playbook**" command:

```
ansible-playbook reqres_token.yml
```

The code produces the following output:

```
TASK [ Reqres token] ***************************************************
**************************ok: [server01.example.com] => {
    "result.json.token": "QpwL5tke4Pnpja7X4"
}
```

## PATCH and DELETE methods

We can use the **PATCH** method to alter the data on the web service or API. In the same way, we can use the **DELETE** method to delete a record on the web service or API. We can automate using the Ansible "**uri**" module setting the relative parameters. The code is similar to the examples already provided.

In summary, the "**uri**" Ansible module is a powerful tool for interacting with APIs. By using this module, Ansible automation experts can easily automate tasks that involve interacting with APIs, such as retrieving data, creating or updating resources, or triggering events.

## Zuul

Zuul is a Project gating system. This is like a CI or CD system, but the focus is on testing the future state of code repositories. It contains Ansible modules and plugins to control the execution of Ansible job content. Zuul provides real-time build log streaming to end users so that users can watch long-running jobs in progress.

Zuul is an open-source CI/CD platform developed by the OpenStack community. It provides a flexible and scalable system for automating the testing, building, and deployment of software projects. Zuul is designed to handle complex CI/CD workflows across multiple repositories and supports integration with various version control systems.

Zuul uses a system of "pipelines" to define the steps involved in the software development process, including code review, testing, and deployment. It integrates with other tools such as Jenkins, Gerrit, and GitHub to facilitate collaboration and automate the software delivery process.

The integration between Zuul and Ansible is performed via an Ansible callback plugin that should be enabled. All jobs run with the "**zuul.ansible.base.callback.zuul_stream**" callback plugin, which writes the build log to a file so that the "**zuul.lib.log_streamer.LogStreamer**" can provide the data on demand over the finger protocol.

# Ansible orchestration

Ansible orchestration refers to the process of coordinating and managing multiple tasks and resources in a systematic and automated manner using Ansible. It allows users to define and execute complex workflows, known as playbooks that involve multiple systems, configurations, and dependencies.

With Ansible orchestration, users can define the desired state of their infrastructure and applications and let Ansible handle the automation and orchestration of tasks to achieve that state. This includes tasks such as provisioning servers, configuring network devices, deploying applications, managing services, and more.

One of the key advantages of Ansible orchestration is its simplicity. Playbooks are written using a declarative language, YAML, which makes them easy to understand, modify, and maintain. The playbooks describe the desired state and the tasks required to reach that state, allowing for consistent and repeatable automation.

Ansible's orchestration capabilities also support parallel execution, allowing multiple tasks to run simultaneously across different systems. This improves efficiency and reduces the time required for large-scale deployments or configurations.

Moreover, Ansible provides a wide range of modules and plugins that can be leveraged in orchestration workflows. These modules enable interaction with various systems, services, and cloud providers, making it possible to orchestrate tasks across diverse infrastructure environments.

Overall, Ansible orchestration empowers organizations to automate complex processes, streamline operations, ensure consistency, and improve productivity. It simplifies the management of infrastructure and applications, accelerates deployments, and enhances scalability and agility in IT environments.

# Fork versus serial

The "**`fork`**" and "**`serial`**" options of Ansible are valuable tools for managing our infrastructure, depending on the purpose of the Ansible Playbooks. The "**`fork`**" option is helpful for running tasks in parallel on multiple hosts (default to 5), while the "**`serial`**" option is helpful for running tasks in sequence on a single host. In Ansible, the concepts of "**`fork`**" and "**`serial`**" are used to control the parallel execution of tasks across multiple hosts. Let us understand each concept:

- **Fork:** Forking determines the number of parallel processes or connections that Ansible will use to manage hosts simultaneously. It specifies how many hosts Ansible can operate on at the same time. By default, the fork value is set to 5, which means Ansible can manage up to 5 hosts concurrently. We can adjust the fork value in the Ansible configuration file (**`ansible.cfg`**) or by using the "**`--forks`**" command-line option. For example, if we have 10 hosts and set the fork value to 5, Ansible will execute tasks concurrently on 5 hosts at a time. Once those tasks are completed, it will move on to the next 5 hosts and so on. The fork value is particularly useful when dealing with large inventories or executing tasks that can be parallelized.

- **Serial:** Serial defines the number of hosts that Ansible will manage in parallel within a group of hosts. It allows us to control the degree of parallelism when executing tasks. By default, the serial value is set to "**`all`**," meaning Ansible will manage all hosts in parallel.

However, in certain scenarios, we might want to limit the number of hosts that Ansible manages simultaneously. This can be useful for tasks that require more controlled execution, such as software updates or sensitive operations. We can control the concurrency by specifying a numeric value for the serial parameter or using patterns to select specific hosts or groups. For instance, if we have a group of 10 hosts and set the serial value to 2, Ansible executes the tasks in our playbook with only two hosts at a time. It will execute tasks on the first two hosts, then move on to the next two, and so forth until all hosts have been managed.

Using the combination of fork and serial parameters, we can fine-tune how Ansible executes tasks across our inventory, balancing parallelism and control according to our requirements.

# Kubernetes

In today's fast-paced and dynamic world of containerized applications, managing infrastructure efficiently is crucial. Kubernetes has emerged as a leading container orchestration platform, providing powerful features for deploying and scaling applications. *Figure 8.2* features the Kubernetes logo:

***Figure 8.2:*** *Kubernetes logo*

Kubernetes is an open-source container orchestration platform for automating the deployment, scaling, and management of containerized applications. Kubernetes is a powerful technology, but it can also be complex. When it comes to Kubernetes, Ansible can be used to automate the management and deployment of Kubernetes clusters and the applications running on them.

Here is a high-level overview of how Ansible can be used for Kubernetes automation:

- **Inventory:** In the case of Kubernetes, the inventory file usually includes **`localhost`**, and we can define the API access (IP addresses or hostnames) of the Kubernetes cluster using environment variables. The authentication is often handled locally via the "**`kubectl`**" command line tool.
- **Playbooks:** These are the key component of the Kubernetes automation containing the tasks to be performed on the Kubernetes cluster.

- **Kubernetes modules:** Ansible provides a set of modules specifically designed for interacting with Kubernetes. These modules enable you to perform various operations on Kubernetes resources, such as creating and managing namespaces, deployments, services, pods, and more. They extract the underlying API calls, making managing Kubernetes resources through Ansible easier.
- **Task execution:** Ansible connects to the target systems using SSH or other transport mechanisms and executes the tasks defined in the playbooks. For Kubernetes automation, Ansible typically runs on a control machine and interacts with the Kubernetes cluster using the Kubernetes modules.
- **Idempotent operations:** Ansible ensures idempotent operations, meaning that if a task has already been executed and the system is already in the desired state, Ansible will recognize this and skip the task in subsequent runs. This ensures that running the playbook multiple times will not cause unintended changes or disruptions.
- **Integration with Existing Tools:** Ansible can be integrated with other tools and processes in your CI/CD pipeline or infrastructure management workflow. For example, you can use Ansible playbooks in conjunction with container build tools like Docker or continuous integration tools like Jenkins.

By leveraging Ansible's automation capabilities and the Kubernetes modules, you can streamline the process of deploying and managing Kubernetes resources. Ansible allows you to define your desired state in a declarative manner and handles the complexities of interacting with the Kubernetes API, making it easier to manage your Kubernetes infrastructure and applications. OpenShift is a container platform created by Red Hat that extends Kubernetes with additional features for enterprise-grade application development, deployment, and management.

All the modules for Kubernetes are included in the "**`kubernetes.core`**" Ansible collection, whereas OpenShift-specific modules are handled by the "**`redhat.openshift`**" collection (available in the Automation Hub, *Chapter 7, Ansible Enterprise,* section *Ansible Automation Platform*). The most important module is the "**`kubernetes.core.k8s`**" Ansible module that interacts with the control plane to execute our automation.

The first step to configure our systems to interact with Kubernetes is to install the "**`kubernetes.core`**" Ansible collection. For the automated way, refer to *Chapter 3, Ansible Language Extended,* section *Ansible collection.* We can install manually using the **`ansible-galaxy`** command:

```
ansible-galaxy collection install kubernetes.core
```

A successful installation can be verified using the command:

```
ansible-galaxy collection list kubernetes.core
```

The output shows the current version of the Ansible collection:

```
Collection      Version
--------------- -------
kubernetes.core 2.3.2
```

## Namespace

Creating and managing Kubernetes namespaces can be a tedious and error-prone task. Ansible can be used to automate the creation of Kubernetes namespaces using the "**kubernetes.core**" module. One of the fundamental constructs in Kubernetes is a namespace. A namespace provides a logical separation and isolation of resources within a cluster. With Ansible's "**kubernetes.core.k8s**" module, we can easily automate the creation of Kubernetes objects, for example, namespaces.

```
---
- name: Kubernetes namespace present
  hosts: all
  tasks:
    - name:  Kubernetes namespace present
      kubernetes.core.k8s:
        api_version: v1
        kind: Namespace
        name: "AutomateEverythingWithAnsible"
        state: present
```

Explanation of the Kubernetes task in the playbook:

- The **name** field within the task provides a descriptive name for the task itself.
- The **kubernetes.core.k8s** module is used to interact with the Kubernetes API server.
- The **api_version** parameter specifies the API version of the Kubernetes resource we want to manage, which in this case is "**v1**".
- The **kind** parameter specifies the Kubernetes resource type, which is "**Namespace**".
- The **name** parameter specifies the name of the namespace to be created, which is "**AutomateEverythingWithAnsible**".

- The **state** field specifies the desired state of the namespace, which in this case is "**present**" to ensure that the namespace exists. On the other hand, the "**absent**" state deletes the namespace.

By running this playbook, Ansible will connect to the target hosts and interact with the Kubernetes API server to create the specified namespace if it does not already exist.

We can easily verify a successful execution using the "**kubectl**" command line utility to list all the namespaces in the Kubernetes cluster:

```
kubectl get namespace | grep AutomateEverythingWithAnsible
```

This output confirms the successful creation of the namespace:

```
AutomateEverythingWithAnsible Active 4m
```

Just like Kubernetes namespaces, we can automate the management of any Kubernetes objects. The benefits of Automating Kubernetes object management are:

- **Consistency:** Automation ensures that the creation of Kubernetes objects follows a consistent and standardized approach across different environments and clusters.
- **Time-saving:** Manually creating namespaces can be time-consuming, especially in large-scale deployments. Automation eliminates the need for manual intervention, allowing teams to focus on more critical tasks.
- **Error reduction:** Human errors are common when performing repetitive tasks. Automation minimizes the chances of errors by consistently applying the desired configuration defined in the playbook.
- **Scalability:** Automation enables the creation of namespaces at scale, making it easier to manage multiple environments or clusters effortlessly.

## Pod

The following "**k8s_pod.yml**" Ansible playbook is focused on deploying a Kubernetes pod. A Kubernetes pod is the smallest and simplest unit of the Kubernetes object model, representing a single instance of a running process within a cluster.

```
---
- name: Kubernetes pod deployment
  hosts: all
  vars:
    my_namespace: "AutomateEverythingWithAnsible"
  tasks:
```

```
- name: K8s namespace present
  kubernetes.core.k8s:
    api_version: v1
    kind: Namespace
    name: "{{ my_namespace }}"
    state: present

- name: K8s pod present
  kubernetes.core.k8s:
    namespace: "{{ my_namespace }}"
    state: present
    definition:
      apiVersion: v1
      kind: Pod
      metadata:
        name: nginx
      spec:
        containers:
          - name: nginx
            image: nginx:latest
            ports:
      - containerPort: 80
```

The playbook starts with a play named "**Kubernetes pod deployment**," which will be executed on all hosts specified in the inventory. It includes a variable section (under the **vars** keyword) where a single variable is defined.

The variable defined in the playbook is:

- **my_namespace**: Specifies the namespace in which the Kubernetes pod will be deployed. It is set to "**AutomateEverythingWithAnsible**".

Following the variable section, there are two tasks defined under the **tasks** keyword. Each task uses the Ansible Kubernetes module (**kubernetes.core.k8s**) to interact with Kubernetes resources.

**Task 1:**

- **name**: Specifies the name of the task as "**K8s namespace present**".

- **`kubernetes.core.k8s`**: Uses the Kubernetes module to manage Kubernetes resources.
- **`api_version`**: Specifies the API version of the resource, which is "**`v1`**" in this case.
- **`kind`**: Specifies the kind of resource to manage, which is "**`Namespace`**".
- **`name`**: Specifies the name of the namespace using the value of the **`my_namespace variable.`**
- **`state`**: Specifies the desired state of the namespace, which is "**`present`**" (to ensure it exists).

Task 2:

- **`name`**: Specifies the name of the task as "**`K8s pod present`**".
- **`kubernetes.core.k8s`**: Uses the Kubernetes module to manage Kubernetes resources.
- **`namespace`**: Specifies the namespace in which the pod will be deployed using the value of the **`my_namespace`** variable.
- **`state`**: Specifies the desired state of the pod, which is "**`present`**" (to ensure it exists).
- **`definition`**: Provides the definition of the pod as a YAML object.
- **`apiVersion`**: Specifies the API version of the pod, which is "**`v1`**".
- **`kind`**: Specifies the kind of resource, which is "**`Pod`**".
- **`metadata`**: Specifies the metadata of the pod, including its name.
- **`spec`**: Specifies the specifications of the pod, including the containers it should run.
- **`containers`**: Specifies the list of containers within the pod.
- **`name`**: Specifies the name of the container as "**`nginx`**".
- **`image`**: Specifies the image for the container using the "**`nginx:latest`**" image.
- **`ports`**: Specifies the ports to expose in the container.
- **`containerPort`**: Specifies port number 80.

Overall, this playbook ensures the presence of a Kubernetes namespace with the specified name and deploys a pod within that namespace. The pod runs an **`nginx`** container using the latest nginx image and exposes **`port 80`**.

# Ansible configuration settings

Ansible has many configuration settings that impact the behavior of the software. We can customize a lot of Ansible behavior by editing the **`ansible.cfg`** in the current project or the default path **`/etc/ansible/ansible.cfg`** in the Ansible Controller. Another option is to define a terminal environment variable with the customized value.

The following command prints the current settings on the screen as set via configuration files or environment variables:

```
ansible-config dump
```

*Table 8.3* summarizes the most used Ansible configuration settings.

| | Section | Key | Environment |
|---|---|---|---|
| role path | `[defaults]` | `roles_path` | `ANSIBLE_ROLES_PATH` |
| collection path | `[defaults]` | `collections_paths` | `ANSIBLE_COLLECTIONS_PATHS` |
| pipelining | `[connection]` | `pipelining` | `ANSIBLE_PIPELINING` |
| dynamic inventory | `[inventory]` | `enable_plugins` | `ANSIBLE_INVENTORY_PLUGINS` |
| keep remote files | `[defaults]` | `keep_remote_files` | `ANSIBLE_KEEP_REMOTE_FILES` |
| timeout | `[defaults]` | `Timeout` | `ANSIBLE_TIMEOUT` |
| verbosity | `[defaults]` | `Verbosity` | `ANSIBLE_VERBOSITY` |
| interpreter python | `[defaults]` | `interpreter_python` | `ANSIBLE_PYTHON_INTERPRETER` |
| remote temp | `[defaults]` | `remote_tmp` | `ANSIBLE_REMOTE_TEMP` |
| paramiko/ssh | `[defaults]` | `Transport` | `DEFAULT_TRANSPORT` |
| host key check | `[defaults]` | `host_key_checking` | `HOST_KEY_CHECKING` |
| fact caching | `[defaults]` | `fact_caching` | `ANSIBLE_CACHE_PLUGIN` |
| fork | `[defaults]` | `Forks` | `ANSIBLE_FORKS` |
| ansible_managed | `[defaults]` | `ansible_managed` | `ANSIBLE_MANAGED` |

***Table 8.3:** Ansible configuration Settings*

We can alter the Ansible behavior when connecting to a target host by customizing the configuration settings. Some people would like to customize the role or collection path or more connection-related behavior. The default behavior for Ansible to connect to any target hosts is to execute the authentication phase and generate a file for each task of the playbook and copy it to the target host. Ansible connects to remote servers and executes code with the same username. The following use cases explain how to customize the default temporary directory for generated files and enable Ansible pipelining and switching between SSH or Paramiko for connection.

# Custom verbosity

As we learned in *Chapter 2, Ansible Language Core,* section *Ansible playbook,* and *Chapter 4, Ansible For Linux,* section *Print Text During Execution,* we execute our Ansible playbooks with verbosity **`level 0`** (zero) by default. We can customize the setting to display more verbose content at each execution using the "**`-v`**" parameter of the **`ansible-playbook`** command or the **`ansible.cfg`** file. For example, let us set the verbosity value to **`level 2`** (two) for every execution.

```
[defaults]
verbosity = 2
```

# Custom role path

We can customize the role path installation directory. The default search path is "**`~/.ansible/roles:/usr/share/ansible/roles:/etc/ansible/roles`**". This means that the first search location is in the current user home directory under the "**`~/.ansible/roles`**", secondly in the "**`/usr/share/ansible/roles`**" and lastly in the "**`/etc/ansible/roles`**" path. For the majority of people, this setting enables them to use the Ansible roles as they want. If we want to customize the search path, we can specify the **`collections_paths`** parameter in the **`ansible-galaxy`** command line tool or **`ansible.cfg`** file.

```
[defaults]
roles_path = "~/.ansible/roles"
```

# Custom collection path

Similarly, we can customize the collection path installation directory. The default search path is "**`~/.ansible/collections:/usr/share/ansible/collections`**". This means that the first search location is in the current user home directory under the "**`~/.ansible/collections`**", secondly in the "**`/usr/share/ansible/collections`**". This setting gives most people enough flexibility. If we want to customize the search path, we can specify the **`roles_path`** parameter in the **`ansible-galaxy`** command line tool or **`ansible.cfg`** file.

```
[defaults]
collections_paths = "~/.ansible/collections/ansible_collections"
```

## Custom username

We can specify the connection account username with the variable **ansible_user** on the inventory, playbook, or **ansible.cfg** file. We can change the running user by specifying the **remote_user** variable in the inventory, playbook, or globally in **ansible.cfg** file. The following example sets the username to "**ansible**" for any connection:

```
[defaults]

ansible_user = ansible
```

## Custom temporary directory

After a successful connection, Ansible creates a temporary directory inside the home of the user of the connection where to copy the task files if it does not already exist. If Ansible is unable to create, or if that user does not have a home directory, or if their home directory permissions do not allow them to write access, we can customize the path of the temporary directory via **ansible.cfg** file. For example, we can use the following path under the **/tmp** directory:

```
[defaults]
remote_tmp = /tmp/.ansible-${USER}/tmp
```

## Enable Ansible pipelining

The Ansible pipelining executes the Ansible modules on the target directly without the prior file transfer, consequently reducing the network operations. Another pleasant side effect is the increase in performance when enabled. By default, Ansible pipelining is disabled. We can enable using the environment variable **ANSIBLE_PIPELINING=True** or setting the **pipelining=true** key in the **[connection]** or **[defaults]** sections of the **ansible.cfg** file as follows:

```
[defaults]
pipelining = true
```

## SSH and Paramiko

Paramiko is a Python native library implementing the SSH protocol. Since it is a native Python, there is no context switching to the system OpenSSH. The drawback is that the Paramiko library is not available for all the target operating systems and has limited ssh options. By default, Ansible adopts the "**smart**" option that toggles between "**ssh**" and "**paramiko**" depending on the controller OS and OpenSSH versions. We can customize the value setting of the transport key in the **[defaults]** section of **ansible.cfg** file as follows, to force only the usage of the **paramiko** library:

```
[defaults]
transport = paramiko
```

# Host key check

SSH host key is a security mechanism to prevent host tampering. The host key is normally generated when OpenSSH is first installed or booted, as we learned in *Chapter 4, Ansible for Linux,* section *OpenSSH configuration*. In a fast pace infrastructure with a fast hostname and IP reuse, we can disable the host key checking to set the appropriate parameter in the **ansible.cfg** configuration.

```
[defaults]
host_key_checking = false
```

# Fact caching

Fact caching could be useful to reduce the time of execution of fact gathering. By default, the value "memory" means that the memory plugin is used, that caches the data for the current execution. Often used are the "**jsonfile**" and "**redis**" which use a JSON file or a Redis server as a caching mechanism. We can also define what values to cache, as we learned in *Chapter 2, Ansible Language Core,* section *Ansible Facts*. The following configuration is often used in conjunction with a local Redis server for fact caching setting the appropriate parameter in the **ansible.cfg** configuration:

```
[defaults]
fact_caching=redis
fact_caching_timeout = 7200
fact_caching_connection = localhost:6379:0:password
fact_caching = namespace.collection_name.cache_plugin_name
```

When used with a Redis server, the "**fact_caching_connection**" parameter expresses the connection parameters in the following format: **host:port:db:password**.

# Fork

In Ansible, "**fork**" refers to the number of parallel processes or connections that Ansible will use to manage hosts simultaneously. It determines how many hosts Ansible can operate on at the same time. The default value for the fork setting is 5. After modifying the value of the fork in the **ansible.cfg** file, Ansible uses the specified number of parallel processes when managing hosts. Remember to restart any running Ansible processes or playbooks for the new fork value to take effect. By adjusting the fork value, we can control the level of parallelism in Ansible host management operations, allowing us to optimize performance based on the available resources and the nature of the tasks being executed, impacting the system resources (CPU, memory, and so on.). We can customize the value setting of the **forks** key in the **[defaults]** section of **ansible.cfg** file as follows, to use **10** forks:

```
[defaults]
forks = 10
```

# Ansible managed

The **ansible_managed** variable is a special variable used in Ansible to indicate that a particular file or template has been managed by Ansible. This variable is typically set as a comment within the managed file. When Ansible performs tasks such as file copying or template rendering (**ansible.builtin.template** and **ansible.windows.win_template** modules), it often creates or modifies files on the target system. The **ansible_managed** variable serves as a marker to indicate that Ansible is responsible for managing that file. It helps in identifying files that were created or modified by Ansible, distinguishing them from other files on the system. The variable is usually set as a comment at the beginning of the managed file and can have different values, but the most common value is a string like "**# Ansible managed**". The specific value and format of the variable are not standardized, and you can customize it to suit your needs or organizational standards. The presence of the **ansible_managed** variable allows system administrators and other users to identify files managed by Ansible quickly. It can be useful for troubleshooting, auditing, or performing manual modifications to files while being aware of Ansible's influence. It also helps prevent accidental modifications to files that are meant to be managed by Ansible, as users can easily identify them based on the presence of the variable.

We can customize the value using the **DEFAULT_MANAGED_STR** environment variable or using the **ansible_managed** key in the **[defaults]** section of **ansible.cfg** file as follows to set the custom text to:

**"This file is managed by Ansible, all changes will be lost.":**

```
[defaults]
ansible_managed = This file is managed by Ansible, all changes will be lost.
```

# Latest trends

In the realm of IT automation, two groundbreaking advancements have emerged that hold the potential to transform how organizations manage and streamline their operations. Ansible Lightspeed and Event-Driven Ansible are pioneering solutions that introduce innovative approaches to automation, revolutionizing the way tasks are executed and orchestrated. These brilliant evolutions were unveiled in the latest *AnsibleFest* part of the *Red Hat Summit 2023*.

Ansible Lightspeed, powered by IBM Watson Code Assistant, represents a focused and purpose-built generative AI service. Unlike the multitude of AI tools flooding the market, Ansible Lightspeed is not aimed at helping write everyday documents or correspondence. Its primary objective is to simplify the creation of Ansible content, specifically Ansible Playbooks, which serve as a cornerstone for IT automation. With a laser focus on delivering an exceptional experience for developers and automation architects, Ansible Lightspeed empowers them to craft Ansible content more efficiently, with heightened speed, improved quality, and reduced effort. By leveraging cutting-edge AI capabilities, this transformative solution aims to save organizations valuable time and resources, enabling domain experts to concentrate on solving critical business challenges using established automation best practices.

Complementing Ansible Lightspeed is the concept of Event-Driven Ansible, an approach that seeks to bridge the gap between traditional automation and real-time event-driven architectures. Traditionally, automation has been executed based on predefined schedules or triggers, operating in a deterministic manner. However, the rise of dynamic and rapidly changing environments has necessitated a shift towards event-driven approaches, where automation responds to events and triggers in real-time. Event-Driven Ansible offers a paradigm shift by enabling the orchestration of automation tasks in response to events, such as system alerts, infrastructure changes, or user interactions. This approach empowers organizations to achieve greater agility, responsiveness, and adaptability in their automation workflows, ensuring that actions are triggered precisely when needed, enhancing operational efficiency, and reducing manual intervention.

We are going to explore the remarkable capabilities of Ansible Lightspeed and Event-Driven Ansible, diving into their unique features, benefits, and the ways in which they reshape the landscape of IT automation. We will delve into how Ansible Lightspeed streamlines Ansible content creation, empowering developers with AI-generated automation code recommendations. Additionally, we will uncover the principles and advantages of Event-Driven Ansible, showcasing its ability to respond dynamically to real-time events and trigger automation tasks. Together, these advancements promise to elevate automation practices to new heights, providing organizations with unprecedented levels of efficiency, flexibility, and adaptability.

# Event-driven Ansible

Event-driven Ansible is an innovative automation approach that allows for faster issue resolution and greater automation in monitoring environments. It utilizes rulebooks, which define event sources, conditions, and actions in YAML format. Ansible-rulebook is the CLI component used to run rulebooks. Event-driven Ansible simplifies troubleshooting and information gathering by automating the process and minimizing manual steps. It offers faster mean-time-to-resolution and opens up possibilities for automated observation of environments. The Ansible-rulebook is easy to learn and work with, and there is a graphical user interface called EDA server available for further simplification.

To get started with event-driven Ansible, follow these steps:

1. Install the **`ansible-rulebook`**.

    a. Using Ansible Galaxy collection: For MacOS and Fedora, run the following command:

    ```
    pip install ansible-rulebook
    ansible-galaxy collection install ansible.eda
    ```

    **Note: This method is supported by MacOS and Fedora.**

    b. Alternatively, we can install "**`ansible-rulebook`**" with **`pip`** and then install the "**`ansible.eda`**" collection. This method requires Java 11+ with "**`openjdk`**".

    c. If we want to contribute to "**`ansible-rulebook`**" via the GitHub repository, set up our development environment and build a test container.

2. **Build a rulebook that defines the event source, conditions, and actions:** Rulebooks are created in YAML format and resemble traditional Ansible Playbooks. The following "**`eda.yml`**" rulebook listens for events on a webhook and triggers an action if a specific condition is met:

```
---
- name: Receive webhook events
  hosts: all
  sources:
    - ansible.eda.webhook:
        host: 0.0.0.0
        port: 8000
  rules:
    - name: Event
```

```
        condition: event.payload.message == "Automate Everything with
Ansible   "
        action:
          run_playbook:
            name: playbook.yml
```

In this example, the rulebook uses the webhook source plugin from the "**ansible.eda**" collection and looks for a message payload from the webhook that contains the string "**Automate Everything with Ansible**". If this condition is met, the defined action (running a playbook named "**playbook.yml**") will be triggered.

3. Once our rulebook is built, we can use "**ansible-rulebook**" to run it and wait for events. Use the following command:

   ```
   ansible-rulebook -r eda.yml -i inventory –verbose
   ```

   This command specifies the rulebook (**eda.yml**) and the inventory file (**inventory.yml**) to use. The **--verbose** option provides detailed output.

With **ansible-rulebook** running, it will wait for events and match them against the conditions defined in the rulebook. If a webhook event is triggered, and the payload does not match the condition, it will continue waiting for the next event. Once the payload matches the condition, the specified action will be triggered.

To simulate a webhook event with the correct payload, we can use the following command:

```
curl -H 'Content-Type: application/json' -d "{\"message\": \"Automate
Everything with Ansible\"}" 127.0.0.1:8000/endpoint
```

When the payload matches the condition, **`ansible-rulebook`** will execute the action (for example, run the playbook) and then continue waiting for new events as shown in *Figure 8.3*:

```
Event driven Ansible — ansible-rulebook -r eda.yml -i inventory --verbose —...
(venv) lberton@Lucas-MBP Event driven Ansible % ansible-rulebook -r eda.yml -i i
nventory --verbose
2023-05-19 16:35:20,893 - ansible_rulebook.app - INFO - Starting sources
2023-05-19 16:35:20,894 - ansible_rulebook.app - INFO - Starting rules
2023-05-19 16:35:20,894 - ansible_rulebook.engine - INFO - run_ruleset
2023-05-19 16:35:20,894 - drools.ruleset - INFO - Using jar: /Users/lberton/prj/
gitlab/OrangeAVA book 26 - Automate Everything with Ansible/code/chapter 7/Event
 driven Ansible/venv/lib/python3.11/site-packages/drools/jars/drools-ansible-rul
ebook-integration-runtime-1.0.1-SNAPSHOT.jar
2023-05-19 16:35:21 210 [main] INFO org.drools.ansible.rulebook.integration.api.
rulesengine.AbstractRulesEvaluator - Start automatic pseudo clock with a tick ev
ery 100 milliseconds
2023-05-19 16:35:21,213 - ansible_rulebook.engine - INFO - ruleset define: {"nam
e": "Receive webhook events", "hosts": ["all"], "sources": [{"EventSource": {"na
me": "ansible.eda.webhook", "source_name": "ansible.eda.webhook", "source_args":
 {"host": "0.0.0.0", "port": 8000}, "source_filters": []}}], "rules": [{"Rule":
{"name": "Event", "condition": {"AllCondition": [{"EqualsExpression": {"lhs": {"
Event": "payload.message"}, "rhs": {"String": "Automate Everything with Ansible
  "}}}]}, "actions": [{"Action": {"action": "run_playbook", "action_args": {"nam
e": "playbook.yml"}}}], "enabled": true}}]}
2023-05-19 16:35:21,224 - ansible_rulebook.engine - INFO - load source
2023-05-19 16:35:21,528 - ansible_rulebook.engine - INFO - load source filters
2023-05-19 16:35:21,528 - ansible_rulebook.engine - INFO - loading eda.builtin.i
nsert_meta_info
2023-05-19 16:35:21,748 - ansible_rulebook.engine - INFO - Calling main in ansib
le.eda.webhook
2023-05-19 16:35:21,749 - ansible_rulebook.engine - INFO - Waiting for all rules
et tasks to end
2023-05-19 16:35:21,749 - ansible_rulebook.rule_set_runner - INFO - Waiting for
actions on events from Receive webhook events
2023-05-19 16:35:21,749 - ansible_rulebook.rule_set_runner - INFO - Waiting for
events, ruleset: Receive webhook events
2023-05-19 16:35:21 750 [drools-async-evaluator-thread] INFO org.drools.ansible.
rulebook.integration.api.io.RuleExecutorChannel - Async channel connected
2023-05-19 16:37:31,319 - aiohttp.access - INFO - 127.0.0.1 [19/May/2023:15:37:3
1 +0000] "POST /endpoint HTTP/1.1" 200 159 "-" "curl/7.87.0"
2023-05-19 16:38:03,917 - aiohttp.access - INFO - 127.0.0.1 [19/May/2023:15:38:0
3 +0000] "POST /endpoint HTTP/1.1" 200 159 "-" "curl/7.87.0"
```

***Figure 8.3:** Ansible event-driven running*

Event-driven Ansible offers the potential for faster issue resolution and greater automation in monitoring environments. It simplifies the lives of engineers by providing an easy-to-learn and work-with solution. Additionally, the graphical user interface EDA server further simplifies the process.

# Ansible Lightspeed

Generative AI has become pervasive in today's technological landscape, offering a myriad of exciting tools and applications. However, Ansible Lightspeed with IBM Watson Code Assistant stands out by adopting a unique approach. While there are numerous AI tools designed for tasks like writing papers or emails, Ansible

Lightspeed is purpose-built for IT automation, focusing on delivering a tailored generative AI experience that saves organizations time and money.

Unlike generalized models, Ansible Lightspeed's superpower lies in its unwavering focus on the development of Ansible content. The ultimate goal is to simplify the creation of Ansible Playbooks, empowering automation architects and developers to produce content faster, better, and with enhanced quality. By minimizing the time spent on writing playbooks, and domain subject matter, experts can concentrate on tackling their most significant business challenges using established automation best practices.

The interaction between the user and the Ansible Lightspeed technology is performed by the Ansible VSCode plugin, an extension for Visual Studio Code that integrates Ansible functionality into the popular code editor, offering features such as syntax highlighting, code completion, and debugging support to enhance the development experience with Ansible. The Ansible Lightspeed offers a prediction to the user based on the context of the code and the name of the task, as shown in *Figure 8.4*.

Ansible Lightspeed with IBM Watson Code Assistant signifies a paradigm shift in IT automation. By combining the power of generative AI with a purpose-built approach, Ansible Lightspeed empowers organizations to accelerate their automation initiatives, optimize resource utilization, and achieve greater operational efficiency. As the automation landscape continues to evolve, the integration of Ansible Lightspeed and Event-Driven Ansible holds the promise of a seamless and transformative automation experience for the future.

Refer to the following *Figure 8.4:*

***Figure 8.4:*** *Ansible Lightspeed code assistant*

# Conclusion

Ansible is a fantastic and powerful automation platform that simplifies and accelerates IT operations by automating tasks, configurations, and application deployments. Many open-source projects and companies create products that integrate and simplify the management of a modern hybrid infrastructure using Ansible as a foundation. We explored cloud computing integration, specifically Amazon Web Services, and used Kubernetes technology to boost our cloud-native application deployment. Teams that embrace automation consistently outperform their low-automation counterparts across a slew of metrics. The sky is the limit, and the key terms are innovating, accelerating, and automating!

# Points to remember

- Ansible could integrate many products and technologies to implement DevOps toolchains, cloud providers, and orchestration technologies.
- Ansible event-driven and Ansible Lightspeed are the latest technologies.
- We can expand and customize many Ansible behaviors using the configuration settings and "**`ansible.cfg`**" file.

# Key terms

- **Callback plugins:** Enable custom handling and formatting of output during playbook execution.
- **Web service:** A software system that allows communication and exchange of data between different applications over the internet.
- **Dynamic inventory:** Allows for automatic generation of Ansible inventory based on external sources such as cloud providers or custom scripts.
- **Amazon Web Services** (**AWS**) is a cloud computing platform that offers a wide range of on-demand services and resources for building, deploying, and managing applications and infrastructure.
- **Kubernetes** is a powerful container orchestration platform that can be seamlessly managed and automated using Ansible, enabling efficient deployment, scaling, and management of containerized applications.

# Multiple choice questions

1. **What is the best place to use the Ansible dynamic inventories?**
   a. Static virtual machines
   b. Static on-premise machines
   c. Static inventory scenario
   d. Cloud computing and containers

2. **What is the default fork value?**
   a. `1`
   b. `5`
   c. `10`
   d. `100`

3. **What is the best way to integrate Ansible with web services?**
   a. Amazon Web Services
   b. API integration
   c. Kubernetes
   d. VMware

4. **How can we enable the `paramiko` connection library?**
   a. Set the "`transport`" value in the "**`ansible.cfg`**" file
   b. Replace the ssh service with paramiko
   c. Execute the "**`paramiko.yml`**" Ansible playbook
   d. Set the "**`ansible_connection`**" to "**`paramiko`**" in the Ansible inventory

# Answers

1. d
2. b
3. b
4. a

# Questions

1. What is an Ansible callback plugin?
2. What is the impact of enabling Ansible pipelining in our system?
3. What is the difference between a **`fork`** and **`serial`** statements?
4. How to integrate Ansible with Kubernetes?
5. What are the most important parameters of the **`ansible.cfg`** file?
6. What are the main advantages of using Event-driven Ansible?

## Join our book's Discord space

Join the book's Discord Workspace for Latest updates, Offers, Tech happenings around the world, New Release and Sessions with the Authors:

**https://discord.bpbonline.com**

# Index